Leadership and Organizational Climate

The Cloud Chamber Effect

by Robert Stringer
Mercer Delta Consulting, LLC

Prentice Hall

Upper Saddle River, New Jersey 07458

Library of Congress Cataloging-in-Publication Data
Stringer, Robert
   Leadership and organizational climate : the cloud chamber effect / Robert Stringer.—1st. ed.
     p. cm.
   Includes bibliographical references and index.
   ISBN 0-13-032187-7
   1. Leadership. 2. Organizational behavior. 3. Corporate culture. I. Title.
   HD57.7 .S783 2001
   658.4'092—dc21

                                            2001036587

Executive Editor: David Shafer
Editor-in-Chief: Jeff Shelstad
Senior Managing Editor (Editorial): Jennifer Glennon
Assistant Editor: Melanie Olsen
Editorial Assistant: Kim Marsden
Media Project Manager: Michele Faranda
Senior Marketing Manager: Shannon Moore
Marketing Assistant: Christine Genneken
Managing Editor (Production): Judy Leale
Production Editor: Michele Foresta
Production Assistant: Dianne Falcone
Permissions Supervisor: Suzanne Grappi
Associate Director, Manufacturing: Vincent Scelta
Production Manager: Arnold Vila
Manufacturing Buyer: Diane Peirano
Design Manager: Patricia Smythe
Cover Design: Jayne Conte
Associate Director, Multimedia Production: Karen Goldsmith
Manager, Print Production: Christy Mahon
Composition: Pre-Press Company, Inc.
Full-Service Project Management: Roberta Peach, Pre-Press Company, Inc.
Printer/Binder: R.R.D. Harrisonburg/Phoenix

Credits and acknowledgments borrowed from other sources and reproduced, with permission, in this textbook appear on appropriate page within text.

Pearson Education LTD.
Pearson Education Australia PTY, Limited
Pearson Education Singapore, Pte. Ltd
Pearson Education North Asia Ltd

Pearson Education, Canada, Ltd
Pearson Educación de Mexico, S.A. de C.V.
Pearson Education–Japan
Pearson Education Malaysia, Pte. Ltd

10 9 8 7 6 5 4 3 2
ISBN 0-13-032187-7

Contents

Series Foreword

The Prentice Hall Series on Organization Development originated in the late 1960s when a number of us recognized that the rapidly growing field of "OD" was not well understood or well defined. We also recognized that there was no one OD philosophy; hence, one could not at that time write a textbook on the theory and practice of OD, but one could make clear what various practitioners were doing under that label. So the original six books in the OD Series launched what became a continuing enterprise, the essence of which was to allow different authors to speak for themselves rather than to summarize under one umbrella what was obviously a rapidly growing and highly diverse field.

By the early 1980s, OD was growing by leaps and bounds and expanding into all kinds of organizational areas and technologies of intervention. By this time, many textbooks existed that tried to capture core concepts in the field, but we felt that diversity and innovation continued to be the more salient aspects of OD. Accordingly, our series had expanded to nineteen titles.

As we moved into the 1990s, we began to see some real convergence in the underlying assumptions of OD. As we observed how different professionals working in different kinds of organizations and occupational communities made their cases, we saw that we were still far from having a single "theory" of organizational development. Yet some common premises were surfacing. We began to see patterns in what was working and what was not, and we were becoming more articulate about these patterns. We also started to view the field of OD as increasingly connected to other organizational sciences and disciplines such as information technology, coordination theory, and organization theory.

In the early 90s, we added several new titles to the OD Series to describe important new themes: Ciampa's *Total Quality* illustrates the important link to employee involvement in continuous improvement; Johansen et al.'s *Leading Business Teams* explores the important arena of electronic information tools for teamwork; Tjosvold's *The Conflict–Positive Organization* shows how conflict management can turn conflict into constructive action; and Hirschhorn's *Managing in the New Team Environment* builds bridges to group psychodynamic theory.

In the mid 1990s, we continued to explore emerging themes with four revisions and three new books. Burke took his highly successful *Organization Development* into new realms with more current and expanded content; Galbraith updated and enlarged his classic theory of how information management lies at the heart of organization design with his new edition of *Competing with Flexible Lateral Organizations*; and Dyer wrote an important third edition of his classic book, *Team Building*. In addition, Rashford and Coghlan introduced the important concept of levels of organizational complexity as a basis for intervention theory in their book, *The Dynamics of Organizational Levels*; in *Creating Labor-Management Partnerships*, Woodworth and Meek take us into the critical realm of how OD can help in labor relations—an area that has become increasingly important as productivity issues become critical for global competitiveness. In *Integrated Strategic Change*, authors Worley, Hitchin, and Ross powerfully demonstrate how the field of OD must be linked to the field of strategy by reviewing the role of OD at each stage of the strategy planning and implementation process. Finally, authors Argyris and Schön provided an important link to organizational learning in a new version of their classic book entitled *Organizational Learning II: Theory, Method, and Practice*.

Now, as we continue to think about the field of OD and what it will mean in the 21st century, we have added several titles that reflect the growing connections between the original concepts of OD and the wider range of the applications of these concepts. Rupert Chisholm's *Developing Network Organizations: Learning from Practice and Theory* explores and illustrates the link between OD and building community networks. In their book called *Diagnosing and Changing Organizational Culture*, Cameron and Quinn explore one model and technique of how to get at the crucial concept of culture and how to make this concept relevant for the practitioner. The theme of process consultation has remained central in OD, and we have found that it continues to be relevant in a variety of helping situations. In *Process Consultation Revisited: Building the Helping Relationship*, Schein has completely revised and updated this concept by focusing on process consultation as a general model of the helping process; his volume pulls together material from previous work and also adds new concepts and cases.

The first member of the OD series to bear a 2000 copyright is *Work-Based Learning* by Joe Raelin. This book shows readers how to acquire learning in the midst of practice by exploring the intersection of knowledge and experience. Intended as a practical guide for a new generation of managers and executive educators, *Work-Based Learning* explores how to learn collectively with others who also wish to develop their own capability and how to engage one's reflective powers to challenge those taken-for-granted assumptions that unwittingly hold us back from questioning standard ways of operating.

The newest member of the series is *Learning Practices: Assessment and Action for Organizational Improvement* by Anthony DiBella. The primary goal of the book is to help readers recognize and use learning capability as a fact of organizational life. It provides practical details and how-tos for team and organizational learning within its Learning Orientations framework. The book guides readers in how to interpret learning profiles, select learning and knowledge management practices aligned with the values and strategic mission of their team or company, and then implement organizational learning capability plans.

Our series on Organization Development now includes over thirty titles. We will continue to welcome new titles and revisions as we explore the various frontiers of organization development and identify themes that are relevant to the ever more difficult problem of helping organizations remain effective in an increasingly turbulent environment.

New York, New York   Richard H. Beckhard
Cambridge, Massachusetts   Edgar H. Schein

As many readers may already know, my co-editor Dick Beckhard passed away peacefully on Dec. 28, 1999 at the age of 81. We all miss his lively enthusiastic insights into the OD field and I will endeavor to keep alive a tradition that he, Warren Bennis, and I started back in 1968 with the launching of the OD series.

E.S.

OD Series

40 years of experience as a consultant, Schein creates a general theory and methodology of helping that will enable a diverse group of readers to navigate the helping process successfully.

Diagnosing and Changing Organizational Culture
Kim S. Cameron and Robert E. Quinn   1999 (0-201-33871-8)
This book helps managers, change agents, and scholars to understand, diagnose, and facilitate the change of an organization's culture in order to enhance its effectiveness. The authors present three forms of assistance for readers: (1) validated instruments for diagnosing organizational culture and management competency, (2) a theoretical framework for understanding organizational culture, and (3) a systematic strategy and methodology for changing organizational culture and personal behavior. This text is a workbook in that readers can complete the instruments and plot their own culture profile in the book itself. They can also use the text as a resource for understanding and leading a culture change process.

Developing Network Organizations: Learning from Theory and Practice
Rupert F. Chisholm   1998 (0-201-87444-X)
The interorganizational network is rapidly emerging as a key type of organization, and the importance of the network is expected to increase throughout the 21st century. This text covers the process of developing these complex systems. The author uses in-depth description and analysis based on direct involvement with three diverse networks to identify critical aspects of the development process. He explains relevant concepts and appropriate methods and practices in the context of developing these three networks, and he also identifies ten key learnings derived from his direct involvement with the development process.

Integrated Strategic Change: How OD Builds Competitive Advantage
Christopher G. Worley, David E. Hitchin, and Walter L. Ross   1996 (0-201-85777-4)
This book is about strategic change and how firms can improve their performance and effectiveness. Its unique contribution is in describing how organization development practitioners can assist in the effort. Strategic change is a type of organization change that realigns an organization's strategy, structure, and process within a given competitive context. It is substantive and systemic and therefore differs from traditional organization development that produces

incremental improvements, addresses only one system at a time, or does not intend to increase firm-level performance.

Organizational Learning II: Theory, Method, and Practice
Chris Argyris and Donald A. Schön   1996 (0-201-62983-6)
This text addresses how business firms, governments, non-governmental organizations, schools, health care systems, regions, and whole nations need to adapt to changing environments, draw lessons from past successes and failures, detect and correct the errors of the past, anticipate and respond to impending threats, conduct experiments, engage in continuing innovation, and build and realize images of a desirable future. There is a virtual consensus that we are all subject to a "learning imperative," and in the academy no less than in the world of practice, organizational learning has become an idea in good currency.

Creating Labor-Management Partnerships
Warner P. Woodworth and Christopher B. Meek   1995 (0-201-58823-4)
This book begins with a call for changing the social and political barriers existing in unionized work settings and emphasizes the critical need for union-management cooperation in the present context of international competition. It demonstrates the shift from confrontational union-management relationships toward more effective and positive systems of collaboration. It is written for human resource management and industrial relations managers and staff, union officials, professional arbitrators and mediators, government officials, and professors and students involved in the study of organization development.

Team Building: Current Issues and New Alternatives, Third Edition
William G. Dyer   1995 (0-201-62882-1)
One of the major developments in the field of organization redesign has been the emergence of self-directed work teams. This book explains how teams are most successful when the team becomes part of the culture and structure or systems of the organization. It discusses the major new trends and emphasizes the degree of commitment that managers and members must bring to the team-building process. It is written for managers and human resource professionals who want to develop a more systematic program of team building in their organization or work unit.

The Dynamics of Organizational Levels: A Change Framework for Managers and Consultants
Nicholas S. Rashford and David Coghlan   1994 (0-201-54323-0)
This book introduces the idea that, for successful change to occur, organizational interventions have to be coordinated across the major levels of

issues that all organizations face. Individual level, team level, interunit level, and organizational level issues are identified and analyzed, and the kinds of intervention appropriate to each level are spelled out.

Competing with Flexible Lateral Organizations, Second Edition
Jay R. Galbraith   1994 (0-201-50836-2)
This book focuses on creating competitive advantage by building a lateral capability, thereby enabling a firm to respond flexibly in an uncertain world. The book addresses international coordination and cross-business coordination as well as the usual cross-functional efforts. It is unique in covering both crossfunctional (lateral or horizontal) coordination, as well as international and corporate issues.

Organization Development: A Process of Learning and Changing,
Second Edition
W. Warner Burke   1994 (0-201-50835-4)
This text provides a comprehensive overview of the field of organization development. Written for managers, executives, administrators, practitioners, and students, this book takes an in-depth look at organization development with particular emphasis on the importance of learning and change. The author not only describes the basic tenets of OD, but he also looks at OD as a change in an organization's culture. Frameworks and models like the Burke-Litwin model (Chapter 7), as well as numerous case examples, are used throughout the book to enhance the reader's understanding of the principles and practices involved in leading and managing organizational change.

Total Quality: A User's Guide for Implementation
Dan Ciampa   1992 (0-201-54992-1)
This is a book that directly addresses the challenge of how to make Total Quality work in a practical, no-nonsense way. The companies that will dominate markets in the future will be those that deliver high quality, competitively priced products and service just when the customer wants them and in a way that exceeds the customer's expectations. The vehicle by which these companies move to that stage is Total Quality.

The Conflict-Positive Organization: Stimulate Diversity and Create Unity
Dean Tjosvold   1991 (0-201-51485-0)
This book describes how managers and employees can use conflict to find common ground, solve problems, and strengthen morale and relationships. By showing how well-managed conflict invigorates and empowers teams and organizations, the text demonstrates how conflict is vital for a company's continuous improvement and increased competitive advantage.

*Leading Business Teams: How Teams Can Use Technology
and Group Process Tools to Enhance Performance*
Robert Johansen, David Sibbett, Suzyn Benson,
Alexia Martin, Robert Mittman, and Paul Saffo   1991 (0-201-52829-0)
What technology or tools should organization development people or team
leaders have at their command, now and in the future? This text explores
the intersection of technology and business teams, a new and largely
uncharted area that goes by several labels, including "groupware"—a term
that encompasses both electronic and nonelectronic tools for teams. This is
the first book of its kind from the field describing what works for business
teams and what does not.

Managing in the New Team Environment: Skills, Tools, and Methods
Larry Hirschhorn   1991 (0-201-52503-8)
This text is designed to help manage the tensions and complexities that
arise for managers seeking to guide employees in a team environment.
Based on an interactive video course developed at IBM, the text takes managers step by step through the process of building a team and authorizing it
to act while they learn to step back and delegate. Specific issues addressed
include how to give a team structure, how to facilitate its basic processes,
and how to acknowledge differences in relationships among team members
and between the manager and individual team members.

Change by Design
Robert R. Blake, Jane Srygley Mouton,
and Anne Adams McCanse   1989 (0-201-50748-X)
This book develops a systematic approach to organization development and
provides readers with rich illustrations of coherent planned change. The
book involves testing, examining, revising, and strengthening conceptual
foundations in order to create sharper corporate focus and increased predictability of successful organization development.

*Process Consultation, Volume I, Second Edition: Its Role in
Organization Development, Second Edition*
Edgar H. Schein   1988 (0-201-06736-6)
How can a situation be influenced in the workplace without the direct use of
power or formal authority? This book presents the core theoretical founda-
tions and basic prescriptions for effective management.

Designing Organizations for High Performance
David P. Hanna   1988 (0-201-12693-1)
This book is the first to give insight into the actual processes you can use to
translate organizational concepts into bottom-line improvements. Hanna's

"how-to" approach shows not only the successful methods of intervention, but also the plans behind them and the corresponding results.

Power and Organization Development:
Mobilizing Power to Implement Change
Larry E. Greiner and Virginia E. Schein   1988 (0-201-12185-9)
This book forges an important collaborative approach between two opposing and often contradictory approaches to management: OD practitioners who espouse a "more humane" workplace without understanding the political realities of getting things done, and practicing managers who feel comfortable with power but overlook the role of human potential in contributing to positive results.

Managing Conflict: Interpersonal Dialogue and Third-Party Roles,
Second Edition
Richard E. Walton   1987 (0-201-08859-2)
This book shows how to implement a dialogue approach to conflict management. It presents a framework for diagnosing recurring conflicts and suggests several basic options for controlling or resolving them.

Process Consultation, Volume II: Lessons for Managers
and Consultants
Edgar H. Schein   1987 (0-201-06744-7)
This book shows the viability of the process consultation model for working with human systems. Like Schein's first volume on process consultation, the second volume focuses on the moment-to-moment behavior of the manager or consultant rather than the design of the OD program.

Stream Analysis: A Powerful Way to Diagnose and Manage
Organizational Change
Jerry I. Porras   1987 (0-201-05693-3)
Drawing on a conceptual framework that helps the reader to better understand organizations, this book shows how to diagnose failings in organizational functioning and how to plan a comprehensive set of actions needed to change the organization into a more effective system.

Organizational Transitions: Managing Complex Change,
Second Edition
Richard Beckhard and Reuben T. Harris   1987 (0-201-10887-9)
This book discusses the choices involved in developing a management system appropriate to the "transition state." It also discusses commitment to change, organizational culture, and increasing and maintaining productivity, creativity, and innovation.

Pay and Organization Development

Edward E. Lawler   1981 (0-201-03990-7)

This book examines the important role that reward systems play in organization development efforts. By combining examples and specific recommendations with conceptual material, it organizes the various topics and puts them into a total systems perspective. Specific pay approaches such as gainsharing, skill-based pay, and flexible benefits are discussed, and their impact on productivity and the quality of work life is analyzed.

Work Redesign

J. Richard Hackman and Greg R. Oldham   1980 (0-201-02779-8)

This book is a comprehensive, clearly written study of work design as a strategy for personal and organizational change. Linking theory and practical technologies, it develops traditional and alternative approaches to work design that can benefit both individuals and organizations.

Career Dynamics: Matching Individual and Organizational Needs

Edgar H. Schein   1978 (0-201-06834-6)

This book studies the complexities of career development from both an individual and an organizational perspective. Changing needs throughout the adult life cycle, interaction of work and family, and integration of individual and organizational goals through human resource planning and development are all thoroughly explored.

Organizational Dynamics: Diagnosis and Intervention

John P. Kotter   1978 (0-201-03890-0)

This book offers managers and OD specialists a powerful method of diagnosing organizational problems and of deciding when, where, and how to use (or not use) the diverse and growing number of organizational improvement tools that are available today. Comprehensive and fully integrated, the book includes many different concepts, research findings, and competing philosophies and provides specific examples of how to use the information to improve organizational functioning.

Feedback and Organization Development: Using Data-Based Methods

David A. Nadler   1977 (0-201-05006-4)

This book addresses the use of data as a tool for organizational change. It attempts to bring together some of what is known from experience and research and to translate that knowledge into useful insights for those who are thinking about using data-based methods in organizations. The broad approach of the text is to treat a whole range of questions and issues considering the various uses of data as an organizational change tool.

Matrix

Stanley M. Davis and Paul Lawrence   1977 (0-201-01115-8)
This book defines and describes the matrix organization, a significant departure from the traditional "one man-one boss" management system. The authors note that the tension between the need for independence (fostering innovation) and order (fostering efficiency) drives organizations to consider a matrix system. Among the issues addressed are reasons for using a matrix, methods for establishing one, the impact of the system on individuals, its hazards, and what types of organizations can use a matrix system.

Introduction

"The Cloud Chamber Effect"

Leadership and Organizational Climate is a book that shows how leaders get people to follow, even when the leaders aren't there. Effective leaders create and direct the motivational energy that compels people to action, and this book explains how this happens even without the leader's constant and personal attention. It is a book about the indirect aspects of leadership: how the "memory" or "shadow" of leadership creates a certain atmosphere or climate within an organization, and how this climate drives an organization's performance. Leadership is too often explained in terms of the leader's direct face-to-face impact on people. This book describes the less dramatic but more lasting impact that certain leadership practices have on people's feelings, motivations, and behavior. General Peter Schoolmaker, commander in chief of the U.S. Special Operations Command, explains, "Ultimately, the most effective measure of a leader is the performance of his unit in his absence." In a very real sense, this book attempts to be a "cloud chamber" for the practice of leadership. It traces the normally unseen, but very real, influence that powerful leaders leave behind when they move through an organization.

In many respects *Leadership and Organizational Climate* completes the story of *Motivation and Organizational Climate* (1968). It does so by expanding the focus from defining and measuring high-performing organizations to understanding *why* these organizations work so well and *how* practicing managers can change their organization's level of performance. This shift from "what" to "how" forces us out of the laboratory and into the field. It forces us to study real leaders, leading real organizations competing in real industries for real performance prizes.

The Original Laboratory Research

During the summer of 1967 a team of researchers from the Harvard Business School, led by George H. Litwin and funded by a research grant from the General Electric Company, hired groups of unemployed students and homemakers to work in three simulated companies. Each company was to build a product line of "radar machines" and sell them to the "U.S. government." These machines represented the very latest in simulated radar technology, and all were carefully engineered and designed to be assembled from Erector Set parts. The purpose of the research was to see if we could create three different kinds of organizations and measure the attitudes and performance of each. To start with, the researchers were very careful to staff each of the three simulated companies with the same kind of employees. We administered psychological tests and balanced the three populations according to the test results, as well as age, gender, and experience.

After two months, the researchers not only succeeded in producing and selling hundreds of Erector Set radar machines, but they also succeeded in creating and sustaining three very different organizations. The quality and quantity of radar machines produced were different, and before-after tests showed that employee attitudes and motivation were also quite different in the three companies. Our most difficult task turned out to be secretly disassembling the Erector Set machines faster than they were being built so the parts could be reused as raw materials inventory for the three simulated companies.

In 1968 I co-authored (with George Litwin) *Motivation and Organizational Climate*, which summarized the results of our Erector Set competitions. This book won the McKinsey award that year for being one of the best books on management. It was a research monograph, with plenty of footnotes, references, and statistics, all aimed at satisfying the inquisitive minds of academia. Perhaps the most memorable parts of the book were those chapters devoted to the description of the three simulated organizations we created. We named the three summer-long companies British Radar, Blazer Radar, and Balance Radar. The British organization was supposed to be a conservatively managed enterprise, a bit on the stuffy and formal side. We tried to create an internal environment in British that aroused employees' need for power (nPow). The Blazer organization was supposed to be superaggressive and competitive. In this company, we tried hard to arouse the need for achievement (nAch). Finally, Balance Radar was to be the most people-sensitive organization where they made most decisions by consensus and emphasized teamwork. Balance was aimed at the need for affiliation (nAff).

The three organizations produced very different results. Employees of British Radar ended up, in fact, more concerned with power, authority, and the formal relationships. At the end of the simulation, members of Balance were more relaxed and more concerned with affiliation and with their informal relationships. Blazer blazed. It proved to be a high-achieving organization, producing more radar machines, more innovation, and employees with a more competitive attitude. As researchers, we were pleased.

Thirty Years of Additional Field Experience

Much has happened in the past 30 years since *Motivation and Organizational Climate* hit the Harvard University Press best-seller's list.

- Research and theories of individual motivation have supplemented what we knew back then about what makes people tick. Studies of the three social motives, nAch, nPow, and nAff, have given way to broader motivational concepts. For example, Ed Deci's book, *Intrinsic Motivation* (1975), greatly expanded our insight into motivation in real work settings. Albert Bandura's *Social Foundations of Thought and Action* (1985) further clarified the motivational effects of goals and the relationship between motivation and self-efficacy. Most recently, Eccles and Nohria (*Beyond the Hype*, 1992) have attempted to capture and summarize the motivational literature and have proposed a theory of motivation that defines what makes us tick in terms of our search for "identity."

- Elaborate laboratory simulations of work environments have given way to a wide range of studies of real-world organizations. What these studies lack in research control they more than make up for in the scope of the variables that can be measured and evaluated. Perhaps the most memorable of the real-world studies was *In Search of Excellence* by Peters and Waterman (1982). Their bold generalities about company environments and performance caught many readers' attention. *In Search of Excellence* broke all nonfiction book sales records in the early 1980s. Ben Schneider's important book, *Organizational Climate and Culture* (1990), describes many of the early, more scholarly studies. His own consulting and research into the design of service organizations illustrates the power of applying research hypotheses to practical business problems. One of the best examples of an in-depth study of a complex organization attempting to change its culture and climate in order to improve performance is David Nadler's study of Xerox, *Prophets in the Dark: How Xerox Reinvented Itself and Drove Back the Japanese* (1992). Nadler concludes that the single biggest factor in Xerox's transformation was the personal leadership exhibited by David Kearns and his group of senior executives.

- The importance of studying the work environment as a determinant of organizational performance is no longer questioned as it was back in the 1960s. No one has demonstrated this more than Edgar H. Schein of MIT. Schein's writings (1980, 1985, 1990,

1992, and 1999) have not only clarified the relationship between the psychological environment and human behavior, but they also have pointed to the central role of leadership as a determinant of cultures in organizations. In 1992, John Kotter and James Heskett conducted a series of real-world research studies involving 207 companies that showed the dramatic relationship between corporate culture and performance (Kotter & Heskett, 1992). Today, discussion of organizational cultures dominates the business literature and culture has become a much more legitimate topic for study. If you search the Amazon.com Web site for the term *corporate culture* you can retrieve 892 separate titles. Linkage, a Massachusetts consulting firm, sponsors an annual conference on "Corporate Culture," and *Fortune* magazine identifies "The World's Most Admired Companies" in terms of their cultures.

Unfortunately, the climate concept has not been similarly exploited or leveraged—either in academic circles or in practice. Perhaps this is because *climate* seems somehow less complete or less profound a term than *culture*. Thanks to authorities such as Schein, organizational cultures are now understood to include the same variables as ethnic or national cultures, such as deeply held beliefs, shared values, unconscious assumptions, and group norms. Culture is a broad and obviously powerful concept. Unfortunately, although everyone knows it is important, nobody knows quite how to measure it or manage it. For most business leaders, it is simply too big to get their arms around. As Schein emphasizes in his latest book, *The Corporate Culture Survival Guide* (1999), the task of understanding corporate culture requires a highly trained observer/consultant. The concept of *climate*, at least the way we defined it in 1968 in terms of the characteristics of the environment that arouse motivation, is a much smaller phenomenon. As such, it is potentially more actionable—and, as this book will show, more manageable— and managing it well can yield significant bottom-line benefits.

One problem with our 1968 concept of organizational climate is that we presented it in academic language. We first described the concept in a research monograph, but we never followed up with our *Harvard Business Review* or *Sloan Management Review* article or our piece in *Fortune* or *The Wall Street Journal*. This book rectifies the situation by updating the research on climate and, more importantly, demonstrating its relevance to real-world management decisions. In doing so, I draw on my personal experience over the past 25 years, as an executive and consultant, to describe how to manage and manipulate organizational climates in order to increase bottom-line performance.

When *Motivation and Organizational Climate* was first published, I was on the staff of the Harvard Business School, writing and teaching in the Philippines. By 1970, I had tired of the routines and the ivory-tower isolation of academia, and I spent the next five years as an entrepreneur. I ran a number of real estate development companies (some of them very successful) and a ceramic technology venture (spectacularly unsuccessful). In 1975 I became a consultant, and for the past 25 years I have had the opportunity to work with many different *Fortune* 100 corporations, as well as a number of smaller firms. Although I walked away from the rigorous research and academic study of human motivation and organizational climates, I became immersed in the high-pressure world of corporate survival, executive egos, powerful emotions, and perform-at-any-cost work environments. On many occasions, I longed for the simplicity and sense of purpose of my Erector Set past. But I enjoyed the complexity, the uncertainty, as well as the pragmatism of business, although I lacked a theory to explain what I was experiencing.

It eventually became apparent to me why our study of climate was not viewed by businesspeople with the same enthusiasm as it was by academics. We had focused on defining and measuring the concept. Business leaders were more interested in *using* the concept. They wanted to know how to manage climate, not just how to measure it! Of course, as both an entrepreneur and a consultant, this made sense. Not surprisingly, my consulting practice has since focused on exactly this topic, and I have had to become an expert on leadership.

Leadership Counts

The "Business" sections of major bookstores today are crowded with titles mentioning leadership, most of them written since 1990. Business leaders are buying them and reading them (or, at least, they intend to read them). And a search under *leadership* at Amazon.com yields an astounding 8,864 titles! People who are interested in organizational performance know that leadership is important, and they read books about it to become better leaders. They are persuaded that leadership consists of learnable skills and practices rather than some sort of innate charisma. And although the concept of organizational climate sounds like the kind of abstraction that makes a pragmatic business leader's eyes glaze over, leadership is practical and real, and it has a more obviously direct impact on the bottom line. So I talk with my clients about leadership practices more often than climate or culture. Leadership practices are things my clients feel they can *do* something about. What they are doing through these practices, in many cases, is managing organizational climate.

Over the past 30 years I have shifted my focus to *improving* organizational performance rather than just *studying* it. I no longer emphasize the intricacies of what makes people tick and how to measure various kinds of work environments that arouse people's motivation. Instead, I emphasize how to change those work environments to make them more productive. My "laboratory" has changed from the classrooms at Harvard to the boardrooms at GE, PepsiCo, Xerox, ICI, Lion Nathan, and General Mills. I recently left Sherbrooke Associates, the consulting company where I have done much of my work, to join Mercer Delta Consulting (MDC), which offers me the chance to meld my thinking with longtime friend and collaborator, David Nadler, MDC's founder. As a consultant, I get paid more for my ideas than I ever did when I was teaching. Why? Because the tools I use help my clients get results that show up in the bottom line.

Organization of the Book

Part I answers the basic question, "What is organizational climate?" Chapter 1 explains why we used the term *climate* as a research concept back in 1968, and why it is even a more useful tool for leaders of today's organizations. *Climate* is a term that describes the way work environments influence people's motivated behavior and, therefore, their performance. In many ways the climate of an organization is like the weather. Some people are made lethargic by cloudy and rainy days, whereas others find them perfect for indoor sports. Many are energized by cool, sunny days, and so on. Like the weather, different climates have a profound impact on the people who experience them. Chapter 1 explains how climate differs from the culture of an organization. This is more than a matter of terminology or theory. We can change and manage organizational climates much more readily than cultures. This distinction makes climate a potentially more actionable tool for leaders who want to know how to influence the behavior of others.

Building on our definition of organizational climate, Chapter 2 reviews what we know about human motivation and how a person's surroundings at work affect his or her motivation. Of course, how much of a person's behavior is determined by immediate environment, by personal history, and by genetics will always be controversial. This chapter discusses the practical implications of this controversy, summarizes the most current research, and proposes a commonsense approach to motivation, based on the research and theories of John Atkinson of Michigan and David McClelland of Harvard, that leaders can use as one part of their performance management strategy.

Chapter 3 describes how we learned to measure climates. Because one of the most important distinctions between climate and culture is the relative ease and specificity with which climate can be measured, it's important to know how to do it. This chapter explains how we developed the climate survey questionnaire for research purposes, and how it has evolved into a tool for practicing managers. The predictive validity of the instrument is discussed as well as its limitations. Chapter 4 continues to explore the evolution of the climate survey as a management tool: how different aspects of climate affect people's motivation, behavior, and performance and how the survey results can be presented so that managers can understand and use them. In this respect, the climate survey functions as a cloud chamber. It actually shows managers what's happening in the work environment. Chapter 4 presents a climate model that has six measurable and actionable dimensions. This chapter also answers the frequently asked question, "Is there a perfect climate?" by illustrating the role each dimension plays in a high-performing organization.

Part II, which includes Chapters 5, 6, and 7, answers the question, "What causes climate?" Chapter 5 reviews the major determinants of climate, pointing out how external forces influence the internal climate. It explains how an organization's response to these forces can radically change how people feel, think, and behave. Chapter 5 also shows how different business strategies create different expectations and how the organization's formal systems change people's aroused motivation. Finally, it points out that one of the most important factors in determining the "weather" inside an organization is its history—the traditions, values, and norms that continue to drive performance.

Chapter 6 focuses on the single most important determinant of climate: the leadership practices of the managers of the organization. This chapter reviews what we've learned about leadership in the last 30 years and provides a practical framework for relating specific leadership practices to each of the six climate dimensions. Examples from both successful and less successful organizations illustrate how leadership impacts climate and how climate influences performance. For those looking for a short list of the most impactful leadership practices, Chapter 7 provides a "hit list" of six key things leaders can do to improve climate and performance. The list was developed from a remarkable regression analysis of climate and practices data and may dispel many of the currently popular myths about effective leadership.

Part III of the book focuses on the most critical issue facing leaders today: "How can we use climate?" Chapter 8 presents four case studies to show different ways we have used climate survey results to manage performance. Chapters 9 and 10 address difficulties associated with two unique kinds of organizations. Chapter 9, emphasizing how schools differ from business organizations, describes my work measuring the climate of two public high schools. The data from schools reveal serious problems lying beneath the surface in these institutions—problems that are manageable if school leadership is willing to address them. Chapter 10 deals with the climate management in health care organizations by discussing the unique challenge of leading health care professionals whose decisions and actions are often matters of life or death.

Chapter 11 discusses the future of the central concepts and themes in the book. Does the climate concept spill out of the organization? If so, are there ways to manage climates experienced by visitors to our organizations, even those who visit via the Internet? And what lies ahead for the practice of leadership? What are the issues, the opportunities, and the psychological demands involved in managing people now that we know how leadership really works?

Part IV, the final section of the book, is the Climate Management ToolKit. Survey questionnaires, climate feedback forms, and diagnostic support materials constitute the section. Guidelines for using each tool are carefully described.

A Cloud Chamber for the Impact of Leadership

Leadership and Organizational Climate illustrates why effective leaders have such a strong influence on the organizations they lead. Although the cause-and-effect relationship between leadership and performance is complicated and often confusing, it is much more understandable when described in terms of climate. This book in one sense moves *backward* from *Motivation and Organizational Climate* because it moves from affect to cause, from motivation to the leadership practices that arouse motivation. With its emphasis on manipulating climate to improve organizational performance, *Leadership and Organizational Climate* looks at the practical side of the climate concept.

Scientists use cloud chambers to identify and make visible the paths that particles take—paths that would otherwise be invisible. Armed with the knowledge gained by studying many cloud chambers, scientists can create more accurate hypotheses about how atomic particles interact, how the world works, and how to harness atomic power. By studying the "cloud chamber effect" of leadership, tracing the impact of leadership on the climates of organizations, we can develop more accurate models of leader–follower relationships and how to build more productive organizations.

Acknowledgments

While I assume total responsibility for the contents of this book, I would like to acknowledge the hard work of others that made it all possible. First, my brother, David. He was my sounding board, my ghostwriter, my editor, my conscience, and my brother. He read every word, wrote many of them, and generally kept me going. George Litwin inspired and helped crystallize my thinking, especially in Chapters 7 and 11. Cindy Simeone, my assistant at Harbridge House, Sherbrooke Associates, and Mercer Delta, prepared the entire manuscript and figured out how to display all the graphs and charts. Without her there would be no book. Finally, I owe my sanity and sense of perspective to my wife, Susie. I have not told her often enough how much her encouragement, emotional support, and patience mean to me. I would bet she's very happy to see this project completed—and can't wait for me to start the next one. This book is dedicated to her.

Boston, Massachusetts   R.A.S.
April 2001

Part I

What Is Organizational Climate?

It's intuitively obvious to anyone who has worked in an organization—and that includes most of us—that we have thoughts and feelings about where we work, and those thoughts and feelings impact how we work. What may not be so obvious is that the collection of these thoughts and feelings—the *climate* of the organization—can be measured and, thus, can be described in hard numerical form. And once measured, organizational climate can be managed in proactive and deliberate ways to improve performance.

The opening four chapters of *Leadership and Organizational Climate* introduce the concept of organizational climate as a way to describe the "internal weather" of an organization. Climate, in this case, is both objective and subjective in that it's an objectively measurable expression of people's subjective perceptions of their work environment. The assumption underlying the concept of organizational climate is that the way people feel about where they work has a powerful impact on how they work and how hard they work. Climate determines the performance of an organization.

Climate drives performance because it is tied directly to motivation, that is, to the energy people put into their work. The theory of motivation that best describes the arousal effects of the work environment points to three main sources of motive energy: the need for achievement, the need for affiliation, and the need for power. Research and experience confirm that these three needs are central to people's thoughts and feelings at work. We know that different organizational climates can arouse these different motives, and we can measure how they do it.

An extensive process of clinical research showed that the ways people describe their perceptions of their organization can be sorted into six climate dimensions:

- Structure
- Standards
- Responsibility
- Recognition
- Support
- Commitment

All of these can be measured using a climate survey. These dimensions have a clear relationship to the three kinds of motivation and give us a tool that combines research-based intellectual rigor with the pragmatic concerns of real-world organizations.

1

1

The Concept of
Organizational Climate

"What's wrong with this place?" Arthur Wilson stands in front of his faculty in the high school cafeteria. It's 3:30 on a Wednesday: time to begin the meeting. He surveys the room. A group is clustered around the coffeepot and cookies. Latecomers straggle in. Wilson is frustrated. These are bright and talented people with years of experience and a lot of success under their belts. Several have their Ph.D.'s, and—unfortunately, he feels—all but a few have tenure. But he has been unable to motivate them to deal with pressing issues that are his top priorities as principal. He does well with them face-to-face when he speaks with them in his office, and they seem to respond well to his formal evaluations of their teaching. But there is no mistaking what happens—and doesn't happen—throughout the large building when he is not around. The same small group of activists volunteer for committees and action teams, but the faculty at large is not moved. Griping and complaining have taken over the faculty lunchroom, and Dilbert cartoons now appear regularly on the bulletin board in the teachers' mailroom. Students are more frequently appearing in his office to complain about teachers who don't care, and parents complain about the lack of standards. When he obliges and transfers them to different sections of the same course, they complain that the curriculum is totally different depending on who the teacher is. And now people are coming late to meetings or skipping them altogether. The school has a good reputation, but Wilson senses that performance is eroding rapidly. "How can I energize these people?"

"This is the same old-same old!" Corinna Tyler is late for the faculty meeting—as usual. She hates these meetings because nothing ever seems to get accomplished. Many issues are proposed, debated, or shoved into committees for further study and discussion, and everything is left hanging. Which, come to think of it, is just fine with her. None of this stuff really matters anyway—at least, not as much as her classroom matters. Why can't the administration just let us teach? Some days she thinks that if it weren't for the cookies and a chance to sit and gossip with her friends, she would skip the meetings entirely. Tyler grabs a cookie and heads for a group of friends who are studying the agenda and encouraging each other to say nothing so the meeting will end sooner. She says to the group, "Why can't they just leave us alone?"

———

The school where Wilson and Tyler work suffers from a problem in its organizational climate. There is something about the work environment that Tyler and her colleagues consistently perceive, and these perceptions to a large extent determine their motivation and performance. That's the bad news. The good news is that the problem can be fixed—if it is analyzed properly and if the leader of the school, Wilson and his bosses on the Board of Education, address it systematically.

———

Origins of Climate

One of the first to study psychological climate was Kurt Lewin in the 1930s. As my colleague George Litwin and I reported in our *Motivation and Organizational Climate* (1968), Lewin, along with Lippit and White, examined climate as an "empirical reality" in an attempt to study the behavioral effects of three different leader-induced "atmospheres." One of their more surprising findings, as Litwin and I reported, was that "the climate itself proved more powerful than previously 'acquired' behavior tendencies, and it was able to change the observed behavior patterns of the group members" (p. 36). In other words, the climate, in this case created by different leadership styles, has a powerful impact on performance. What Wilson does—and does not do—to create the climate of the school can be more important to Tyler's performance as a teacher than what she has learned from all her previous experiences. Surprising but true, though there will be individual exceptions.

Another important finding of Lewin's work was more conceptual. Again, from my collaboration with Litwin: "In Lewin's theory of motivation, the concept of 'atmosphere' or 'climate' was *an essential functional link* between the person (P) and the environment (E)" (Litwin & Stringer, 1968, p. 37). This concept of the functional link evolved in the 1960s to our emphasis on subjective reality: "The realities of the organization are understood only as they are perceived by members of the organization, allowing the climate to be viewed as a filter through which objective phenomena must pass" (pp. 42–43).

The term *organizational climate* fully emerged in the 1960s. In his introductory essay, "The Concept of Organizational Climate," Renato Tagiuri points out, "the way an individual carries out a given task depends upon what kind of person he is, on the one hand, and the setting in which he acts, on the other" (Tagiuri & Litwin, 1968, p. 11).

The distinction between individual and setting, especially the setting within an organization such as a business, a hospital, or a school, is as important as it is problematic. The distinction is important to leaders of businesses and other organizations because, outside of selective firings and hirings, it is very difficult to change the individuals working within an organization. Moreover, even with those firings and hirings, the newly hired will find themselves working in a pervasive situation that will, to a large extent, arouse or squelch their motivation and, thus, "the way an individual carries out a given task." In other words, climate arouses motivation, and motivation determines performance, no matter who is shuffled into or out of the organization. In the next chapter I will explore the distinction between *motivation,* a general term that describes the network of a person's potential motive energy, and *aroused motivation*, the source of energy that drives behavior at any given point in time. I will also examine the precise ways that climate is linked to motivation and motivation to performance. But in the preceding example, even if Wilson could fire Tyler and people like her (he can't because of tenure laws and contractual language), and even if he could change the fundamental psychological motive profile of "difficult" staff members (he can't because of human nature), these changes might not be enough. He will need to change something in the setting in which his staff acts, or the new people will soon fall into "the same old-same old."

The problem, however, is that what is important about this setting—what gives it such a crucial importance in determining the motivation and, thus, the performance of people working within this organization—is *how that setting is perceived.* Tagiuri (Tagiuri & Litwin, 1968, p. 13) describes this problem in terms of "the distinction of objective and subjective environments," and he uses the term *organizational climate* to capture this elusive but very powerful concept. He says of organizational climate: "It is in the actor's or observer's head, though not necessarily in a conscious form, but it is based on characteristics of external reality" (p. 25). In other words, although the subjectivity of organizational climate suggests that it might be a product of feelings, past history, or genetics that the individual brings to the organization, it is in fact a response to actual characteristics of the organization itself.

How do we know this? We know it when we see a pattern of agreement about those perceptions. How do we know that the sun really appears in the morning and that it is not just a subjective delusion—a product of toilet training and ingested drugs? Philosophers tell us that if people agree then it is not simply an individual delusion, and if the event is predictable, then it is most likely an external event operating by its own mechanical laws. And even if we can't know with any certainty that an event is not a collective delusion with unusual regularity, it makes sense to act as if the event is real. The sun may be only an illusion, but it's best to put on sun block in the middle of the day. Pragmatically, it works.

Tagiuri (Tagiuri & Litwin, 1968) again: "It [organizational climate] is capable of being shared (as consensus) by several persons in the situation, and it is interpreted in terms of shared meanings (with some individual variation around a consensus)" (p. 25). Organizational climate exists simultaneously as a set of characteristics of the organization and as a set of insider perceptions of those characteristics. It describes the organization *as experienced* by its members, and this is what makes it such a powerful influence. At the same time, those perceptions of the organization are grounded in what the organization actually is and how it got to be that way. We will see that the most powerful determinants of this subjective organizational reality that we call climate are the day-to-day practices of the leaders of the organization. And this means that the perceptions and the consequent motivation and performance can be managed by changing leadership techniques.

Wilson does not have to fire Tyler, nor does he have to subject her to a personality transplant. What he needs to do is manage the climate of his organization. To do this, he needs to learn how to lead.

The Bridge

It is precisely this distinction between the individual in an organization and the organizational setting in which the individual operates that explains why George Litwin and I were drawn to the concept of organizational climate in 1968. During the 1950s and 1960s, scientists made significant advances in the systematic study of human motivation. Especially noteworthy was the work of psychologists David C. McClelland at Wesleyan University and later Harvard University, and John W. Atkinson at the University of Michigan. What is known as the McClelland–Atkinson formulation appealed to us because it is scientifically based and derived from a number of empirical studies, many of them experimental. In fact, now in the twenty-first century, more than 35 years after their original work, the body of confirming evidence has steadily mounted. It is useful, and it is good science. Chapter 2 presents our version of that motivational theory more fully.

That was the human motivation piece. Equally important were the developments in organizational theory going on at the same time, especially the work of Edgar H. Schein, whose *Organizational Psychology* (1965) remains a standard text in the field. We'll examine what came to be Schein's area of expertise, "organizational culture," later in this chapter. Schein and others were seeking to explain what happens in organizations in terms of properties or constructs of the organization itself. What is most significant to our work is that most organizational theorists, including Schein, examine this question objectively through their own expert eyes. They typically view the perceptions of individual members as an unreliable way to discover objective truths about the organization being studied.

Litwin and I, along with Tagiuri and others working with organizational climate in the late 1960s, saw in the concept a vital link between motivational theory and organizational theory. As we stated in 1968:

> The concept of climate provides a useful bridge between theories of individual motivation and behavior, on one hand, and organizational theories, on the other. Organizational climate, as defined here, refers to the perceived, subjective effects of the formal system, the informal "style" of managers, and other important environmental factors on the attitudes, beliefs, values, and motivation of people who work in a particular organization. (p. 5)

What many see as an epistemological problem, the relationship between objective reality and subjective experience, became the subject of our research. This same bridge, because it dynamically combines the power of subjectively experienced life with the stubbornness of objective reality, has become the tool we have used for 25 years to impact motivation and, thus, to manage performance.

The Weather of the Workplace

Tagiuri notes a number of words that have been used to identify the setting in which the individual acts, among them *environment, milieu, culture, atmosphere, situation, field, setting, behavior setting,* and *conditions.* He distinguishes organizational climate from a number of these terms that have subsequently fallen by the wayside. *Environment* is widely used as a natural science analogy for what surrounds an individual in an organization; however, it is too broad, too all encompassing, for what we have in mind. Instead, we choose to focus on a particular aspect of an environment—its climate—to describe the interface between the individual and the setting in which the individual acts. In order to have a concept that is useful, we need a tighter focus.

The word *climate* carries a rich, metaphorical power, at the same time lending itself to a more or less precise definition. We have experience with weather and climate on a daily basis, and we know that "it does something to us." We respond to a climate. We are probably less tuned in to our milieu or our behavior setting.

The subjective aspect of organizational climate makes it fitting that we use a term that carries connotations of personal emotional response. We know that hot, humid weather makes many people feel lethargic, and that a prevailing climate of such weather can impact the way people living there behave. Similarly, a prevailing climate of crisp, cool days can inspire an emotional response and, thus, behavior. It is often the case that our response to weather is indirect. That is, a storm will cause others to act differently and this (rather than the storm itself) will influence our own behavior. Although this kind of psychology is obviously simplistic, ignoring many other factors and encouraging a dangerous kind of stereotyping, it illustrates the analogy implicit in the term *organizational climate.* Tagiuri (Tagiuri & Litwin, 1968) simplifies when he says, "In meteorology climate is the average condition of the atmosphere (in a particular locality) . . . Climate is a convenient way of referring simultaneously to various atmospheric features and to a typical series of events" (p. 19). But this is not my main point. *Organizational climate* is a term that has worked for us for the past 25 years in a utilitarian way because of its connotative power—it makes sense to people.

Another problem with the climate analogy is that it is very difficult to change the weather, no matter how clever or charismatic our political and scientific leader may be (although our global warming may in fact reflect the quality of our world leadership). An organizational climate, however, is much more changeable. As Litwin and I wrote about organizational climates: "Climate conditions . . . are assumed to show properties of cyclical change, time decay, and fairly rapid temporary shifts (with return to base levels and basic cyclical patterns)" (Litwin & Stringer, 1968, p. 39). The analogy between the weather and organizational climate is quite strong, as both allow for variations and cycles while at the same time emphasizing underlying consistencies and patterns.

Definitions

We are now ready to move to a definition of organizational climate. Let's begin with the one that Tagiuri so carefully developed in 1968:

> Organizational climate is a relatively enduring quality of the internal environment of an organization that (a) is experienced by its members, (b) influences their behavior, and (c) can be described in terms of the values of a particular set of characteristics (or attributes) of the organization. (p. 27)

Here we see, first, that organizational climate is a "quality of the internal environment," *internal* meaning that it is within the boundaries of the organization. It is part of the organization itself. It is real. He moves from this objectification of climate to emphasize its subjective reality: It exists as it is perceived by the members of the organization. In other words, climate is part of the experiential reality of the organization's members. It is a perception. Without getting under the tree falling in the woods with nobody to hear it, we can define reality as a set of collective perceptions. This is a pragmatic definition. Whatever the epistemological status of organizational climate may be, we can know it only indirectly by means of the perceptions of the members of the organization. What is important in a pragmatic sense is that if we can measure these perceptions and understand how they relate to motivation, we can begin to manage them. And if we are smart, we can change those perceptions in a way that changes motivation and, thus, performance. This is more than sleight of hand, for those perceptions are perceptions of something—organizational climate—and that is what we change.

Tagiuri goes on to say that organizational climate "influences" the behavior of the members of an organization. Our research has taken this a step further. We see it as a **determinant.** But note that we do not say that it determines behavior, which would be a bold claim to make in freedom-loving America, but that it determines **aroused motivation.** We have ample evidence to back that claim from more than 25 years of successful work with clients in a variety of organizations. We will explore this in subsequent chapters of the book.

Tagiuri's definition of organizational climate places a great deal of importance on measurement. Although the characteristics of climate that we want to measure are part of the organization, we can only define them indirectly through the lens of the perceptions of the organization's members. This has at least three practical implications: (1) It is necessary and worthwhile to identify the specific characteristics that seem to impact people the most, so we can ask the right questions. (2) We must ask people about their perceptions in a way that doesn't influence those perceptions. We want to minimize distortions and bias. (3) We want to develop a definition of climate that works across organizations, so that we can compare climates and apply what we've learned in one organization to improve the motivation and performance in others.

Next, let us repeat our definition from *Motivation and Organizational Climate* (Litwin & Stringer, 1968):

> Organizational climate is a concept describing the subjective nature or quality of the organizational environment. Its properties can be perceived or experienced by members of the organization and reported by them in an appropriate questionnaire. (p. 187)

In 1968 we were still working on defining the most important dimensions or characteristics of the organizational environment, and we hadn't figured out the best approach to measuring climate. Since then I have focused more time and attention on uncovering the most critical aspects of the work environment—the elements of the clouds that have the greatest impact on people's aroused motivation. I have also tried to tackle the measurement issue. I have developed a climate survey that produces consistently replicable results in many different settings, is easy to administer, and generates data that allow us to predict organizational performance.

We can move finally to the definition of organizational climate that is central to the argument of this book:

> Organizational climate is the collection and pattern of the environmental determinants of aroused motivation.

The language here is mercifully brief. The focus on the environmental determinants of motivation is central to the definition and will be outlined more fully in Chapter 2. Subjectivity is still crucial to my use of the concept, although it does not explicitly appear in the definition. You will see how I make subjectivity a reliable basis for analyzing climate in Chapter 3, in which I discuss how we measure organizational climate through the use of surveys.

Climate Dimensions

Organizational climate exists objectively in the organization, but it can only be described and measured indirectly through the perceptions of the members of the organization. Over the years, we have found it useful to focus on climate as an "it," existing in the organization independent of the perceptions through which we know it. The tree falling in the woods does make a sound. Try this analogy: Even with nobody in the woods to actually hear the tree's falling, we can place tape recorders in the woods to "hear" the sound indirectly. The perceptions of people in an organization provide a similarly indirect medium by which we can measure the climate of that organization. And like the tape-recorded sounds, we can analyze the climate data we gather into a discrete number of meaningful dimensions. These are what Tagiuri (Tagiuri & Litwin, 1968) earlier called "a particular set of characteristics (or attributes) of the organization" (p. 25).

Common sense tells us that almost all aspects of the work environment will likely have some influence over how we act. The trick is to figure out which dimensions really count—which factors have the most impact on people's motivation and performance. Our original research, described more fully in Chapter 3, identified a number of characteristics of climate that seem to correlate with certain types of aroused motivation. More importantly, our consulting experience has shown that specific dimensions of climate have a predictable impact on motivated behavior and can be measured and managed by those accountable for organizational performance. We have found that climate can best be described and measured in terms of six distinct dimensions: **structure, standards, responsibility, recognition, support,** and **commitment.**

1. **Structure** reflects employees' sense of being well organized and of having a clear definition of their roles and responsibilities. Structure is high when people feel that everyone's job is well defined. It is low when they are con-

fused about who does what tasks and who has decision-making authority. Even in high-tech industries in which temporary or horizontal organizational arrangements predominate, a sense of appropriate structure has a large impact on people's aroused motivation and performance.

2. **Standards** measure the feeling of pressure to improve performance and the degree of pride employees have in doing a good job. High standards mean that people are always looking for ways to improve performance. Low standards reflect lower expectations for performance.

3. **Responsibility** reflects employees' feelings of "being their own boss" and not having to double-check decisions with others. A sense of high responsibility signifies that employees feel encouraged to solve problems on their own. Low responsibility indicates that risk taking and testing of new approaches tend to be discouraged.

4. **Recognition** indicates employees' feelings of being rewarded for a job well done. This is a measure of the emphasis placed on reward versus criticism and punishment. High-recognition climates are characterized by an appropriate balance of reward and criticism. Low recognition means that good work is inconsistently rewarded.

5. **Support** reflects the feeling of trust and mutual support that prevails within a work group. Support is high when employees feel that they are part of a well-functioning team and when they sense that they can get help (especially from the boss) if they need it. When support is low, employees feel isolated and alone. This dimension of climate has become increasingly important for today's e-business models in which resources are severely constrained and a premium is placed on teamwork.

6. **Commitment** reflects employees' sense of pride in belonging to the organization and their degree of commitment to the organization's goals. Strong feelings of commitment are associated with high levels of personal loyalty. Lower levels of commitment mean that employees feel apathetic toward the organization and its goals.

These six climate dimensions are what allow us, in our consulting practice, to get a handle on the otherwise vague concept of organizational climate. Wilson, as principal of the school, can improve the climate for teachers such as Tyler by improving the levels of support that employees feel, by setting and enforcing high professional standards, and by establishing a clearer sense of purpose and structure. Improving the climate means a lot more than providing cookies at meetings or removing Dilbert cartoons from the bulletin board in the teachers' mailroom.

The Determinants of Climate

But what, exactly, causes organizational climate? Ongoing research, confirmed by my experience in the field, has identified five major determinants of organizational climate. It's important to think of them in terms of which causes are under the direct or indirect control of an organization's leadership and which are outside of that control. This distinction will help leaders to focus their energies. At the same time, they need to be aware of the factors that cause the climate of their organization, even though they cannot control those factors.

The first three determinants that follow are *controllable;* the last two are not.

Leadership Practices

Most studies have shown that the single most important determinant of an organization's climate is the day-to-day behavior of the leaders of the organization. The manager of a work group has a powerful influence on the expectations of its members. Managers often control rewards, establish work rules and structures, enforce performance standards, and set the informal rules in the workplace. Often the quickest way to change the climate of the organization is to change the way the managers are managing.

Organizational Arrangements

The second most powerful determinant of climate is what we call organizational arrangements—the formal aspects of the organization including the design of tasks and jobs, the reward systems, the policies and procedures, and the physical location of the people in the organization. It is clear that these factors influence the tone of the workplace and that they create strong barriers or incentives to employee behavior. Formal organizational arrangements often determine the flow of information as well as perceptions of opportunities for advancement, and all of these affect climate.

Strategy

An organization's strategy can have a profound impact on its climate and can influence how employees feel about achievement opportunities, rewards, obstacles to success, and sources of satisfaction. If a corporation has chosen an aggressive, growth-oriented strategy, for example, and has successfully communicated this strategy to people, the organizational climate will, over time, begin to reflect the strategic priorities. Standards and responsibility would likely be high in this case. The absence of a clearly articulated strategy also has implications for the organization's climate. Often, low levels of structure and commitment are the measurable indicators of unclear strategic guidance from management.

External Environment

The external environment in which an organization competes often plays an important role in determining the organization's climate. Factors such as government regulation, economic conditions, competitive industry forces, and changing technology create pressure on organizations and their managers. All of these external forces manifest themselves in measurably different climate profiles. For example, the climate that characterizes a team of engineers working in a fiercely competitive high-technology industry will be markedly different from the climate of a similar team of engineers working in a conservative, semimonopolistic public utility in which technology is not changing.

Historical Forces

An organization's history has a strong impact on its climate. People's expectations regarding future rewards, punishments, and consequences are often a reflection of what they think occurred before. It is hard to develop a complete checklist of important historical forces, but our consulting experience has led us to focus on four that seem to be consistently relevant: (1) perceptions of how crises were handled, (2) traditions regarding rewards for performance (especially executive promotions or separations), (3) the organization's memory of past leaders and role models, and (4) the pattern of business investments (that is, the history of resource allocation).

These five variables, we have found, determine an organization's climate. We have also found, fortunately, that the most important of these are the day-to-day practices of the leaders of the organization. This is fortunate because, although it is impossible to change the external environment or the historical forces, and it is difficult and time consuming to change the strategy and modify all of the formal organizational arrangements, a leader can change his or her own leadership practices. Wilson cannot change the amount of funding that the school district receives from the state, and he cannot change his school's history. But he can work with the teachers and the school district's central administration to change organizational arrangements and strategy, and he certainly can change how he operates as a leader.

To summarize: Although climate is a largely subjective phenomenon, we know how to measure it accurately. We also know how climates are created. Of all the factors that determine climate, the most important are the practices of the leaders of the organization. Different climates arouse different kinds of motivation and stimulate different kinds of behavior. Thus, by changing how the organization is managed we can change the climate, and this will change the direction and persistence of people's energy and have a profound impact on the organization's performance.

Climate and Culture

The concept of organizational climate has often been confused with the term *organizational culture*. The two are very different. Culture emphasizes the unspoken assumptions that underlie an organization, whereas climate focuses on the more accessible perceptions of the organization, especially how they arouse motivation and, thus, impact performance.

The work of Edward Schein has been central to bringing the concept of culture to the main stage of organizational development. Schein, an anthropologist by training, has brought that perspective to his work with corporations. This is both a strength and a weakness.

The strength of Schein's work lies in the depth of his analysis. With an anthropologist's sensitivity and a scholar's thoroughness, he works through the multiple and complex layers of an organization's culture. He sees culture in terms of "shared basic assumptions" (1992, p. 12), distinguishing basic, underlying assumptions from espoused values, which he further distinguishes from the visible artifacts of the culture. It takes a knowing eye and a long period of time to decipher the artifacts—the organizational structures and processes—and to probe beneath the values espoused in strategies and mission statements, reaching down to the unconscious beliefs and feelings. At that level, with a lot of hard work, we find what Schein calls in two of his chapter titles, "Assumptions About Reality, Truth, Time, and Space," and equally profound, "Assumptions About Human Nature, Activity, and Relationships." Heavy stuff.

Schein goes on to point out the deeply conservative function of organizational culture. He sees it as rooted in the values and assumptions that the founders of an organization embed in their creation from the outset. The voice of an organization's founding father (rarely, founding mother, although this is changing—Martha Stewart, Inc., will bear her stamp long after she has passed from the scene) is never silent—no more than it is in our American culture today in arguments about gun control or free speech.

Schein (1992) is very explicit about this conservatism:

> All human systems attempt to maintain equilibrium and to maximize their autonomy vis-à-vis their environment. Coping, growth, and survival all involve maintaining the integrity of the system in the face of a changing environment that is constantly causing various kinds of disequilibriums. The function of cognitive structures such as concepts, beliefs, attitudes, values, and assumptions is to organize the mass of environmental stimuli, to make sense of them, and to provide, thereby, a sense of predictability and meaning to the individual. The set of shared assumptions that develop over time in groups and organizations serves this stabilizing and meaning-providing function. The evolution of culture is therefore one of the ways in which a group or organization preserves its integrity and autonomy, differentiates itself from the environment and other groups, and provides itself an identity. (p. 298)

An organization's culture, then, is conservative by nature. Conserve is what a culture does.

One of the implications of Schein's insights is, unsurprisingly, that cultural change is slow and difficult. Schein (1992) invites us to see culture as "in part a learned defense mechanism to avoid uncertainty and anxiety," both of which are inevitable consequences of change (p. 307). Without disagreement, he cites the conclusion of J. W. Lorsch (1985) that the companies described in "Strategic Myopia: Culture as an Invisible Barrier to Change" took 10 to 15 years to accomplish cultural change. That's too long a time for organizations that need to change quickly to adapt to rapidly changing business and social conditions.

It is hard to disagree with Schein's thorough analysis. Yes, organizational culture is deeply complex, and so change seems discouragingly slow. As pragmatists, we look at the problem from a different angle. The point is not to change culture; it is to change performance. More specifically, the point is to focus on those aspects of culture that most directly impact the kinds of performance we want to improve. We can do this by working with climate, a more tightly focused set of variables within the messy reality of culture. We know from established research and from more than 25 years of experience that organizational climate is manageable and, thus, changeable. We know how to do it. The right kind of organizational climate can lift performance in the way that a sunny spring day can lift our energy level and motivate us to plant a garden.

We have found it useful to divide corporate culture into five components: **values, beliefs, myths, traditions,** and **norms.**

Values are the ways in which employees evaluate or assess certain traits, qualities, activities, or behaviors as good or bad, productive or wasteful. A high level of customer service, for example, is a core value of organizations such as Nordstrom's or Dell Computer. This value might be reflected in such aspects as the company motto, measurement systems that focus on response time and reliability, the proportion and seniority of the staff who are available to respond to customer questions and complaints, and the frequency with which senior executives comment on quality service.

Beliefs, although frequently unstated, reflect people's understanding of the way the organization works and the probable consequences of the actions they take. For example, in some organizations people champion new-product ideas in the belief that innovation is the way to get ahead. In other organizations, people emphasize quantitative analysis in the belief that controlling risk is the way to get ahead. These generally held beliefs are rarely based on a clear statement of values; more often, they are based on recognition of patterns in the career paths taken by successful and unsuccessful executives over the years.

Myths are the stories or legends that persist about an organization and its leaders, reinforcing the core values or beliefs. For example, in McKinsey, the international consulting firm, myths surround "close calls" in making travel connections. These myths symbolize the emphasis on spending the most possible time with clients and minimizing time wasted in transit. Such stories are not pieces of trivial information; they are part of a body of clues or signals that transmit the culture to new members of the organization and reinforce that culture for existing members.

Traditions are repetitive significant events in an organization, including such rituals as welcoming luncheons, promotion celebrations, special awards, retirement parties, and twenty-fifth anniversary dinners. These events inject a predictability into the organizational environment and are a basic means of perpetuating cultural values, whether they honor tenure, advancement, or a special accomplishment that is held in high esteem by the organization.

Norms are the informal rules that exist in organizations regarding dress, work habits, work hours, and implicit codes of interpersonal behavior. For example, at Cisco Systems, the senior executives answer their own telephones; at IBM, all phone calls are screened by secretaries. Cisco is known for its open-door policy and for the openness of communications among levels of management. At Sherbrooke Associates, the consulting firm I used to own, it was expected that all business travel be done either before or after business hours. This rule of conduct was not written down in any employee handbook or policy guide, but it was generally accepted as representing "the way things are done around here."

Exhibit 1.1 summarizes the way organizational climate and corporate culture fit into the organizational performance model used in this book. The problem is that culture is too big to be managed in the normal sense. There are too many variables, too many things to pay attention to. As one manager at Colgate-Palmolive expressed it: "It's like punching a pillow. . . . You exert a lot of energy, but the results are so transitory. Nothing seems to really change, and you never know what to do next" (personal interview, 1992). The behavioral consequences of organizational culture are more tangible and observable than the culture itself. As a result, executives who are trying to change the direction of an organization—and know that they need to change the behavior of managers—will be frustrated and discouraged if they focus too much attention on modifying or creating new values, beliefs, norms, and so on. What is required is a more manageable task but one that still affects all of the important cultural variables.

Measuring the Unmeasurable

In contrast to culture, the broadest and least tangible organizational influence on managerial behavior, organizational climate offers a more clearly definable and measurable vehicle for assessing and changing behavior in the workplace. The act of measuring it makes it

Exhibit 1.1
An Organizational Performance Model

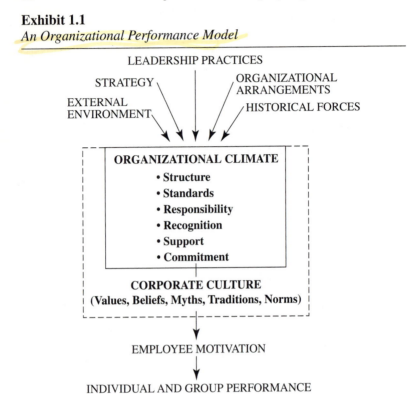

more real, more tangible, and, therefore, more manageable. We have developed an easy-to-complete questionnaire that measures the current state of the organization's climate. Think of it as a kind of "organizational cloud chamber." Analysis of climate survey results creates a climate profile based on the relative strength of each of the six climate dimensions. Climate profiles allow a company to size up its overall climate as well as the climates of various departments or divisions. The survey gives the company a language for managing the corporate culture. Climate, again, is more manageable than culture. Therefore, one way to change corporate culture is to focus on changing organizational climate.

For any of this to work, we need to peer into the engine that makes organizations run: motivation. Motivation is the fundamental energy to do something. People who lead organizations must bend the motivation of its members in the direction that serves the organization's needs. It does so, ironically, by catering to the needs of individuals. Chapter 2 explains how this works in our theory of motivation.

2

Motivation: "What Makes People Tick?"

"What's gotten into her?" Ed Chang stared at the door of his office. His protégé, Julie Goode, had just gone out the door, and Chang was totally confused and frustrated. He had promoted her to the position of lead researcher because she had been the "star" of a number of the organization's research teams—a bright young woman whose energy seemed to bring out the best in everyone around her. People loved her—colleagues and supervisors alike. But now that she had been given more responsibility, including her own office and a set of performance incentives that would allow her to shine in comparison with others at her level, she seemed to be lost. Her energy simply was not there any more. Work was piling up on her desk, and she seemed to be spending more time talking to people rather than getting her work done.

"What's going on here?" Chang wondered. "What's motivating her?"

The Human Mystery

Everyone wants to be an expert on human motivation:

- Why does my wife seem so unhappy? What does she want? Why can't I see it?
- Why is our teenage son sulking in his room with his headphones on instead of studying?
- How can you motivate that cute little three-year-old who refuses to be potty trained?

- What can I do to earn the praise of my boss? Why do I want that praise so badly?

- How can I motivate my research team to collaborate on a project that's important—to me, anyway? And why don't they see it as important?

- What will be the next trend in business-to-consumer e-commerce?

- How can I motivate my mother to express love for me? Why do I want it so badly?

- How can I motivate the members of my staff to think more creatively and independently?

In both the family and work arena, trying to understand what moves people to action—to specific types of actions—has long been an obsession. We spend a lot of time wondering what makes people tick—during quiet moments of solitary reflection ("Why does he keep *doing* this?"), in gossip sessions at lunch ("What's up with her?"), in late night discussions ("Is he *trying* to flunk out of high school?"), and in personnel evaluation meetings in businesses and organizations ("Does he have what it takes to be a contributor here?").

Efforts to solve the puzzle of motivation are the core of what happens in the offices of psychoanalysts, marriage counselors, high school guidance counselors, and successful executives. Sometimes the subject matter is not just the motivation of *other* people but our *own* motivation as well ("Why do I keep doing this?" "What do I really want?" "How do I feel about what I am doing?"). *Time Magazine* estimates that 30% of all Americans will see a shrink before they're 50 years old. Personnel managers cite employee motivation as their most vexing people problem. Federal and state governments spend hundreds of millions of dollars a year on programs to motivate schoolchildren to learn. Retaining talent, which is a serious problem for an increasing number of companies in the United States, usually comes down to understanding what *really* motivates people. And books about motivation often dominate the *New York Times* nonfiction best-seller list.

Unraveling the mysteries of human motivation is important not only to the individual but also to those who are accountable for the collective actions of individuals in organizations. In fact, the success of organizations—whether they are businesses, schools, government agencies, or hospitals, and however that success might be measured—frequently comes down to *how well that organization understands and manages the motivation of its members.* Our most well-educated leaders of organizations now know this, but they didn't always. Each class of the Harvard Business School (HBS) has a reunion every five years. When queried about the HBS course thought to be most valuable, members of the five-year and ten-year reunion classes typically name finance or marketing. At the twenty-fifth reunion, this perspective changes dramatically. The most valuable course after 25 years of experience is judged to be human behavior.

More and more companies, especially in the information age, cite human capital as their most important resource. When General Electric (GE) trumpets, "People are our most important product," the "people" it refers to are not just consumers—they are the people working within the GE organization. Many of America's highest-performing business leaders, including Jack Welch, Bill Gates, Andrew Grove, Scott McNealy, and Lou Gerstner, know that motivation is the most important mystery for leaders to solve. Andy Grove, for example, devotes most of his book, *High Output Management,* to the dilemmas and challenges of managing human motivation.

But the answer to the question of what makes people tick remains elusive and mysterious. Richard Alexander in *Darwinism and Human Affairs* theorizes that we have evolved to make it this way for a reason. For thousands of years we needed to keep our motives a secret in order to protect ourselves from our competitors— both those outside of our social group and those within our group against whom we compete genetically. We have evolved to do just that. It's a familiar negotiation strategy: If you reveal your deepest motives, you will be revealing your weaknesses. This competitive situation has created an elaborate dance marked by increasingly sophisticated mechanisms of disguise in order to keep our motives hidden. Because of the depth of this cat-and-mouse game, our true motives are often unknown, even to ourselves.

In today's society, the situation has changed. Successful competition relies on successful cooperation within increasingly complex organizations. In order for this cooperation to occur, for people to work together toward a common goal, we need to know how to tap into their productive energy. We need to know how to motivate them. Chang needs to know how to get the best out of Goode's talent and turn her energy back on again.

This is exactly what makes human motivation so fascinating and so important. We want and need to know, in order to meet our own personal needs and desires as well as the goals of the organization, "what really does make people tick."

Most people view motivation as energetic behavior toward some goal. Under the surface lies a feeling of need, want, or desire. When people feel a *lack* of something they do not have, this feeling leads them to *act* in ways that will *satisfy* the feeling.

In business and other organizations, the term *motivation* usually has a narrower meaning. Employees are said to be motivated if they show the energetic behavior desired by management; otherwise, they are unmotivated. Typically the most common tool that management used to generate the desired behavior was money, and if employees do what the boss expects, the boss pays. A lack of financial incentives, however, is not the reason for Goode's lack of energy and success in her new job.

If motivation were as simple as the preceding discussion suggests, the mechanics of motivation would work easily—we would all be experts, problems would disappear, and the topic would cease to be interesting. But because human motivation remains complex and mysterious, expertise is elusive.

Historical Perspective

This curiosity about human motivation has prompted a rich history of literature on the subject. It has fascinated us with good reason, for motivation gets at the core of who we are and how we lead others. We have literary works that function as case studies of individuals whose motivation the authors probe and reveal. We have religious writing that evaluates human motivation and its results. We have psychological research that poses theories about human motivation. And we also have philosophical writings that speculate about human nature.

Many of Shakespeare's characters, especially the tragic heroes, grip us today because of our fascination with their motivation, especially as they seek to manipulate (or "manage") other people or are manipulated by them. Consider Hamlet, stalled in enacting the revenge he has sworn to fulfill, deeply puzzled about his own motivation (or lack of it) and bent on manipulating King Claudius into revealing his role in the murder. Macbeth is skillfully led by his power-hungry wife, just as the evil Iago twists the virtuous Othello into murdering his innocent wife. These plays, like much Renaissance writing after Machiavelli, focus on the dynamics of power and the lengths people will go to in order to fulfill their power motives.

Centuries earlier, Plato formulated a theory of motivation based on the split between the body and the soul. While the soul, aroused by philosophy, yearns for the good, the body, aroused by the senses, is forever dragging us into temptation and error. His management solution is a rather totalitarian republic led by a philosopher king. It features eugenics, censorship, education, and a highly selective caste system designed to protect us from our baser half and achieve twin goals of justice and order. Although Plato's vision may seem chilling, at its core is his view of human motivation and the importance of managing it.

Christianity underscores this struggle between our divine and our devilish selves with a system of ethics that rewards unselfish virtues (charity, love, forgiveness, patience) with the kingdom of heaven. In doing this, Christianity, like Buddhism and Hinduism, creates a difficult agenda: to supplant an essentially selfish system with an essentially selfless one. We may be motivated by *this,* but we should be motivated by *that.* The essence of Christian ethics is an assumption about the value and centrality of social motivation, with particular emphasis on people's need for love and affiliation. The unselfish virtues noted previously all serve to motivate people into a closer relationship with one another.

Psychologists in the nineteenth and twentieth centuries continue our fascination with motivation by applying the methods of science to the problem. The attempt is to generalize about human nature in a systematic way based on careful research. Freud, most notably, saw many of our motivations as unconscious—acknowledging their essentially hidden and mysterious quality. Furthermore, he argued that they are frequently a result of unremembered childhood experiences. B. F. Skinner, working in another direction, argued that our behavior is motivated not by our unconscious dynamics but by our conditioned responses to stimuli from our external environment. We want to do something, he says, because we have been trained to want it. Behaviorists argue that we can ignore Freud's unconscious motivations and simply shape the behavior of individuals or groups by properly arranging the way behavior is reinforced. Little wonder that most leaders can recall and apply Skinner's principles of positive or negative reinforcement—think of the almost universal use of grades in school and financial incentives in business. And little wonder that so few leaders turn to Freud, whose theories of motivation do not offer useful leverage points for managing people in organizations.

Our approach to leadership and organizational climate combines the directness of Skinner's behaviorism with Freud's complex truth that the sources of people's actions often lie beneath the surface.

I believe that the ultimate truth about human motivation is, finally, unsolvable, although we may approach it much the way we approach a limit in quantum physics or a calculus problem. More important than which view is true is which theory we can apply to get the results we want. This is not Plato's philosophy and it's not Freud's theory. It's American pragmatism that asks, "What works?"

A Workable Framework

I know what works. At least I know what works for me and what has worked for my clients.

My colleagues and I have studied the topic of human motivation for the past 40 years, including the recent research. The framework proposed and validated by the late David McClelland of Harvard and John Atkinson at Michigan continues to make the most sense to me. I acknowledge that absolute facts about the human psyche, including what makes people tick, are wonderfully elusive. But the McClelland–Atkinson approach was based on extensive research and has been overwhelmingly confirmed both by common sense and real-world experience. Their approach is *coherent*—it holds together. To make an analogy: A carpenter may understand the mysteries inherent in quantum mechanics, the uncertainty principle, and chaos theory, but this does not stop him from measuring, cutting, and nailing accurately enough to build a solid house. This is workable. The trick is to be sensitive to the complexities of human motivation without simply throwing up your hands in despair and saying, "It's a mystery."

I think I've built that house. For the past 27 years as a consultant I have been applying the McClelland–Atkinson approach to human motivation, and it has yielded *results* for the executives and organizations that have been my clients. These include large American and international corporations, hospitals, and schools. This approach works because people intuitively grasp it. Not only can they understand the theory but they also can easily apply the theory to their everyday relationships. And they can use it to understand and manage the motivation of larger groups of people by means of the concept of organizational climate.

Let me cite an actual example. Greg managed a regional sales force that sold off-the-shelf training programs to hospitals. Because his region was underperforming, I was asked to work with Greg to see how we could increase sales. After observing how he managed his sales team (made up mostly of young, aggressive women), I suggested that he drastically change his leadership techniques and style. Instead of emphasizing teamwork, social rewards, and group incentives, we shifted to an approach that stressed individual goal setting, rigorous measurement of performance, and high personal responsibility. Greg had been using the former strategy because it was consistent with what his hospital customers expected. (In a moment, we will label this an affiliative approach.) Our new strategy worked better because it was consistent with the actual motivational needs of his sales force. (This will be called an achievement approach.) The performance of Greg's region improved dramatically after only three months. Two salespeople (who complained about the lack of team spirit) left, but the others were revitalized and energized to sell more training programs than they had ever sold before. All it took was a basic understanding of the psychological profile of his sales force and the skill to modify his leadership practices so that the proper motivational environment was established in the region. Greg figured this out in less than a month.

In commonsense terms, here are the basic principles of the McClelland–Atkinson approach to motivation:

1. All adults have certain basic motives, needs, or energy sources that provide a reservoir of potential energy.
2. Whether or not this potential energy is actualized or finds its way into useful work or behavior depends on the specific situations in which a person finds himself or herself.
3. Certain characteristics of each situation "cue off" or arouse different motives or energy sources.
4. By changing the nature of the person's environment, different kinds of motivation can be stimulated; this is because different cues arouse different motives, needs, or energy sources.
5. Because each kind of motivation is directed at the satisfaction of a different kind of need, the direction and persistence of human behavior change with the change in motivation.

In other words, all adults carry around with them the *potential* energy to behave in a variety of ways. Whether or not they do behave in these ways depends on (1) the kinds of motives or needs a person has and (2) the characteristics or opportunities presented by the environment. It is the environment—or climate as we call it—that determines which motives will be aroused and which needs can be most readily satisfied.

What exactly is it in the environment or climate that arouses a person's motivation? McClelland, Atkinson, and their colleagues (including myself) conducted years of experiments to pinpoint the environmental determinants of aroused motivation. In the end, they developed a formula to explain what makes people tick:

Aroused Motivation $= M \times E \times I$

where M is the strength of the motive or need, E is the expectancy of attaining the goal, and I is the perceived incentive value of that particular goal.

People will invest energy if they have a need (M) and they think that by doing something they have a chance (E) of reaching a goal they desire (I). If the basic need (or strength of the motive) is low, there won't be much aroused motivation. If you don't think that an activity gives you a decent chance to get to a goal, there won't be a lot of motivation to engage in that activity. And if you don't value the goal itself, then there won't be as much energy invested in the task of reaching it. If the motive (M) is strong and the environmental conditions (E and I) are right, you have a formula for high levels of aroused motivation. Stand back and watch the work get done!

These principles and this formula oversimplify things. But, without some simplification, the complexity of human motivation can be overwhelming.

In our simplified model of motivation, we understand and accept the fact that people have hundreds, perhaps thousands, of needs, wants, or motives. They want or desire lots of things. There are "positive" wants that people strive for, such as wanting to eat, to be liked, or to be praised. And there are "negative" wants that people wish would go away, such as wanting a headache to end or wanting to avoid failing at some task.

As it turns out, although the two kinds of wants may be equally strong in people, it's the positive wants that are the key to effective leadership. Positive motivation, by definition, involves people striving to attain a positive outcome or goal. Leaders who learn how to arouse and engage positive motivation can confidently predict the persistence and direction of people's behavior once they understand the goal that is being sought. Negative motivation is quite different. It involves avoiding something, not attaining something (other than relief from what one wants to avoid). When leaders focus on negative motivation, they are attempting to influence behavior by manipulating what people want to avoid. The persistence and direction of behavior are often impossible to predict or control because, when the goal is to avoid something, there are usually numerous avenues available to a person to do this.

Leadership strategies that rely on negative motivation are inherently unproductive. Positive incentives are always better motivational tools than negative punishments. A person can avoid punishment by doing what the leader wants or by doing something totally different. For example, when companies keep strict track of the hours employees work and punish those who arrive late, they assume that the threat of punishment for tardiness will lead to higher levels of productive work. But employees can avoid the penalties by simply "showing up." And showing up does not always translate into productive work. How many times have we tried to construct punishment programs for our sons and daughters in order to motivate them to behave the way we want, only to discover how creative they are in avoiding the punishments *and* misbehaving?

Intrinsic Motivation

Many wants are not material in nature. In other words, they are not aimed at getting something such as money but are intrinsic, that is, satisfied by engaging in certain kinds of activities. For example, exploring new territory or doing original research might satisfy a person's curiosity. Solving a difficult problem or completing a difficult task might satisfy another's need to accomplish things and take pride in doing so. Here the external or material rewards are not important; the activity generates inner or intrinsic satisfaction. Thus, the behavior can be rewarding in itself.

This idea of intrinsic motivation is at the core of the McClelland–Atkinson model. It can be validated by personal experience and common sense. Think of the things you do that bring no material reward and may, in fact, count against such rewards. Think of the time spent lingering with colleagues at lunch when you could be doing the kind of work that earns raises and promotions. Or the way you take a "back road" off the expressway, just to see what the countryside is like, even though it may make you late for an appointment. Or think of the time you spend figuring out how to perform some minor operation on your computer that is unrelated to any productive work for which you will be rewarded but which you just want to figure out how to do. Or the time you volunteer to captain your department's softball team and how long you spend working out the positions and batting order. Activities such as these are driven by powerful forces of intrinsic motivation.

Contrary to the extrinsic motivational systems currently used in schools (where grades are presented as deferred income) and the workplace (work for money), research shows intrinsic motivation to be a much more powerful motivator. The work of Herzberg and Myers in the 1960s demonstrated that material and object-centered extrinsic wants serve mainly as dissatisfiers. That is, they lead to dissatisfaction and frustration if *not* met, but they do not account for very much variation in performance levels. A person who does not get a raise will be frustrated, but a raise—or even the prospect of a raise—will not have much impact on performance. More recently, Ed Deci (1995) in *Why We Do What We Do* takes the matter a step further. His research shows that extrinsic rewards actually *discourage* performance, and he argues persuasively for greater reliance on intrinsic motivation.

If the source of a person's satisfaction is "inside" the person and comes from engaging in an activity rather than being "outside" (getting something material for doing the activity), how can we accurately see what motivates the person? How do we know what makes the person tick, what is driving the person to action? It's so much easier to analyze and manage extrinsic motivation. We manipulate the material rewards—the things that are "outside" of the person—and we watch people energetically striving to get those rewards. But how can we *understand* intrinsic motives or needs, and how can we *use* this understanding to manage the energy investments people make in their activities?

The Intrinsic Motives of Achievement, Affiliation, and Power

The McClelland–Atkinson framework and my consulting work based on that framework focus on three intrinsic motives that are important determinants of work-related behavior. They are the *need for achievement* (nAch), the *need for power* (nPow), and the *need for affiliation* (nAff). These three broad categories of positive, intrinsic wants are associated with feelings of satisfaction derived from particular kinds of activities. Lunchtime conversation with close friends makes you feel satisfied by being connected to others. Solving that computer problem is very satisfying because it was a difficult task and you were able to do it. Taking charge of other people makes you feel satisfied by demonstrating your influence over others. Because not everyone feels the same sense of satisfaction from these three activities, not everyone is motivated to chitchat at lunch, solve computer problems, or boss others around. These three intrinsic motives are certainly not the only ones that need to be managed by successful leaders, but they are the most important.

Need for Achievement

People with a high need for achievement are easy to spot. They are competitive. They always seem to be working toward an achievement goal. Not only do they think and talk about winning, but they also focus on *how* to win. These people seek out and enjoy jobs that are entrepreneurial in character, for example, businesspeople in start-up companies, in sales positions, or in jobs where they are their own boss. We used to call them "go-getters." What makes the high achiever tick? What kinds of activities allow high achievers to feel really satisfied? What turns them on?

1. *High achievers try to outperform someone else.* They thrive on situations in which they can prove themselves by doing better than others do. Winning makes them feel good. They get satisfaction from succeeding at a task or a contest that others can't do. High achievers are very competitive people.

2. *High achievers try to meet or surpass a self-imposed standard of excellence.* Often this standard does *not* involve competition with others. It is a personal sense of what is high-quality performance. It is an internal standard of excellence. Situations in which goals or standards are imposed on high achievers may or may not stimulate their nAch. Achieving a prescribed sales quota, for example, will be satisfying to them only if they internalized the quota as a moderately risky and challenging standard of excellence. (See later for more about calculated risk taking.)

3. *High achievers like situations in which they can take personal responsibility for their actions and the results of their actions.* That way, they have only themselves to blame—

and only they can take the credit. That's a turn-on to the high achiever. High nAch people are not gamblers—they do not want the outcome of their actions to depend on luck or on factors beyond their control. They are especially satisfied, not just by winning, but by winning through their own efforts. High achievers do not always perform well as part of a team. They often are loners. Team success satisfies the achievement motive when individual contributions can be clearly identified.

4. *High achievers are calculated risk takers.* A degree of difficulty is necessary if the situation is going to arouse the achievement motive. If the task is too easy, high achievers won't feel a sense of accomplishment. If it is too difficult, they will attribute success to luck or good fortune. Moderate risk simultaneously maximizes the expectancy of success ("I can do this if I really try!") with the incentive value of accomplishing the task ("Doing this will be an important test of my competence and my ability to accomplish something!").

A classic experiment demonstrates this aspect of nAch. A child is told that she scores when she succeeds in throwing a ring over a peg on the floor and that she can choose to stand anywhere she pleases to toss the ring. Obviously, if she stands next to the peg she can score a ringer every time, but if she stands a long distance away, she will hardly ever get one. The curious fact is that children with a high need for achievement quite consistently stand at moderate distances from the peg, for this is where they are most apt to get achievement satisfaction. They prefer a situation in which there is a challenge, with some real risk of not succeeding, but in which that risk is not so great that they might not overcome it with their own efforts. (In experiments, this turns out to be situations in which the high achiever feels there is a 50-50 chance of succeeding.) What is true for children is, of course, true for adults with high nAch. The goals and risks need to be calibrated so that personal satisfaction of the need to achieve can be met.

So don't waste too much time feeling sorry for the entrepreneur who constantly complains that he is overworked. His high need for achievement suggests that he loves the challenges he complains about—in fact, he probably creates most of them for himself. Feeling stressed and overextended is precisely the way he wants to feel because overcoming difficulties maximizes his achievement satisfaction. His real problem is to keep the challenges from getting too big and beyond his ability to manage or too small and, thus, not worth testing himself against.

5. *High achievers seek to make a unique contribution.* They want to be involved in accomplishing more than an ordinary task. They are attracted to jobs and situations in which they can apply unique methods or approaches to doing the work. They are innovators. Not surprisingly, McClelland found that Nobel prize winners were extraordinarily high in nAch.

6. *High achievers set long-term goals and develop plans to overcome personal and environmental obstacles to achievement.* High achievers carefully plan for the future by trying to anticipate any barriers to achievement of their goals. This makes goal accomplishment more satisfying for them. It also enables them to be successful where others (not as high in nAch) may fail because they have developed better plans and have thought through their actions more thoroughly than others.

7. *High achievers thrive on concrete feedback.* High achievers always want to know how they're doing. Sales figures, production figures, profit figures, grades, objective measures of performance—any of these will suffice. The business world typically supplies this kind of feedback in abundance. Many professions, such as law, education, or medical research, do not supply this kind of constant, specific, concrete feedback. Not surprisingly, these professions do not attract the number of high achievers that business does.

Need for Affiliation

High affiliators are going to be your best friends. People who spend their time thinking about developing warm, friendly relationships are high in need for affiliation. These people focus on restoring relationships that have been disrupted, consoling or helping someone, or participating in bull sessions, reunions, and parties. We used to call them "people persons." What makes these folks tick? What situations arouse nAff and provide high affiliators with the greatest sense of satisfaction?

1. *High affiliators strive to be part of a group or team.* They seek out situations that allow them to be with others. They will often sacrifice their own needs for the good of the team, and they enjoy the relationships and companionship that group activities can bring.

2. *High affiliators gain their greatest satisfaction from being liked and accepted.* People with high need for affiliation are joiners. They think about, care about, and act to establish, restore, or maintain a close, warm, and friendly relationship with other people. Because of their nAff, they tend to pay more attention to the feelings of others. In meetings they try to establish close relationships, often by agreeing or giving emotional support.

   I can remember a staff meeting I once facilitated for a Pepsi-Cola division president who was very high in nAff. It was in my opinion a total disaster, a waste of time. Nothing was accomplished. The team danced around a number of issues, came to no conclusions, made no decisions, and failed to confront or resolve any of the pressing matters the meeting was called to address. As the hired gun consultant, I felt terrible. I had let my client, the division president, down. Silly me. After the meeting, he thanked me for a job well done. He praised me for supporting various members of his team, even though (I thought) we were going around in circles. I still remember his most sincere complement: "You were able to guide us through all of the negative feelings without losing anyone." That's a high affiliator speaking.

3. *High affiliators seek to maintain positive interpersonal relationships.* They are walking case studies of separation anxiety. They hate to be by themselves and they fear rejection. High affiliators will engage in even the most competitive of activities if doing so will bring them closer to the people they want to be with. The most attractive job situations for high affiliators are those with opportunities for friendly interactions, for example, grade school teachers, nurses, counselors, or staff positions in business where maintaining relationships is valued. They are true team players because maintaining their membership on the team is the source of their greatest motivational satisfaction.

It is interesting to note that students with high needs for affiliation will perform better in the classroom when the teacher provides affiliative rewards. Teachers who simply ask high nAff students to "help out" by doing well on a test will motivate these students. Teachers who create an atmosphere or climate that stresses warmth, friendliness, and a relaxed approach to learning, therefore, may get more out of high affiliators than high achievers.

4. *High affiliators hate conflict and avoid conflict situations.* High affiliators gain tremendous satisfaction from positive interpersonal relationships, so they will do almost anything to maintain the positive and eliminate the negative. Conflict is anathema to nAff. It is to be avoided, denied, suppressed, smoothed over, and ignored. Affiliators are quite sensitive to the feelings of others. They know all about conflict, but their need for affiliation does not drive them to confront or actively manage conflict—it drives them away from it. Affiliators are what I call "master smoothers" when it comes to conflict.

It once was thought that the need for affiliation was unrelated to effective leadership and managerial performance and might even be a detriment. Recent work by Goleman (*Emotional Intelligence*), Katzenback (*The Wisdom of Teams*), and Nadler and Spencer (*Executive Teams*) has emphasized the importance of leaders who are natural team players and especially sensitive to the needs and feelings of others. In many organizational situations the need for affiliation provides a valuable reservoir of motivational energy for those who must engage in close, sensitive interpersonal relationships. Because being involved with others and maintaining a positive connection with others is the heart of nAff, this motive is particularly relevant in matrix or complex horizontal organizations.

5. *High affiliators maintain robust interpersonal networks.* They talk to other people a lot. Their e-mail address books are larger and longer, and they are likely to be active communicators on the Web. They're also constantly on the telephone. Affiliators learn about other people more quickly and they work hard to maintain their connections to others. This makes them perfect network managers in task force or

committee situations. They are motivated to keep others informed, to build bridges to others, and to preserve and strengthen the cooperative spirit of the group or team.

Need for Power

We all know people with a high need for power, and there is a good chance we don't always like them. These are people who spend their time thinking about how they can use their influence over others to win an argument, to change another person's behavior, or to gain greater authority or status. We label these types of people as being on "a power trip." And we're right.

High power people usually try to influence others directly by making suggestions, by giving their opinions and evaluations, or by trying to talk others into changing their views or actions. They are forceful, argumentative, and even pushy. Depending on their social skills, they may be seen as bossy, domineering autocrats or inspirational leaders. Think of Lucy from the *Peanuts* comic strip.

What makes these people tick? What kinds of situations stimulate nPow and provide those high in need for power with intrinsic satisfaction?

1. *High power people are concerned about influencing others by means of powerful actions.* These actions in themselves express a person's concern for power. For instance, a person might use strong, forceful actions that affect others, such as verbal attacks, threats, or reprimands. Power-motivated people love to give advice and to "help out" when the intention is not so much to assist or support as it is to express their own opinion. Powerful actions include efforts to impress others and to influence or persuade others through argument.

2. *High power people strive to arouse strong positive or negative emotions in others.* When people around them react with emotion (be it fear, pressure, delight, awe, anger, or offense), the power motive is satisfied. So power people try to provoke strong reactions in others. They love a good fight, a good argument, and a good "attention getter," and they seek out situations in which they can manipulate other's reactions.

3. *High power people are interested in acquiring a reputation or position.* People high in need for power are very concerned about public evaluations. They seek prestige. They

care deeply about what others see or think of their power. Power people are social climbers. They are acquisitive, especially with respect to those symbols we associate with success, status, and importance. Their power motive is best satisfied when others can affirm their power, their social position, their high status, or their reputation.

4. *High power people like to be in control of situations.* The power motive is all about control and influence. People high in nPow, therefore, will seek jobs or roles in which they can attain and exercise control over others. Studies by McClelland and others have shown that politicians, high school and college teachers, ministers, psychologists, and journalists all have very high levels of nPow. Politicians, teachers, and members of the clergy are attracted to those fields in part because they offer great scope for power and influence. Psychologists and journalists, on the other hand, have access to more inside information. They know what other people don't know and they are in a better position to influence others through this special information.

   Like affiliators, people high in nPow are quite sensitive to the emotions, needs, and feelings of others. They develop behaviors in response to what they sense in order to control others, but they are "sensitive."

With our strong democratic traditions and with our experiences with totalitarian abuses of power in the twentieth and the twenty-first centuries, we tend to be suspicious of people with high nPow. We toss around labels such as *fascist* and *authoritarian personality.* Although such watchfulness is healthy and necessary, I should note that the need for power does not always mean abuse of power. Many of history's greatest leaders were very highly motivated by nPow. A leader with no compassion for others and intolerance for disagreement may indeed become an autocrat, but a person who combines a healthy need for power with sensitivity to others' feelings and a desire to serve others might become a Peace Corps worker, a missionary, or an inspirational role model.

McClelland and others have carefully studied the power motive and its relationship to what is called social-emotional maturity. They have discovered that many of our most successful leaders have developed high levels of socialized power motivation. That is, their basic nPow is channeled into more socially acceptable goals. To illustrate the difference, McClelland (1987) cites the example of the plot summaries of two stories. The first story is written by a person high in personalized power (in which the goal is exclusively personal); the second is written by a person high in socialized power (in which the goal seems to be socialized in the service of others).

a) "He is fighting the champ—a chance to win a big purse, retire to a beach in Tahiti."

b) "He is fighting the champ—a chance to win a big purse. His kid is in the hospital and needs an expensive operation." (p. 298)

It is not hard to see how much more likable and culturally acceptable the socialized power motivation is. As we will see later, nPow is an important determinant of leadership effectiveness, but socialized power motivation is what we want to arouse, not personalized power.

The Role of the Environment in Arousing Motivation

It is important to note that the McClelland–Atkinson theory describes motivation as much more than a function of "who you are." People's basic *motives* for achievement, affiliation, or power are established early in life (and are largely a function of a person's exposure to socialization and child-rearing practices), but demonstrated or *aroused motivation* differs from situation to situation.

This is an important addition to our understanding of what makes people tick. We all know how immediately after we have smelled popcorn we crave it much more powerfully than we did a moment before. Or how, for many, playing tennis against a skilled opponent brings out our best game, or how a football team (usually the one you are rooting for) can let down and lose to a weak opponent—a team they could defeat if they were playing their hardest. Obviously, although many people skip over this fact, human motivation varies in response to situations. In other words, different environments, or *climates* as we are using the term, can arouse different kinds of motivation. The McClelland–Atkinson theory is powerful and useful because of the importance it assigns to immediate environmental influences on motivation. The result is *aroused* motivation.

As leaders, we want to know what a person's motive profile is (i.e., which of the three motives are strongest or weakest in a person). But it is far more important to know how to arouse the different motives. Everyone has a bit of each motive in his or her personality.

Most people have a dominant motive, say nAch, but also have sufficient nAff and nPow to allow these motive energy sources to be tapped or aroused in any given situation.

The Future of Motivation

Ten years ago I was teaching a leadership training program at GTE. After running three very successful programs (all of them had received rave reviews from GTE's skeptical managerial population), the head of GTE's training department audited the fourth session, in his words "to see what was going on." When he saw me teach students to analyze and manage motivation by using the McClelland–Atkinson model, he was shocked. Afterward he came up to me and said, "I'm not paying top dollar for a consultant to teach nAch, nAff, and nPow. That's old hat." No matter that almost every single participant had rated that particular part of the program as the most valuable. No matter that graduates of the first three programs had reported being immediately able to apply what they'd learned. And no matter that several program participants had even reported interpersonal break-throughs in their personal lives partially due to a new insight about what makes people tick. There's nothing out-of-date about this theory. It's the best the science of psychology has produced. Have the basic needs of people really changed in the last 10 years? In the last 100 years?

I never taught another program at GTE. But whenever I can, I build a McClelland–Atkinson Motivational Management Unit into my leadership training. It works! My clients and students pick it up quickly. They find it useful. In the future, I believe more and more practicing managers, school administrators, health care leaders, and public servants will rediscover the usefulness of this model of motivation. "Old hat" or not.

Here's what's really "old hat": Today's business organizations still rely heavily on extrinsic motivation, using money and ever-fancier job titles to try to retain valuable people and stimulate their performance. But this is changing. The technology explosion and the proliferation of high-tech start-ups and e-businesses are a window to the future. Intrinsic motives are much more obvious at Cisco and Sun than they are at Fleet Bank or General Motors. How many of us really think that Bill Gates is in it for the money?

The future may include identifying new motives, or coming up with new definitions of old motives. For example, in recent years our understanding of the development of nPow has expanded, and future leaders will need to take advantage of these new insights. As originally formulated, nPow referred to power over other people. People with high nPow want to be the boss who organizes others, usually from a position at or near the top of a hierarchy. As we understand the development of nPow, we see that the first stages have to do with power over oneself rather than power over others. As nPow evolves, we learn to enjoy status and a certain degree of control over other people and events around us. But only certain people get "stuck" here— we call them "control freaks." The mature person can continue to enjoy power but in the form McClelland called "socialized nPow." For such people, the real power stems from their ability to build a team and from the nPow and nAch they can induce in others. In the diverse people environments of today, with more women, African Americans, Hispanics, and Asian Americans in the workforce, understanding and arousing socialized nPow will be the key to leadership success.

High schools are, in many ways, models of how to misuse motivation. On the one hand, today's grade-based system of motivation used to stimulate student academic performance is entirely extrinsic and, as the work of Ed Deci suggests, ultimately destroys intrinsic motivation. In one famous experiment, he had two groups of students working to solve a difficult puzzle. He paid one group for their efforts but not the other. The crux of the experiment was when he had the students take a "break." He secretly observed their behavior, and he noted that those who were being paid stopped working at the puzzle, while those who were not given this extrinsic reward continued to work because of intrinsic factors. Deci repeated this experiment with different tasks and various age groups of people—always with the same result. It's no surprise that few students continue on their own to read and write, or explore the worlds of history and science, after schools have unintentionally but consistently extinguished their inner motivation to do so.

Recent research reported by Kenneth W. Thomas in *Intrinsic Motivation at Work* (2000) questions the validity of some of Deci's conclusions for work in an organizational setting. Thomas finds that "there is no inherent conflict between intrinsic and extrinsic rewards" (p. 116). But, he emphasizes, people generally do not work hard because of financial incentives. As he aptly states, "Wanting fair 'pay for performance' is not the same as 'performing for the pay'"(p. 120). Provided that pay for performance is seen as equitable and fair, then intrinsic motivation plays a dominant role.

Thomas's main thesis is that intrinsic motivation can and should be managed. That's also my main thesis. In early 2001, I worked with a small, privately owned company that illustrates the future of motivation. Called Whole Health Management (WHM), it operates a dozen health and wellness clinics for large, self-insured organizations. Based in Cleveland, WHM is led by Jim Hummer. Jim is a great leader. He probably comes by his leadership naturally, although two years at the Harvard Business School did him no harm. Jim knows the importance of motivation and spends an inordinate amount of time arousing nAch, nAff, and nPow. He doesn't use the term *organizational climate* very often, but he knows what it is, and he knows how to manage it.

Jim's leadership style dramatically impacts the thoughts and feelings of others. At his semiannual WHM advisory board meeting, Jim invites six distinguished outside advisers to comment on WHM's operations and advise the company about future trends in occupational health and wellness. First, Jim includes not only his top management team but also a half dozen other key managers in the meeting. This in itself is a huge motivational plus. Exposure to the WHM advisory board (which happens to include well-known doctors and several HBS professors) arouses everyone's nPow. Then Jim manages to publicly compliment each and every person in the room during the course of the meeting. This isn't easy. The conversations are often difficult and lots of people want to talk. But Jim does it. And people notice. You can almost physically see the motivation levels rise around the room. In addition, Jim turns each conversation into a project. People are given tasks, assignments are made, goals are set, and nAch is aroused. Finally, there is the luncheon and the schmoozing. If nPow and nAch were the unconscious targets of Jim's formal meeting, nAff is not forgotten at the lunch.

WHM is a high-performing company in a very competitive business environment. The company has incentive programs. It has bonuses and a few perks. But 99% of what Jim Hummer does as a people manager is focused on intrinsic motivation and creating the right kind of organizational climate. That's the future of motivation.

In the future, it will be impossible to ignore the fact that the highest and best energy at work comes from intrinsic motivation—the pleasure of doing science, solving a technological problem, bringing a business to life, or working with a cool group of people or with your own dress code, clock, and background music. Future business organizations, large and small, will need to be led by people who know how to expand the ways they manage these powerful intrinsic motives. They may not be referred to as nAch, nAff, or nPow, but that's what they are.

Think back to the case of Julie Goode and Ed Chang with which this chapter began. Goode apparently has a strong need for affiliation, a need that contributed to her success on teams in her previous position. But since she has been promoted to a situation that is more competitive, one that arouses the need for achievement, her performance has fallen off. Why? The situation she is in, working alone in her office in competition with her co-workers, does not tap into her dominant motive and, thus, does not *arouse* or harness her dominant energy source. To make matters worse, her boss does not understand what is going on. Chang apparently has a high need for achievement, and he is puzzled that everyone is not like him. But at least he is asking the right questions.

3

Measuring Organizational Climate

"What's wrong with this place?" Bob Potts paced in a circle around his desk—something he did frequently when feeling stressed. In fact, he wondered if he were wearing a path in the carpet. As vice president of human relations for the entire Metropolitan Health Care System (MHCS), he had a lot to worry about. On his desk was a report on the customer satisfaction scores for the last quarter, and they were down at Metro General Hospital, although the scores remained stable at some of Metro's smaller satellite hospitals and clinics. And in the Metro Children's Center, satisfaction scores were actually rising.

Potts knew that MHCS was experiencing a budgetary crisis, but this was nothing new. No, the reports seemed to indicate that the problem was with the people working at Metro. Patients and their families did not feel they were being treated right by hospital personnel, and this, Potts knew from experience, meant that the personnel probably felt that they were not being treated right by their managers. In some of Metro's hospitals, you could tell how bad it was just by walking through the wards.

"If only . . ." he thought. "If only I could figure out what is really going on in the various parts of the organization—what is hurting morale and employee motivation." He sat down at his desk and started to look through the papers again. "Something is definitely working at Metro Children's," Potts mused. "I wonder what it is."

Maybe he should find out.

The Need for a "Thought/Feeling Meter"

If Bob Potts were to read the previous chapter, he would know better what makes people tick. He could start defining the MHCS morale problem in terms of people's needs for achievement, for affiliation, and for power, and their inability to satisfy those needs on the job. He would know the magic formula:

Aroused Motivation $= M \times E \times I$

where M is the strength of the individual's motive or need, E is the expectancy of attaining the goal, and I is the perceived incentive value of that particular goal. In other words, people will invest energy if they have a need (M) and they think that by doing something they have a chance (E) of reaching a goal they desire (I). But it would be far too complicated, time consuming, and expensive for Potts to administer motivation tests to all Metro Children's Center employees (to define the Ms) and then figure out all the environmental factors (the Es and Is) that aroused people's motivation at any particular time at the center. Even more daunting would be to figure out the patterns of aroused motivation for every person in the MHCS organization.

E and I are highly individualistic variables that are unique to each person and each situation. Two nurses at MHCS, one high in nPow and the other high in nAff, might have very different thoughts, feelings, and reactions (E / I) to a bossy head nurse. And these might change very quickly as the work context changes. For example, in a crisis situation, the bossiness might arouse a different motivational response from each nurse, and this response could vary greatly from the pattern of aroused motivation we observed during a quiet time on the night shift. In order to truly understand what motivated his work-force, Potts would have to attach some kind of "thought/feeling meter" to everyone and constantly monitor these meters.

Individual expectancies and incentives are almost impossible to measure except in rigorously controlled laboratory studies, in which we can put strict limits on the situation and the various inputs. Then, if we are careful, we can experimentally determine the expectancies and incentive values associated with an individual motive or cluster of motives. We can also make reasonably reliable estimates of an individual's general expectancies and incentives through the use of interviews by professional counselors (although accurate prediction of situational changes in Es and Is are harder to identify by means of such interviews).

When we try to identify and understand the Es and Is for people outside the lab in a normal work environment, the problem of measurement becomes substantially more difficult. Even if we limit ourselves to the three important motives of nAch, nAff, and nPow, we need a way to generalize, combine, or summarize the influence of the work environment on aroused motivation. Potts needs a way to group all of the readings he takes from each person's "thought/feeling meter" into meaningful patterns. Otherwise, he would never be able to act on what he learned.

In order to be actionable, his measurements of E and I must also allow him to describe and compare different organizations. If Potts really wants to know what is working at Metro Children's Center, he needs a common measurement tool to use with all of the parts of the MHCS organization.

There are additional measurement problems. First, people don't think in terms of specific expectancies and incentive values. Even if people carry around in their heads the definitive expectancies and incentive values described in the McClelland–Atkinson model, asking them to articulate what those Es and Is are would drive you—and them—crazy. Reflect back on your own personal experience, using common sense. Most of the time we react to more general impressions of what is likely, possible, or valuable in a given situation. We may, in everyday terms, say that our situation is stressful or unfriendly, or that we feel unappreciated or lost. On a more positive note, we may say our situation is stimulating or warm, or that we feel supported or committed. We think, feel, and respond to situations in terms of bigger, more integrated chunks of experience. A nurse in Metro Children's Center may feel as if she is being given a lot of personal responsibility for how she does her job, but she does not experience this in terms of discrete E and I variables. Or a lab technician in the same facility might respond well to the clearly stated procedures and structure in his unit without being aware of the specific expectancies and incentive values involved in each immediate situation. We describe our experience in terms of generalized or summarized patterns, not in terms of specific, discrete situational variables.

Finally, there is the problem of language. Because E and I are subjective things, we must *ask* people what they are. We must *ask* people to describe what it is in the environment that is arousing their interest and motivation. Research and experience tell us how difficult it is to get people to agree on the precise meaning of words. Somehow, Potts's "thought/feeling meters" have to be calibrated in a way that makes sense to everyone. Those who have the thoughts and those who are trying to read the thoughts must all agree on a common language of environmental determinants. Good luck!

What we need, then, is a more general concept, one that describes a set or cluster of individual expectancies and incentive values. We need a tool that characterizes the most important (but not all) situational determinants of aroused motivation, a concept that uses common words that most people can relate to, and a construct that will apply to multiple organizations and lots of different people. This is our concept of organizational climate. It's a general construct that represents a property of organizational environments that is perceived directly or indirectly by the individuals within the environment.

Bob Potts is too busy to hook up and monitor hundreds of individual "thought/feeling meters," even if such a tool were in existence. But maybe he could use an organizational thought/feeling measurement device—one that doesn't pretend to capture specific E and I values but that tries to describe the general forces that arouse motivation in the workplace. Armed with one of those, our vice president at MHCS would not only better understand what was going on at Metro Children's Center but he could also use this understanding to solve the performance problems in other parts of his organization.

Climate Dimensions and Aroused Motivation

What is the most effective way to come up with an organizational thought/feeling measurement device, one that captures those "bigger chunks of experience"—the clusters of expectancies and incentives— that lead to aroused motivation? In the work that George Litwin and I did at Harvard in the 1960s, we felt we needed to group the various Es and Is into useful categories. By *useful* I mean that they pass tests of scientific rigor and common sense and also that they also yield insight into the way members of an organization actually experience and respond to their environment. Furthermore, we had to come up with a set of dimensions that was measurable and consistent enough to use in a variety of organizations.

Before going any further, however, I want to make it clear what I mean by *dimension*. Think in terms of a two-dimensional (flat) drawing or the three-dimensional way we view the depth of a scene. Or we may add a fourth dimension by conceptualizing the scene as it moves through time. The emphasis is on the function of a dimension—its usefulness in viewing and understanding.

When we are discussing organizations and organizational climates, the complexity can be overwhelming. Because climate represents a set of subjective perceptions of an organization, there may be an infinite variety of organizational climates. That's why we need a way to sort the features of climates into useful groupings—useful in characterizing each organization and in comparing different organizations. Most importantly, the groupings need to be useful to those leading and managing organizations by providing a guide to arousing people's motivation and energizing their performance.

In our 1965–1966 research for our book, *Motivation and Organizational Climate,* George Litwin and I focused most of our attention on achievement, affiliation, and power motivation. If nAch, nAff, and nPow are the source of many people's on-the-job performance energy, then it stands to reason that the way organizations do and do not address and arouse these needs is the way to describe their climates. In other words, different organizational climates push different people's motivation buttons in different ways, and we were looking for a pattern in the climates that had at least a rough correspondence with the dominant motive patterns that McClelland and Atkinson had discerned in human motivation.

Thus, the nature of nAch, nAff, and nPow pointed us toward the clusters of expectancies and incentive values that we wanted to measure. And this, in turn, helped us figure out where to start.

For example, we saw that people with a high nAch value such things as:

- A sense of personal responsibility
- Quality of feedback on performance
- Specific goals
- Importance of standards of excellence

We reasoned that one or more of the important dimensions of an organization's climate would center on meeting these needs.

Similarly, we saw that people with a high nAff value:

- Rewards and warmth
- Supportive relationships
- Emphasis on teams
- Avoidance of conflict
- Sense of belonging and commitment

Exhibit 3.1
Original Climate and Motivation Hypotheses

1. Structure (arouse nPow, reduce nAff)
2. Emphasis on individual responsibility (arouse nAch)
3. Warmth (arouse nAff)
4. Support (arouse nAff and nAch)
5. Reward vs. punishment (arouse nAch and nAff)
6. Conflict and tolerance of conflict (arouse nAch and nPow; reduce nAff)
7. Performance standards and expectations (arouse nAch)
8. Organizational identity and group loyalty (arouse nAff)
9. Risk and risk taking (arouse nAch)

And we reasoned that one or more dimensions of an organization's climate ought to address these needs.

Finally, people with a high nPow value:

- Hierarchy and structure
- Formal systems and rules
- Sense of boundaries
- Control tools and influence mechanisms

Again, we hypothesized that these values should be an important part of at least one dimension of climate.

With this framework of the McClelland–Atkinson theory of aroused motivation as a start, we reviewed dozens of previous studies of work environments and employee motivation. We then created a theoretical description of climate made up of nine different dimensions, each with strong ties (either positive or negative) to at least one of the three motives. Our initial hypotheses are outlined in Exhibit 3.1.

Let's take a look at the way Litwin and I saw these dimensions and their potential for motive arousal. Although not all of the hypotheses that lay behind this theoretical description of climate were ultimately confirmed, our logic was 90% right, and it provides a clear picture of the link between the climate dimensions and the three key motives.

Structure

It helps to see Structure in two ways. First, there is the structure of the task situation—the perceived limitations in terms of the amount of detailed information available and the constraints placed on behavior. You are in a structured task situation if the operating procedures are rigorously spelled out for you, and you have all the information needed to make the decisions you need to make. We hypothesized that this kind of structure would fail to arouse the motivation of people with a high nAch.

Second, there is the structure of the interpersonal situation—the perceived hierarchy of status and authority. You are in a structured interpersonal situation when there is a clearly defined chain of command that is reinforced by job titles, organizational charts, and a variety of other cues. We hypothesized that cues suggesting a competition for recognition and status would arouse nPow and generate power-related behavior.

We also thought that both task and interpersonal structure would reduce (or have a negative effect on) nAff because the formality and social distance tend to increase as the hierarchy and work rules become more explicit. People high in nAff prefer closer relationships.

Emphasis on Individual Responsibility

Some situations allow people to choose their own operating procedures and to accept responsibility for the consequences of their actions. You are working in a climate that emphasizes individual responsibility if your success (or failure) depends more on your own efforts rather than on pure chance. It's important that you can control the means of attaining your achievement goal and that you receive concrete feedback on your progress. We hypothesized that people with high nAch thrive in such a climate. But if they feel constrained, so that the success is not their success, the incentive value is greatly reduced.

We reasoned that climate emphasizing individual responsibility could arouse people with high nPow in two ways. First, if "being your own boss" is given a lot of importance and status, then these people will be motivated whereas the freedom and feedback aspects will motivate high nAch people. It's all in how you present it.

Second, people with high nPow can be motivated if it is made clear that if they do not take control of their own actions, then somebody else will take control of them—and that is precisely what they fear. Again, it's in how you present the responsibility.

As far as we could tell, Emphasis on Individual Responsibility would not arouse nAff. This is not surprising, for the competitive aspects of both nAch and nPow work against the need for connection and relationship that is so important to people with high nAff.

Warmth and Support

These two dimensions are very closely related. In 1966, we thought it would be important to distinguish between them. On the one hand, there is Warmth: a jocular and friendly environment—you know you are working in one if there is a lot of informal socializing, use of first names or nicknames, and conversation about personal lives that have little to do with the workplace. We doubted that this kind of atmosphere arouses the need for achievement, although it does, of course, arouse the need for affiliation.

Much more important in arousing nAch, we hypothesized, is the creation of positive helping relationships preferably expressed in the form of encouragement rather than the kind of dominance that turns off nAch. This was our original Support dimension. Setting high standards arouses nAch, as long as those high standards are not accompanied by strict directions on how to achieve them. An employee-oriented supervisor can appeal to nAff along with nAch by taking a personal interest in his or her people and being understanding of their situations, and by expressing personal appreciation and support for their efforts and achievements.

We did not think that either Warmth or Support would arouse nPow. A feeling of warm affiliation contradicts the competition for status in a hierarchy and a supportive environment would not be on the "radar screen" of a personality dominated by nPow.

Reward Versus Punishment

George Litwin and I distinguished climates marked by what we called *rewards* from those marked by the more general term, *approval*. In our early studies, however, we often lumped them together into a Reward versus Punishment dimension. Rewards, whether in the form of pay raises, bonuses, promotions, or formally or informally given praise, are performance based. As such, they should arouse the nAch motivation. If the reward system is perceived as objective, specific, prompt, and performance oriented, people high in nAch will strive for those rewards as symbols of their success and personal achievement. This kind of performance-based reward climate will not stimulate people with high nAff. Instead, they need to perceive that their hard work will lead to warm, close personal relationships.

Climates marked by approval do not discriminate. You are working in a high-approval climate if positive reinforcement is given in a general, nondiscriminatory way for task- and non-task-related behavior. High achievers, we reasoned, will not be interested in general approval unrelated to their personal accomplishments, much the way that a warm and friendly atmosphere would not arouse nAch. The affiliation motive, however, is aroused in an approving climate, for it signals to the person high in nAff that close friendships are important and that such relationships are being encouraged.

We also hypothesized that the power motive would not be aroused in a climate of performance-based reward unless the reward takes the form of an increase in status and power. But nPow would be aroused in an approving climate because general social and personal approval tends to increase cues associated with personal recognition and influence.

The negatives—punishment and disapproval—do little to arouse any of the three primary motives. High achievers fear the punishment that comes with failure and would, thus, avoid risks, and disapproval leads to social distance and weak affiliation, demotivating people with a high need for affiliation. People seeking to gain power, status, and influence will also be discouraged by the prospect of losing these important qualities.

Conflict and Tolerance of Conflict

How an organization deals with conflict has a lot to say about that organization's overall climate. Litwin and I were aware of three ways that organizations deal with conflicts: (1) avoiding them, (2) compromising them, or (3) confronting them.

We focused our attention on the benefits of confronting conflicts by bringing them out into the open. We hypothesized that doing so would arouse achievement motivation because it would increase the flow of relevant information—both factual and emotional information. Doing so makes the performance standards more clear and realistic, clarifying achievement goals. Confronting conflicts is also a way to increase the promptness and concreteness of performance feedback, so the individual can learn "how well he or she is doing"— another aspect of climate that arouses nAch.

Tolerance of conflict should have a negative effect on nAff because confrontation threatens the warm and friendly relationships so important to individuals with a high need for affiliation. These people naturally shy away from conflict.

On the other hand, people with a strong nPow will be aroused by conflict because the confrontation provides them with a direct opportunity to influence other people—something that is very important to them.

Performance Standards and Expectations

The establishment and communication of high performance standards plays an important role in arousing nAch, for the whole theory of achievement motivation is built around the notion of achievement relative to a standard of excellence. Research shows that these standards are not simply expressed in terms of explicit criteria but also through very subtle and often unconscious cues. Expectations that are embedded in organizational climate can have a powerful impact on achievement motivation.

We did not expect a direct relationship between high performance standards and the arousal of nAff or nPow. But it may work indirectly. If high performance leads to greater warmth, friendliness, and personal support, then people with high nAff will respond to the performance standards in order to please their boss or co-workers. In much the same way, if the organizational climate leads people to perceive that high performance leads to status and influence, then people with high nPow may respond. But these are indirect responses that are mediated through other climate mechanisms.

Organizational Identity and Group Loyalty

In many organizations individuals work with others on a common task. When this happens, it's important that individuals identify with the group goal. People with high need for affiliation will respond to an environment that emphasizes group cohesiveness and loyalty, along with close, interpersonal relationships and mutual support. And when the climate of the organization emphasizes these things and gives feedback only on the performance of the group as a whole, the result is increased group performance, less concern about personal rewards, more mutual trust, and less strain in personal relationships.

People with high nAch, however, are unlikely to be motivated by such a climate unless they identify so strongly with the group goal that their nAch is aroused. When these people are working as part of a team, it's important to give feedback on both how the group and individuals are doing. The result is the greatest increase in personal performance and group productivity.

Most climates that emphasize group loyalty and identity tend also to emphasize friendliness, warmth, and mutual support. Because of this, we hypothesized, people who are power-oriented and striving to obtain individual prominence are likely to be frustrated by the emphasis on group identity. They have no way to achieve personal power, status, and personal dominance.

Risk and Risk Taking

It is obvious from what I said earlier about the need for achievement that environments that emphasize moderate, calculated risk taking will most likely arouse nAch. Climates that are very conservative or that legitimize blind speculation—not enough risk or too much risk—will frustrate and weaken achievement motivation. Perceived risk should have little impact on nAff or nPow.

In tracing the logical connections between the dimensions of climate and aroused motivation, we made several simplifications:

- We categorized individual effects of each dimension independently of other climate factors. In reality, climate dimensions interact with each other in more complex patterns. For example, high Structure tends to have a negative effect on achievement motivation. But if high Structure were coupled with high performance standards and an emphasis on risk taking, achievement cues might be extremely salient and achievement motivation aroused. Litwin and I knew at the time that we needed to do considerable research in order to identify the patterns of climate that arouse the highest levels of achievement, affiliation, and power motivation in different types of organizations.

- We spoke of the effects of climate dimensions on particular motives as if some people were simply high in nAch, others high in nAff, and others high in nPow. Although this may work as a simplification, in reality individuals have configurations or combinations of these motives, arranged in a hierarchy. People's behavior emerges from the ways these configurations respond to the complex cues that situations present.

- Finally, we tended to speak of achievement-related behavior, affiliation-related behavior, and power-related behavior as if they could only emerge by arousing the appropriate motives. In reality, of course, the causes of behavior are complex, often with multiple and disguised causes. We have to be careful not to look only at the behavior and assume the person's motivation. As I explained in Chapter 2, understanding must come from an analysis of behavior and an assessment of the configuration of motives and other personality factors.

The First-Generation Climate Questionnaire

Litwin and I wanted to test our hypotheses and construct a measurement instrument that would collect members' perceptions and subjective responses to the organizational environment. We were also interested in developing an instrument that was workable, that is, one that didn't require a Ph.D. to fill out and could be completed in a reasonable length of time. Our first step was to collect descriptive material about an organization's internal environment. Under the guidance of Dr. Herbert H. Meyer of GE, we distributed an open-ended questionnaire to about 25 managers and personnel specialists in several departments of the General Electric Company, and to about 20 men with experience in other kinds of organizations, such as the military and research. We then analyzed the responses and identified 44 specific questionnaire items that were candidates for our initial questionnaire.

If you take a quick peek at the sample Climate Questionnaire in the ToolKit in Part IV of this book, you will see what we mean by the term *questionnaire item*. Depending on the survey format, an item can be either a question or a statement. In almost all of the generations of our climate survey, people filling out the questionnaire respond in one of four ways to each item:

1. DA = If they definitely agree; that is, the statement definitely expresses how they feel about the matter.
2. IA = If they are inclined to agree; that is, they are not definite but think that the statement tends to express how they feel about the matter.
3. ID = If they are inclined to disagree; that is, if they are not definite but think that the statement does not tend to express how they feel about the matter.
4. DD = If they definitely disagree; that is, the statement definitely does not express how they feel about the matter.

Next, we asked three judges with experience in content analysis to sort the 44 items into categories or dimensions. We ended up with a first-generation questionnaire that included six dimensions and 31 items. Brief definitions of the initial climate dimensions are shown in Exhibit 3.2.

Exhibit 3.2

Preliminary Scale Descriptions (Form A)

1. *Structure*—the feeling the workers have about the constraints in their work situation; how many rules, regulations, and procedures there are.
2. *Responsibility*—the feeling of "being your own boss"; not having to double-check all of your decisions.
3. *Risk*—the sense of riskiness and challenge in the job and in the work situation.
4. *Reward*—the feeling of being rewarded for a job well done; the emphasis on reward versus criticism and punishment.
5. *Warmth and support*—the feeling of general good fellowship and helpfulness that prevails in the organization.
6. *Conflict*—the feeling that management isn't afraid of different opinions or conflict with the emphasis placed on settling differences here and now.

We tested this questionnaire for scale consistency and scale independence at the Harvard Business School. Sixty first-year M.B.A.'s used the instrument to describe organizations in which they had worked. We found a reasonable degree of consistency among the items grouped for each dimension, although two scales, Responsibility and Conflict, were less consistent than the others. Unfortunately, we discovered there was a lot of scale overlap, with the Responsibility and Risk scales strongly related, and both of these strongly related to the Reward scale. Also, Conflict was strongly related to Warmth and Support. The most serious overlap was between the Reward scale and the Warmth and Support Scale, and we saw this as a serious deficiency. We decided to rearrange and revise some of the items, especially those under the Reward and the Warmth and Support scales.

We also wanted to see what the questionnaire showed about how different climate conditions might be compatible with different kinds of individual motivation. So we administered a Thematic Apperception Test (TAT) to 52 M.B.A. students to measure the strength of their nAch, nAff, and nPow. Using the questionnaire, we then asked them to describe the kind of climate in which they would ideally like to work. We correlated the motive scores with the measures of preferred or ideal organizational climate, and these correlations were further compared with the original hypotheses about which types of people would respond to which climate dimensions, as outlined in Exhibit 3.1. We learned that the majority of our hypotheses were supported, and the findings on several others were in the hypothesized direction, although not to a statistically significant degree. Where we thought motivation would be aroused, it was, and where we thought there would be no effect, there was none. Only two hypotheses were not supported, both of them regarding reduction of motivation.

It is important to point out that the original hypotheses concerned the influence of certain climate properties on the level of aroused motivation. But the results I just described deal with the preferences of people with different motive patterns for certain climates. We had not hypothesized about that, but the results indicated that people are attracted to climates that arouse their dominant needs. We were encouraged that evidence lent credibility to our concept of climate.

There were, however, some dramatic and unexpected results, especially the positive relationship of nAch and a preference for Structure. We expected and found a strong positive relationship between nPow and Structure, but the nAch figures surprised us. An examination of other correlations suggested an explanation. People with high nAch prefer climates with a high Reward dimension, so we reasoned that their preference for Structure derived from a desire for a way to get feedback and reward for excellent performance. Perhaps naively, the M.B.A. students in our sample may have felt that a highly structured environment would satisfy their desire for feedback and reward. People with high nPow, on the other hand, want a status-based rather than a performance-based reward system and we found a higher correlation with the Structure scale than with the Reward scale (which emphasizes rewards for excellent performance).

Over all, we were pleased with the results. We saw that our first-generation questionnaire indicated that people preferred climates that seemed most likely to satisfy their needs. We were on the right track.

The Next Generation of the Questionnaire

We used the first-generation climate questionnaire (Form A) to study the impact of organizational climate on the development of aroused motivation in two groups of salesmen in two sales organizations that we thought were quite different in terms of organizational climate. One was an electronics components firm that seemed to value interpersonal skills more than aggressive salesmanship. They believed that the technical quality of their product was their most important selling point.

The second group sold computer time. They seemed to emphasize aggressive selling techniques, characterizing their organization as "on the move." They stressed achievement.

The results of the climate surveys, although not dramatic, did confirm that the computer time sales organization has established a more achieving climate—one favorable to the development of achievement motivation. And when we tested the motivation of the salespeople, we found that the nAch of the computer time sales force was significantly higher than that in the electronics components sales force.

However, we were not satisfied with the climate questionnaire itself. Although we were pleased that the initial measure showed that the scale properties made sense, and several studies established reasonable validity for the measure—one that was generally consistent with the theoretical model and our hypotheses—we knew we could do better.

We dropped some items or rewrote them to make them more scale specific. We decided to separate Warmth from Support, with the former measuring the amount of warmth and friendliness and the latter measuring task-related support and encouragement.

We also added two new scales: Standards and Identity. The first dealt with the emphasis management placed on attaining high standards of excellence in performance. The second dealt with feelings of involvement in and belonging to an organization, and with team spirit. Our second-generation questionnaire was imaginatively called Form B, and the dimensions are described in Exhibit 3.3.

This second-generation climate measure, with 50 items grouped among these nine climate dimensions, was administered to over 500 people in a wide variety of roles in a wide variety of business organizations. We also used it in the two-week experimental study I described in the Introduction, the one involving three "companies" ("British Radar," "Balance Radar," and "Blazer Radar") with very different leadership styles and climates. We found that scale consistency—items on a single scale and, thus, measuring aspects of the same climate dimension—improved considerably. The Standards scale had some consistency problems, but we felt a rewording of items would solve this problem. The Conflict scale showed the poorest consistency, and the open-ended responses attached to the questionnaire suggested that many people were describing the existence of conflicts rather than how conflicts were accepted and confronted. We decided to drop the Conflict scale from the questionnaire. It was too ambiguous.

Exhibit 3.3

The Revised Scale Descriptions (Form B)

1. *Structure*—the feeling that employees have about the constraints in the group, how many rules, regulations, procedures there are. Is there an emphasis on "red tape" and going through channels, or is there a loose and informal atmosphere?

2. *Responsibility*—the feeling of being your own boss; not having to double-check all your decisions; when you have a job to do, knowing that it is *your* job.

3. *Reward*—the feeling of being rewarded for a job well done; emphasizing positive rewards rather than punishments; the perceived fairness of the pay and promotion policies.

4. *Risk*—the sense of riskiness and challenge in the job and in the organization. Is there an emphasis on taking calculated risks, or is playing it safe the best way to operate?

5. *Warmth*—the feeling of general good fellowship that prevails in the work group atmosphere; the emphasis on being well liked; the prevalence of friendly and informal social groups.

6. *Support*—the perceived helpfulness of the managers and other employees in the group; emphasis on mutual support from above and below.

7. *Standards*—the perceived importance of implicit and explicit goals and performance standards; the emphasis on doing a good job; the challenge represented in personal and group goals.

8. *Conflict*—the feeling that managers and other workers want to hear different opinions; the emphasis placed on getting problems out in the open rather than smoothing them over or ignoring them.

9. *Identity*—the feeling that you belong to a company and you are a valuable member of a working team; the importance placed on this kind of spirit.

We also evaluated scale independence on the revised (Form B) questionnaire. We found the degree of scale overlap to be considerably lower than Form A, although there was still a strong relationship between scores on the Warmth, Identity, and Support scales. We concluded that these three scales tap a common dimension of climate, and they should probably be combined in future research.

We also replicated our previous study of the kind of work climate people would prefer or ideally like—this time using a group of 59 M.B.A. students and 42 managers from different companies. We again used a Thematic Apperception Test to measure their nAch, nAff, and nPow, and we measured the correlations between these scores and their preferences for different climate characteristics.

We found the same strong relationships that we found with the first-generation questionnaire, with most of our hypotheses supported, especially those dealing with arousal. We did, however, find some disparities between the scores for students and the scores for businessmen. Previously we were surprised to learn that achievement-oriented men expressed a preference for a structured climate. In this case, however, we found that the achievement-oriented managers, with experience in business organizations, preferred not to work within that kind of structure, whereas the less experienced students did prefer it. We thought that experience within structured organizations helps shape more realistic preferences.

We also found, from the differences in student and manager scores, that the experience of achievement-oriented managers led to an increased preference for climates emphasizing responsibility, just as we had hypothesized. Experience also led managers who were more power oriented to prefer *not* to work in such a climate. In both cases we compared the scores of experienced managers with the scores of less experienced students.

Finally, our hypothesis that the Identity scale would be positively related to nAff was confirmed. But we also found, to our surprise, a strong preference for climates characterized by group identity and loyalty among those with high nAch. Those with high nPow expressed a weak preference for this dimension, where we thought there would be distaste.

Managerial Validity

Based on what we learned in 1967 and 1968, Litwin and I constructed a third-generation climate survey that had 33 items organized into the following six dimensions:

1. Organizational Clarity
2. Responsibility
3. Reward
4. Standards
5. Conformity
6. Team Spirit

We were still unsure exactly how much emphasis to put on the issues of rewards, support, and teamwork, but we were increasingly certain that further climate research would have to be done in nonacademic settings. Students simply did not have sufficient organizational experience to provide us with the data we needed.

Over the next 10 years, the basic challenge of measuring organizational climate shifted from research validity to managerial validity. We knew we had a way to capture people's thoughts and feelings about their work environment, and we knew we could organize our measurements into relatively stable and reliable dimensions. But we weren't sure how practical and useful our measurement system was to businesspeople struggling to improve the performance of their organizations. When apprised of our climate research, the business community's first question always was, "So what?"

In order to answer the "so what" question, we had to venture out of the classroom where leadership and climate are theoretical constructs into the world of business and management consulting where leadership and climate are critical components of the day-to-day challenge of improving organizational performance.

4

The Climate Survey

"So what?"

Bob Potts hurled his copy of *The Journal of Irrelevant Psychology* across his office, where it crashed into his statue of Tom Peters.

"What a bunch of crap! Another article full of so-called 'valid' studies, done in some lab at Harvard 20 years ago! What does that have to do with my problems at the hospital here in the real world, where I need answers, not academic hairsplitting and hypotheses? I need answers about real people who have had some experience in real organizations—like mine here at Metro Health Care. That's what's 'valid.' Enough about motivational theory applied to graduate students! Enough about correlations and interitem consistency! Just help me solve my problems with customer satisfaction scores at Metro General Hospital."

He picked up his frazzled copy of JIP and tossed it in the wastebasket. "I'm a leader here—but I need help. Just tell me what works."

Although I disagree with Bob Potts's view that academic research is irrelevant to his immediate needs, I certainly understand his frustration. Solid grounding in research that involves careful definition, statistical calibration, and patient revision until we "get it right" is needed to ensure that we are dealing with knowledge rather than unsubstantiated feelings or opinions. But still, he is right that all the careful research counts for little in his world unless he can see a pragmatic application outside the lab. This means the *data* that are collected must be turned into actionable *information*.

And that is where we turned next.

Soon after *Motivation and Organizational Climate* was published, George Litwin and I left the Harvard Business School and Herbert Meyer (our primary corporate research sponsor) retired from GE.

Before leaving Harvard, Litwin collaborated with Stevan K. Trooboff and Jeffery Timmons in conducting five field research studies that explored the relationship of our list of six climate dimensions to organizational performance. These five studies covered very different organizations: a medical technology sales company, several life insurance agencies, a stock brokerage firm, a number of broadcasting organizations, and an airline. In every case, the high-performing units had measurably higher levels of the climate dimensions.

Their unpublished research monograph entitled *Organizational Climate* points out that within each of the various organizations, certain climate dimensions were clearly more important than others in contributing to high performance. The differences in "healthy" climate patterns, they concluded, were primarily a function of the differences in the organizations' competitive situation and task structure. That is, what would be the best for a sales organization may not be appropriate or as "healthy" for an airline. I will explore this idea later in this chapter.

In addition, the Litwin–Trooboff–Timmons work highlighted the need for a more purposeful climate questionnaire, one that not only measured dimensions of the work environment but that also measured people's perceptions of *how* and *why* that environment was created. As soon as executives realized that certain patterns of climate were strongly related to high levels of performance, they wanted to know how to *create* these kinds of climates. Companies were increasingly asking climate researchers to justify their interventions and provide useful feedback, advice, and counsel regarding the managerial implications of their research.

Given these shifting expectations and the fact that Litwin, Trooboff, Timmons, and I no longer had a home at Harvard Business School, it is not surprising that the next generations of the climate questionnaire were developed by several Boston-based consulting firms. In the early 1970s, firms such as Humana, Inc., The Forum Corporation, and McBer and Company started marketing climate surveys as a tool to help companies assess the effectiveness of their organizations. These consulting companies were not only searching for answers to the "so what" question, but they were also learning and teaching their clients a language of climate. This language was focused less on motivation theory and more on models of organization performance. For the first time, leadership variables were considered to be as important as climate variables.

Perhaps the most widely used version (and the one I was most familiar with, since I joined the company in the late 1970s) was The Forum Corporation's "Organization and Management Audit." The Forum Corporation questionnaire utilized most of the items Litwin and I developed, but they relabeled and redefined the six dimensions. (See Exhibit 4.1.)

The main focus of The Forum Corporation's and other consulting companies' climate surveys was organizational performance improvement rather than simply aroused motivation. As a practical matter, few business organizations would let us administer Thematic Apperception Tests (TATs) to calculate levels of nAch, nAff, and nPow. The tests were considered too "psychological" and too "academic," and clients couldn't see how the results of the TATs would add much value to solving their performance problems. From my earlier perspective, the logic was reversed. Whereas Litwin and I were interested in climate as the embodiment of the environmental determinants of aroused motivation, I was now viewing climate in terms of its power to predict organizational performance.

Exhibit 4.1
The Six Dimensions of Forum's Climate Survey

CLARITY	How well people understand an organization's goals and policies and the extent to which they understand the requirements of their jobs.
COMMITMENT	How strongly employees identify with and are dedicated to goal achievement.
STANDARDS	The perceived emphasis that management places on high standards of performance and the degree to which pressure is exerted to improve performance.
RESPONSIBILITY	The degree to which people feel personally responsible for their work.
RECOGNITION	The degree to which individuals feel they are recognized and rewarded for doing good work.
TEAMWORK	The degree to which individuals feel they belong to an organization characterized by cohesion, mutual warmth and support, trust, and pride.

The Final Phases of Development
of Our Climate Survey

In the 1980s, my climate survey work moved from The Forum Corporation to Harbridge House, Inc. (another consulting firm in Boston), and I began a long and stimulating collaborative relationship with David Nadler, founder of Delta Consulting Group, Inc. (now Mercer Delta Consulting). In fact, as this book goes to press, I am leaving Sherbrooke Associates, the consulting company I founded after leaving Harbridge House in 1986, to work with my friend and colleague at Mercer Delta Consulting. At the time, Nadler and his colleagues at Columbia University and Delta were interested in developing a broad assessment tool that matched their "congruence model" of how organizations work. This model, fully explained in his 1998 bestseller, *Champions of Change,* attempts to describe the multitude of factors that contribute to organizational performance and has proved to be an extremely useful managerial framework. Nadler hypothesizes that the better the "fit" or congruence between all of the parts of the model, the higher the organization's performance will be.

Nadler and I called the survey instrument the "Organizational Assessment Questionnaire" (OAQ), and we conducted a number of validation studies of the OAQ at AT&T, Westinghouse Electric Corporation, and Union Carbide Corporation. As shown in Exhibit 4.2, organizational climate was considered a key indicator of the nature of the fit that exists between the different organizational components.

As you can see from Exhibit 4.2, the climate section of the OAQ placed greater emphasis on cross-department cooperation than did previous instruments. This was because Delta's and Harbridge House's clients—the validation study sites for the OAQ—were traditional, vertically organized companies that were struggling to improve organizational performance by increasing the level of cross-boundary collaboration. Nadler and I frequently discussed this phenomenon. We concluded that the key to success for hard-charging employees at AT&T, Westinghouse, and Union Carbide in the 1980s was demonstrating executive maturity and recognizing and accepting the importance of corporate-wide goals. Achievement motivation and climates that aroused nAch were less relevant. Because we were more focused on the determinants of organizational performance (so we could score points as high-impact consultants), our climate measurement system shifted. For two years while I was consulting for Harbridge House, I

Exhibit 4.2
The OAQ Conceptual Structure

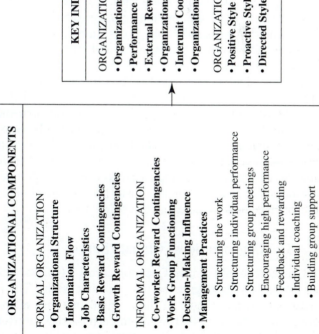

ORGANIZATIONAL COMPONENTS

FORMAL ORGANIZATION
• **Organizational Structure**
• **Information Flow**
• **Job Characteristics**
• **Basic Reward Contingencies**
• **Growth Reward Contingencies**

INFORMAL ORGANIZATION
• **Co-worker Reward Contingencies**
• **Work Group Functioning**
• **Decision-Making Influence**
• **Management Practices**
  • Structuring the work
  • Structuring individual performance
  • Structuring group meetings
  • Encouraging high performance
  • Feedback and rewarding
  • Individual coaching
  • Building group support
  • Encouraging participation

KEY INDICATORS

ORGANIZATIONAL CLIMATE
• **Organizational Clarity**
• **Performance Standards**
• **External Rewards**
• **Organizational Support**
• **Interunit Cooperation**
• **Organizational Commitment**

ORGANIZATIONAL STYLE
• **Positive Style**
• **Proactive Style**
• **Directed Style**

OUTPUT

INDIVIDUAL OUTCOMES
• **General Work Satisfaction**
• **Basic Reward Satisfaction**
• **Social Satisfaction**
• **Growth Satisfaction**
• **Turnover**

EFFECTIVENESS
• **Managerial Effectiveness**
• **Work Group Effectiveness**
• **Organizational Effectiveness**

used a version of the climate questionnaire that had a dimension called Cooperation, in addition to the standard dimension called Support. After several years, I realized that this approach tended to confuse many of my clients. Survey respondents reported over and over again that they couldn't distinguish the difference between interunit cooperation (Cooperation) and intraunit teamwork (Support).

A Real-World Climate Measurement Tool

By the mid-1980s, it became clear to me that the complexity of real-world organizational life was too great to capture by means of one measurement instrument or survey methodology. Academic researchers could administer monster instruments and justify doing so in the "interests of research." But management consultants were generally paid to solve problems, not just define them. My clients were demanding quick answers and inexpensive solutions. I was stuck. I was either going to have to take a few diagnostic shortcuts or rejoin academia.

So, in 1986, I left Harbridge House, Inc. and started my own consulting firm, Sherbrooke Associates, Inc. One of the first things I did was review all of the previous climate survey instruments and develop one that worked for me. It contained only those items and scales that had proven to be consistent and relatively independent. It contained a section on leadership practices, but I did not try to measure the other factors that might influence climate or organizational performance. It also was flexible and user friendly in that the survey form allowed clients to add their own items or add open-ended questions in order to collect information they deemed to be especially relevant or important. But, most importantly, it was shorter and easier to administer than earlier versions of the survey. This made it more usable, more manageable, and easier to explain to practicing managers and my consulting clients. I was back in the climate business with a management tool, not just a research tool.

The Organizational Climate Survey

The Organizational Climate Questionnaire I have used for the past 15 years has 24 items grouped into six dimensions. The items and dimensions preserve most of the original integrity of the earliest generations—the ones tied to the three powerful motivation syndromes of nAch, nAff, and nPow. They also reflect what we learned using later-generation climate measures. Most importantly, the climate questionnaire incorporates my consultant's sensitivity to measuring factors that predict high performance—whether or not the item has a high statistical correlation to aroused motivation. It's a pragmatic instrument.

Here are the actual climate questionnaire items organized into the six dimensions of climate that each describes. You will note that some of the items are worded in a negative way. That is, instead of being scored 1-2-3-4 (as I explained in Chapter 3), the scoring is reversed. We found that certain aspects of climate were better expressed and easier to describe if we asked people to comment on their absence.

1. *Structure* reflects employees' sense of being well organized and of having a clear definition of their roles and responsibilities. Structure is high when people feel that everyone's job is well defined. It is low when there is confusion about who does which tasks and who has decision-making authority.

   - The jobs in this organization are clearly defined and logically structured.
   - In this organization, it is sometimes unclear who has the formal authority to make a decision.
   - In some of the projects I've been on, I haven't been sure exactly who my boss was.
   - Our productivity sometimes suffers from a lack of organization and planning.

2. *Standards* measure the feeling of pressure to improve performance and the degree of pride employees have in doing a good job. High standards mean that people are always looking for ways to improve performance. Low standards reflect lower expectations for performance.

   - In this organization we set very high standards for performance.
   - In this organization people don't seem to take much pride in their performance.
   - Around here there is a feeling of pressure to continually improve our personal and group performance.
   - Our management believes that no job is so well done that it couldn't be done better.

3. *Responsibility* reflects employees' feelings of "being their own boss" and not having to double-check decisions with others. A sense of high responsibility signifies that employees feel encouraged to solve problems on their own. Low responsibility indicates that risk taking and testing new approaches tend to be discouraged.

- We don't rely too heavily on individual judgment in this organization; almost everything is double-checked.

- Around here management resents your checking everything with them; if you think you've got the right approach you just go ahead.

- You won't get ahead in the organization unless you stick your neck out and try things on your own.

- Our philosophy emphasizes that people should solve their own problems by themselves.

4. *Recognition* indicates employees' feelings of being rewarded for a job well done. This is a measure of the emphasis placed on reward versus criticism and punishment. High-recognition climates are characterized by an appropriate balance of reward and criticism. Low recognition means that good work is inconsistently rewarded.

- In this organization the rewards and encouragements you get usually outweigh the threats and the criticism.

- There is not enough reward and recognition given in this organization for doing good work.

- We have a promotion system here that helps the best person rise to the top.

- In this organization people are rewarded in proportion to the excellence of their job performance.

5. *Support* reflects the feeling of trust and mutual support that prevails within a work group. Support is high when employees feel that they are part of a well-functioning team and when they sense that they can get help (especially from the boss) if they need it. Support is low when employees feel isolated and alone.

- You don't get much sympathy in this organization if you make a mistake.

- When I am on a difficult assignment, I can usually count on getting assistance from my boss and co-workers.
- People in this organization don't really trust each other enough.
- I feel that I am a member of a well-functioning team.

6. *Commitment* reflects employees' sense of pride in belonging to the organization and their degree of commitment to the organization's goals. Strong feelings of commitment are associated with high levels of personal loyalty. Lower levels of commitment mean that employees feel apathetic toward the organization and its goals.

- Generally, people are highly committed to the goals of this organization.
- People here feel proud of belonging to this organization.
- People don't really care what happens to this organization.
- As far as I can see, there isn't much personal loyalty to the organization.

To my knowledge, this climate questionnaire (which is copyrighted by Mercer Delta Consulting Group, LLC) has been successfully translated and used in at least six different languages, including Spanish, French, German, Japanese, Chinese (Mandarin), Portuguese, and, most recently, Dutch.

What Is the Organization Being Measured?

Our climate questionnaire begins with the following instructions:

This questionnaire is designed to measure how people feel about their work environment. You will be asked to describe the kind of working climate that has been created in your organization. By "organization" we mean the smallest work unit that is meaningful to you.

In laboratory and tightly controlled research settings, these instructions proved adequate. However, as I began to administer hundreds or thousands of questionnaires to employees in different parts of large organizations, more and more people started asking me, "What organization should I be thinking of when I answer the questions?" In our questionnaire, when we don't refer to "this organization," we use phrases such as "around here" or "our management" or "our philosophy." We want people to characterize their *immediate* work environment. But, as organizations become flatter, more fluid, and more complex, this environment doesn't always lend itself to exact boundaries. Although this has been a source of confusion to some of my clients, it is not a major measurement issue.

Climate is a summary of people's perceptions of their work environment. It is what people sense and think and feel. We don't ask people to try to imagine or guess what another person—in another part of the organization—might sense or think or feel about his or her own work environment. We want people to stick with what they really know or sense. Then, and only then, are their responses going to be valid.

That is not to say that what goes on in the larger organization doesn't have an impact on the individual's own organizational climate. It usually does. As the diagram in Exhibit 4.3 illustrates, each member of an organization is embedded in a work group or unit, which is part of a larger unit, and so on. We want to measure people's perception of their immediate environment. We will get a picture of the larger unit's climate by rolling up the climates of the various work groups. And we will describe the overall organizational climate by adding up all of the unit climates.

Exhibit 4.3
The Embedded Organization

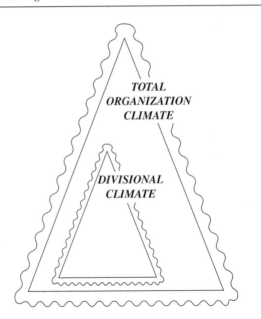

So, although our Organizational Climate Questionnaire may look a bit sloppy at first, it works quite well, even in highly matrixed or horizontal organizations.

Measuring Leadership

One of the most important developments in the way we measured climate after I left the Harvard Business School was the inclusion of a separate section in the same questionnaire that measured management practices. As soon as George Litwin and I started using climate measurement as a consulting tool, we realized that business leaders wanted to know how to *change* climates that were less than healthy. And you can't deal with climate change without dealing with leadership.

The way we approached measuring leadership and the evolution of our list of important leadership practices I discuss in greater detail in Chapter 6. The important points to note here are:

- Real-world clients want to *improve* climate, not just measure it.
- Real-world clients understand that leadership influences performance. Therefore, they view the measurement of leadership practices as a practical and welcome part of our consulting assignments.
- They also want the consultants to "get it over with" as quickly and efficiently as possible. The "it" I refer to is the surveying and the measuring. My clients are less than comfortable having consultants hanging around passing out different surveys every time a new problem arises.
- Therefore, including leadership practices in our climate questionnaire makes both conceptual and practical sense.

So, we have been including leadership practices in our climate surveys for the past 15 years.

The Feedback Report

When your goal is performance improvement, not just research, how the climate and leadership practices survey data are reported is almost as important as the information that is collected. Over the years I have developed a Climate and Practices Feedback Report that seems to work. It contains enough information to satisfy the curious executive who wants to know lots of details about the survey but not so much as to be confusing.

A sample of the feedback report is provided in the ToolKit. As you can see, it has four essential features:

1. *It is roomy.* We don't cram all the numbers onto one page. We don't use tiny columns and small print. We use simple graphics. Paper is cheap, so we use six pages of it. That means executives have plenty of room to jot notes or mark their thoughts on the report itself.

2. *It displays both the climate profile and leadership practices results in terms of percentile scores, not raw scores.* Although the climate questionnaire utilizes a 4-point scale and the leadership practices section of the survey utilizes a 5-point scale, we show survey results for both climate and practices as a score between 1 and 100. These percentile scores tell the person we have just surveyed how his or her results compare to all the other results we have kept track of in our norm base. For example, if a person received a score of 37%, it would mean that he or she scored *higher* on that item or scale than 37% of all the others we have measured and included in our database. (Of course, it also means he or she scored *lower* than 62% of others we have surveyed.)

3. *The percentile scores are derived from a robust norm base.* I have been doing climate surveys for 30 years. The climate norm base consists of a sample of the surveys I have done for the past 20 of these years. Over 1,000 separate organizations and almost 10,000 individual climates or leaders are included. Most are from American companies. Most are from business organizations (between 5% and 10% of the norm base comes from health care and educational work groups). Most are from middle management and executive populations, although approximately 10% of the database is made up of first-line or factory-level work groups. I'd like to say our norms are of only high-performing organizations. I'd like to say that, but I can't. Our norms are composed of my climate clients. Although they include such obviously successful organizations, such as Gillette, Rockwell, Citibank, Pepsi, Sony, and GE, they also include companies that have struggled to improve climate and performance, such as Union Carbide, Xerox, and Long John Silver's.

4. *Practices data include an indication of respondent consistency as well as a measure of the median raw score in the norm base.* The column labeled "spread" is derived from a statistic called the standard error. (It's something like the standard deviation.) If all of the people filling out a questionnaire about a manager agreed and gave the manager the same score, the spread would be "narrow." If there were some disagreement, the spread would say "medium." And if respondents were not at all in agreement (i.e., the manager got scores that ranged from 1s and 2s all the way to 5s) on the same question, then the spread would be "wide." The report also gives the 50th percentile raw score for each of the 18 leadership practices. This is the median score in our norm base and it gives recipients a sense of "how high the bar is" for each practice. For example, the number in parentheses on leadership practice 4 is 4.14. This means that many managers in our norm base received scores of 4 or 5 (half of them received scores higher than 4.14). Armed with this information, a person looking at a 35th percentile score on practice 4 will understand that he or she received average scores closer to 4, not closer to 1 or 2.

Is There a "Perfect Climate"?

You may know the cynical joke about the difference between a good marriage and a perfect marriage: A good marriage exists. I'm not so cynical about perfect climates, for as a researcher and a consultant I know that there are a number of different "perfect climates." Although there may not be *one* climate profile that is best for all organizations, we *can* identify profiles that are more or less healthy or suitable for different organizations.

The perfect climate profile depends on the answers to two questions:

- What are the dominant motive profiles of the people in the organization?
- What is the nature of the work to be done by the organization?

To the extent that people's energy to perform work stems from their nAch, nAff, and nPow, then the most productive climate would be one that arouses the most dominant motives of the organization's members. However, since each motive syndrome has its own characteristic pattern of behavior, we must understand which patterns are best suited to the work to be performed by the organization. For example, high affiliators will naturally engage in cooperative, collegial activities. If such behavior contributes to effective task performance, then the "best" climate profile would emphasize Support and deemphasize Responsibility. Power motivation is aroused by climates that stress formal power relationships. If rigorous discipline and adherence to prescribed hierarchies are critical success factors, the perfect climate would be high in Structure. If entrepreneurial initiative (closely tied to nAch) is called for, lower levels of Structure and higher levels of Responsibility would work best. And so on. The best climate depends on both the kind of work to be performed and the dominant motives of the organization's people. When you ask, "What is the perfect climate?" you first have to answer "Perfect for whom?" and "Perfect for doing what?"

Do Climate Survey Results Predict Organizational Performance?

Of course, the bottom-line question for practicing managers is "Will the survey help me manage the performance of my organization?" This entire book is my attempt to answer "yes" to this important question. But perhaps a study I conducted in 1999 with Carter Holt Harvey (CHH) will emphasize this point. CHH is a large forestry products and paper company based in Auckland, New Zealand. Its largest shareholder is International Paper (IP). When I did my study, John Faraci, an up-and-coming IP executive, was in charge. CHH is now led by Chris Liddell, a dynamic young Kiwi executive. Both Faraci and Liddell are converts to climate management. Exhibit 4.4 tells you why.

Carter Holt uses CFROI as its most important measure of organizational performance. CFROI stands for "cash flow return on investment" and represents each business's total annual value to the corporation (and to IP). Since that was the number Faraci and Liddell were looking at, that's the number I used to rank the performance of the 19 different CHH business units. I had conducted climate surveys at CHH for several years, so I was able to access lots of climate data. I not only wanted to see if Total Climate (the sum of the scores of all six dimensions) was correlated with performance, but I also wondered if one or more individual dimensions were a better performance predictor. I was particularly interested in the predictive power of the first

Exhibit 4.4

1999 CHH Performance and Climate Comparisons

BUSINESS UNIT	CFROI PERFORMANCE RANKING	RANKING BY OVERALL CLIMATE SCORE*	RANKING BY THE PERFORMANCE DIMENSIONS*
CHH Panels	1	4	2
Paper Bag	2	2	3
Tissue	3	11	12
Plastics	4	12	13
EWP	5	5	4
Raleigh	6	3	11
Continental Cup	7	1	1
Carton NZ/Aust.	8	9	9
Timber	9	7	5
Whakatane	10	18	17
Case	11	15	15
B.J. Ball	12	10	8
Business Forms	13	17	18
Forests	14	8	7
Penrose	15	19	19
Kinleith	16	16	16
Carters	17	14	14
Mataura	18	6	6
Distributors	19	13	10

*Both measures of climate are correlated with performance (over all at .01 significance level; performance dimensions at .05 level).

three climate dimensions (Structure, Standards, and Responsibility). Taken together, they are sometimes referred to as the "performance dimensions" of climate because intuitively they seem to be what leaders stress when they seek to squeeze more short-term performance from their organizations. As you can see from Exhibit 4.4, we learned that Total Climate is a better predictor of performance than any single dimension or group of dimensions. The correlation study showed that Total Climate was correlated with performance at the .01 level, whereas the performance dimensions correlated at the .05 level.

Our climate survey measures stuff that makes a difference—at least at Carter Holt Harvey.

The Practical Benefits of Our
Approach to Measuring Climate

Our techniques and methods of measuring climate have evolved since George Litwin and I began our work in the mid-1960s. I am sure others will find new ways to describe work environments in the years ahead. But for now, as both a researcher and consultant, I am satisfied. Our approach and our Organizational Climate Survey are not perfect. Neither is our Climate and Practices Feedback Report. But I believe there are at least three practical benefits of our approach to measuring organizational climate:

1. *It is relevant.* The six dimensions we use are tied to things that are important. All six dimensions have been linked, not only to patterns of aroused motivation, but to high performance as well. This linkage has been validated in laboratory and real-world organizations. Our climate measure has predictive validity. We're not searching for things that *might* make a difference. We're measuring things that do.

2. *It is useful.* Our approach turns what is murky and fuzzy and hard to comprehend into something that is quantitative and relatively clear and easy to grasp. Our approach allows you to *compare* the climate profile of one organization to that of another. It allows you to *benchmark* different work environments against each other and against high-performing organizations. When you use the same questionnaire over and over again, you can develop robust normative data that enhance its benchmarking usefulness. Our feedback reports take advantage of this. They organize the survey results into numbers and graphs that help people understand what the survey measured.

3. *It is easy to use.* Our 24-item questionnaire takes less than 10 minutes to complete. It is not laden with jargon. When people read the questions, they find they can answer them. Although the theory behind the climate measurement process may be complicated, the measurement tool isn't. This means that busy people in real-world organizations will find the time to candidly describe their thoughts and feelings. And, once we collect the data, the results are displayed in simple, easy-to-understand reports.

If Bob Potts, from the example I used to open this chapter, wants to attack the performance and morale problems of the Metropolitan Health Care System, he should begin by using our approach to measuring the climate of the organization. He should start by surveying his successful Metro Children's Center. Then he should compare its climate to the climate profiles of his less successful units, including the troublesome Metro General Hospital. These climate surveys would provide him with snapshots of how people think and feel about working at MHCS. He would know how challenged, how confused, how distrustful, or how frustrated the different employee groups were. He might not like what he learns, but he would know what and where the problems are.

Measuring the climate isn't going to fix it, but Potts—and any leader in Potts's situation—will be much better prepared to fix things once armed with our kind of climate data. At a minimum, he will be working on the right issues and he will have a tool to calibrate his ongoing impact as a leader.

The next step, then, will be to learn what factors cause different climates to be the way they are. This means understanding the determinants of organizational climate. When Potts knows this, he can figure out which determinants he can control and which he's got to learn to live with. Then he can set about improving both the climate and the performance of his organization.

Part II

What Causes Climate?

Climate doesn't just happen—it is caused. And the more we know about the causes of climate, the better able we will be to successfully manage it to improve organizational performance. Chapters 5 to 7 explore the primary causes of organizational climate.

Research with a variety of organizations has identified five determinants of climate:

- External environment
- Strategy
- Leadership practices
- Organizational arrangements
- Historical forces

Each of these is important, and anyone who wants to change an organization's climate should carefully evaluate the role of all five of these factors. But research has consistently shown that by far the most important determinant of climate is leadership. And we have found that it's most useful to approach and describe climate leadership in terms of specific practices that can be taught and learned by leaders at all levels of an organization.

Further research with different types of organizations has established a connection between certain leadership practices and the six dimensions of climate. This means that we know what practices to focus on in order to improve the climate dimensions that will have the greatest impact on performance. Over the years, I have relied on a list of 18 leadership practices that have proven to be the most workable. But, through a process of statistical analysis, we have also developed a shorter "hit list" of six practices that have the greatest impact on all of the climate dimensions. We all know that effective leadership cannot be boiled down to six practices. Nevertheless, our "hit list" provides leaders with basic behavioral strategies that will maximize their motivational impact.

5

The Determinants of Climate

Stuck in traffic while driving home, Maria Lopez uses the time to reflect on the state of her business. She can't tell if her frustration is more the result of the road construction delays or her own situation as president of Eagle Exports.

Maria inherited the family export business from her father, Jerry, who died when she was 30. At first things went well. She enjoyed being "the guy in charge," and she had big plans to expand the business. For the first eight months Eagle Exports was making money by emphasizing high-quality packaging and service to its loyal customers in the automotive industry. But recently Maria has been feeling that something is wrong, and she's puzzled as to what and why. Her 30-person company is experiencing labor problems, with high absenteeism and two men whom she feels sure are abusing workmen's comp. While she was negotiating a new labor contract, her car was "keyed" in the company parking lot, and the tires were flattened on the trailer carrying her large powerboat temporarily stored in the shop. She administered a climate survey she saw in a magazine, and the low numbers confirmed her suspicions. The people at Eagle Exports are not happy.

In response to the results of the climate survey, Maria made a few changes. She shifted some of the organizational arrangements in the shop, putting Ed, a 30-year veteran, in charge of internal operations so she can focus on suppliers and customers. She also appointed one of the hardworking younger employees to the position of shop steward. The company has responded to the entry of a number of nonunion competitors by lowering costs and increasing volume, and she hired a salesperson who is working on straight commission. She also invested in a new computer system for the office, as well as in new technology on the shop floor in an effort to speed up production. In anticipation of increased productivity, she rented a second building, but so far it stands idle.

Sensitive to the fact that she is a woman in a male-dominated industry, Maria has been paying a lot of attention to her leadership style. She is not her father, a gregarious and charismatic man who sometimes seemed to run the business by the sheer force of his personality. But Maria has worked hard to lead by example, putting in long days, and she has established systems of internal communications. As often as possible, she eats lunch in the small company cafeteria. She has instituted a highly visible company bulletin board and has encouraged employees to post items of interest on it. For her part, she has posted monthly Eagle Exports performance statistics.

Despite her efforts, productivity has remained constant—but it should be increasing! In fact, Eagle Exports lost money in the last quarter, even though the auto industry, a major client, is booming, and the state's economy is at an all-time high. And she readministered the climate survey last week, but the results are about the same.

The traffic inches ahead. Maria feels that the key to the success or failure of her business lies in the people working for her, especially their attitude toward their work. But what causes that attitude to be what it is? And what can she do to change it?

———

———

Causing Climate

As soon as we shift our attention from *defining* and *measuring* climate to *creating* and *controlling* it—or managing it—we have to answer the question, "What *causes* climate?" Or as Litwin and I stated the issue in 1967: "What are the *determinants* of climate?" This is the question that Maria is asking. And in a sense she is on the right track because she is examining her organizational arrangements and her leadership practices—two important factors—but she needs a more systematic approach.

This is not an easy question to answer, largely because of the issue of causality. When there is a direct correlation between two factors, it is not necessarily clear which one causes the other, or if some third factor is causing the other two to move together. For example, we might see that one group of workers is happy and productive and another group unhappy and unproductive. But is the first group productive because they are happy, or are they happy because they are productive? And we can ask a similar question of the second group. When we observe that the first group is also well paid, then we might ask if that is what causes them to be happy and productive, or are they well paid because they are productive? As I said, causality can be difficult to determine, even in a simplistic example such as this one.

One way to understand how causality works in the laboratory is to hold constant as many of the variables as you can. Manipulate one and see what happens. Or using a more scientific method, make a prediction about what will happen if your hypothesis is true, and then see if the results confirm your hypothesis. You can do this in the lab because you can control all or most of the factors, while in the messy real world factors are coming at you from all directions, and in fact one of the challenges is to determine which ones you really can control.

When Litwin and I did our 1967 research at Harvard described in the Introduction, we tried to hold constant most of the variables. We staffed each of the three simulated companies ("British," "Blazer," and "Balance") with the same kind of employees by administering psychological tests and balancing the three populations according to the test results, as well as age, gender, and experience. We also controlled factors such as the economic and market forces, competitive rivalry, and technology. In our experiment, these were all "make-believe" and were only visible to Blazer, British, and Balance employees through the actions and comments of the presidents of these make-believe organizations. And the three presidents were members of our research team. The purpose of the research was to see if we could create three different kinds of organizations and measure the attitudes and performance of each. It would be both self-serving and inaccurate to say we knew exactly what we were doing back then. But we assumed (correctly, as it turns out) that leadership was a major determinant of climate. And, therefore, we focused mainly on manipulating leadership practices to alter climate while holding other factors constant.

This is a luxury that is not available in real-world organizations, but it served our purposes well. We succeeded in creating and sustaining three very different organizational climates that led to differences in the quality and quantity of "radar machines" produced. Employees of British Radar, with a climate designed to arouse nPow, ended up, in fact, more concerned with power, authority, and the formal relationships. Members of Balance, whose nAff we had aroused, were more relaxed, and more concerned with affiliation and with their informal relationships. And Blazer's aroused nAch created a high-achieving organization, producing more radar machines, more innovation, and employees with a more competitive attitude.

So in our laboratory study we clearly established that leadership practices are a significant determinant of climate. By varying leadership practices we caused changes in climate. And the different climates led to different behaviors and performance. In addition to leadership, we also assumed that the formal organizational structures, policies, procedures, the way jobs are defined, and the reward and communication systems—what we now call organizational arrangements—are important determinants. So we had our three presidents modify those aspects of each of the three experimental organizations. For example, the president of British Radar established written job descriptions and instituted very strict rules about who could talk to whom. The chain of command was clear and it was enforced. The president of Balance, on the other hand, described jobs largely in terms of relationships and implemented a policy that once each morning and once each afternoon there were to be small group meetings to "build team spirit." And the Blazer president used a rigorous system of performance measurement. He had all sorts of information posted on the workplace walls such as production statistics, competitive data, results of quality audits, and so on.

We pretty much stopped there. As we reported in *Motivation and Organizational Climate,* by manipulating (1) leadership practices and (2) organizational arrangements, we successfully created three distinctive climates. These three climates, and the kinds of performances aroused by each, confirmed our hypotheses about motivation, climate, and performance. We established the causal links between these two determinants and climate, and between climate and performance. In doing this, we gave managers an important tool they could use to arouse motivation and stimulate productivity.

Determinants Inside and Outside of the Organization

Over the years, however, I have had to expand the list of important climate determinants. In the real world where it is difficult to control the variables, a good way to approach causes or determinants is to divide them into two categories: factors that are *outside* of the organization and factors that are *inside* the organization.

Those that are outside the organization—the category we came to call "external environment"—include such things as government regulation, economic conditions, competitive industry forces, technology, and the overall pace of change in the world that surrounds the organization. As I said earlier, in our laboratory experiment we held these constant while manipulating inside variables.

But I have seen the need to identify and take into account a few climate determinants in addition to leadership and organizational arrangements. These two continue to prove to be the most powerful determinants, but I have seen the importance of two other inside factors.

The first is the "strategy" of the organization—the understood direction and purpose of the organization, the way it sets goals and priorities, and how it allocates resources and tries to "win" in its chosen industry or marketplace. I'll examine the impact of strategy on climate in a variety of organizations later in this chapter.

The second additional internal factor in determining climate I call "historical forces." This is a broad category, almost a catchall in our climate model. In a sense it's the collective memory of the people who live and work in the organization. It includes the norms and values that have grown up over time, along with the traditions, work habits, and general expectations regarding future rewards or consequences based on what has happened in the past. This category has a lot in common with what Edgar Schein calls "culture," the often unspoken assumptions that lie deep in the history and, thus, the psyche of an organization. I'll say more about this as well. Suffice it to say that historical forces, like Schein's culture, are very difficult to change.

What we have, then, is a model that includes five main determinants of organizational climate.

If you look at these five determinants in Exhibit 5.1, you can see why Maria has been frustrated in her attempts to change Eagle Exports. Although the first and the last (external environment and historical forces) are much less controllable than the middle three (strategy, leadership, and organizational arrangements), her approach to climate management must take all five determinants into consideration.

Maria is properly focusing her attention on her own leadership practices—the single most significant determinant of climate and the

Exhibit 5.1
The Determinants of Climate

subject of my next chapter. But she is not paying much attention to what is an apparent shift in strategy from a customer service orientation to one that emphasizes higher productivity, lower costs, and more aggressive corporate growth. Maria must also be more sensitive to the influences of historical forces, that is, what Eagle Exports has always been and what this means to employees. She is aware of the change in leadership practices involved when she took over from her father, but she needs to understand this change more fully in the context of the history of the company and the norms and assumptions held by the members of the organization, especially among longtime employees. But it's not limited to old-timers, for these norms and assumptions are passed along to newer members of the organization.

Maria also made changes in the organizational arrangements at Eagle Exports. These changes impact how people think and feel. For example, Ed's new role and the use of a shop steward to deal directly with the guys on the floor, something that Jerry used to do himself, represent an entirely new organizational structure. Patterns of decision-making authority, and perhaps policies and procedures have all changed. And although Maria can't do anything to manage the external environment, she certainly can better understand how it might be affecting her organization. For example, the globalization of the auto industry, the tight labor market, and the state's economic prosperity all have to have an impact on Eagle's employees. Perhaps they are aware of brand-new employment opportunities outside of Eagle. Or perhaps they are bewildered and confused by the new technology or Maria's reaction to new and foreign competition.

Let's review each of these major climate determinants to understand how they influence climate. Let's see how each has operated in some of the organizations with which I have worked in the last 20 years. And let's see how Maria might leverage her understanding of these determinants to improve her effectiveness as a change agent.

External Environment

One of the first things you notice as a climate consultant is the broad similarity of climates among organizations in the same industry. Insurance agency climates are often quite similar. Radio station climates aren't that different from one another, but they are quite different from insurance agencies. High school climates tend to have similar features, and the climates of hospital emergency rooms tend to have the same high and low dimensions, even though the overall level of the dimensions might be quite different.

In 1984, I was part of a consulting team that helped figure out how the Bell Operating Companies (BOCs) were going to function after they split off from the old AT&T. As part of our work, we conducted climate surveys of all five original BOCs. The "typical" climate profile is shown as Exhibit 5.2. I say "typical" because they were all largely the same. Not identical, but pretty close.

Why is this? Granted, the BOCs were part of Ma Bell. But why do we tend to find the same patterns of climate in the same industry? This is partly due to the similarity of the external environments in which these organizations are forced to operate. The question isn't *does* the external environment influence organizational climate, but *how.* What aspects of the outside cause climate patterns on the inside? And what patterns seem to contribute to high levels of organizational performance?

It's difficult to conduct rigorous quantitative research to answer these questions, especially when dealing with real-world organizations outside of the lab. However, I have a wealth of personal, anecdotal data that leads me to the following four conclusions about the causal relationship between the external environment and organizational climate.

1. *Although the external environment influences all six climate dimensions, it seems to have the most direct impact on only three of them: Structure, Responsibility and Commitment.* In other words, these three dimensions define *Es* and

Exhibit 5.2
Bell Operating Company (BOC) Climate Profile

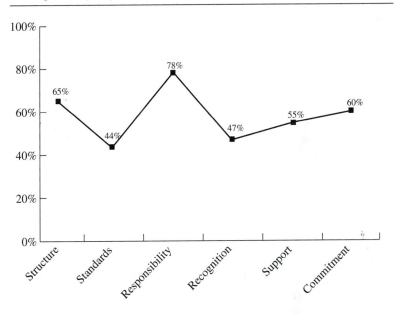

*I*s that are most closely related to factors outside the organization. The other three, Standards, Recognition, and Support, tend to vary more with the inside determinants of climate.

2. *The pace of change in an industry is the biggest single external environmental determinant.* I am talking about all kinds of change—technology change, the emergence of new customers, new competitors, new rules of engagement, new products, and new business models. Any one of these will shape how people think about their work, their relationships, and the likely consequences of their actions. And this will happen no matter what else is going on with the other four determinants of climate.

   - As the pace of change increases, I have found that successful, high-performing organizations have lower Structure and higher Responsibility. A lower sense of Structure allows for more nimble and immediate responses to changing circumstances. High Responsibility encourages individual initiative and this usually means those closest to the outside (think "customer") make more of the decisions.

- Over the long term, high-performing organizations facing rapid external change must have a strong sense of teamwork, trust, and support to go with their low Structure and high Responsibility. Although not caused by the pace of external change, high Support allows people to function effectively when roles and relationships are unstable or unclear.

Misys, a highly successful and rapidly growing information technology (IT) company based in the United Kingdom, is a perfect example of what can happen in a company competing in an industry marked by a number of rapid changes. Listed on the London Stock Exchange, Misys develops and sells software. It has grown an average of 30% per year for the past 10 years by entering new geographic markets and adding new products. In addition to these technological and customer changes, the company faces a bewildering array of new competitors each year.

The Misys climate is as distinctive as it is successful. Our surveys revealed that Structure is low and Responsibility is high. The long-term climate and leadership challenge for Misys is in the Support dimension. In 2000, Misys had over 6,000 employees, but fewer than 50 of them were in the corporate headquarters. Individual Misys businesses were often so independent that they considered each other their main competitors. Large banking customers would apologize to one Misys division when it lost a contract without realizing that the bank's new IT supplier was another Misys division. The feelings of support at Misys are only moderate, and they are limited to supporting others within each narrow business unit. The five top executives have worked together for years and trust one another explicitly. But their feelings of mutual support are not reflected further down in the Misys organization. Internal competition has reinforced a silo mentality and a business unit selfishness. Lower-level Misys managers often discourage their people from "wasting time" (their term) on collaborative efforts. This, in turn, has inhibited marketing synergies and technology transfer between Misys businesses. Support is the climate dimension that must be improved if the company's climate is going to drive performance in an external environment that continues to change rapidly.

3. *High levels of industry consolidation and regulation with the absence of competitive rivalry in an industry often have a profound impact on the patterns of organizational climate.* In industries dominated by a few large players, competition often amounts to what strategy guru Michael Porter calls a "gentleman's game." When industries are heavily regulated, everyone knows the rules. There is a predictability about things, and I have found that the most successful organizations have climates that are higher in Structure and lower in Responsibility.

- It is the opposite of the "pace of change" logic. A well-oiled bureaucracy contributes to success in highly regulated industries because it is easier to predict and, therefore, proscribe what to do to maximize efficiency or performance. Clarity is a virtue when navigating well-defined paths with severe penalties for breaking the rules and, consequently, individual initiative, when it leads to "outside the box" approaches, is a vice.

- The higher-performing climate profiles of high-Structure environments usually include higher levels of Recognition. I am sure this is related to the need to arouse both nAch and nAff. High Structure and low Responsibility arouse nPow.

A vivid example of this was provided by a 1998 climate study of the Attorney General's Office (AGO) of the Commonwealth of Massachusetts. Then attorney general, Scott Harshbarger had an enviable track record of success. Under his leadership, violent crime in Massachusetts hit a 30-year low, the state recovered $7.6 billion from big tobacco companies, over 200 public corruption cases were prosecuted, and the AGO was able to successfully negotiate a $50 million recovery program for low- and moderate-income loans and save business over $2 billion in excess workmen's compensation costs. Judged to be a high-performing organization by almost any standard, the AGO climate profile appears as Exhibit 5.3.

Exhibit 5.3
AGO's Climate Profile

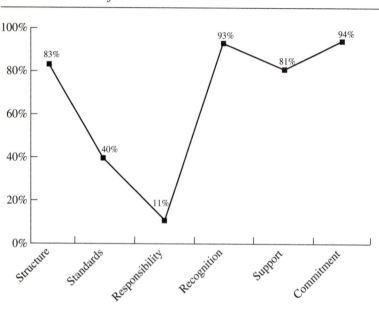

As one of the largest "law firms" in the common-wealth, many of the AGO's activities are explicitly pre-scribed and relatively predictable. There is no real competitive rivalry and the industry has to be considered highly consolidated. Attorneys are discouraged from "sticking their necks out" and taking risks with the commonwealth's legal system. The profile described in Exhibit 5.3 may look atypical, but it matches the demands of the external environment.

In 1998, Harshbarger had been the commonwealth's attorney general for eight years. Harshbarger's leadership clearly impacted the climate of the AGO. But no amount of leadership can alter the fundamental role or constraints placed on that office by the external environment and, thus, the climate profile is the result of those constraints.

4. *A strong economy and buoyant job market influence the Commitment dimension of climate.* When employees feel they have opportunities and career options separate from their existing organization, Commitment is lowered. In such external environments, high levels of performance depend on having high levels of Commitment. A climate that

emphasizes employee pride, personal loyalty, and goal attachment provides the glue that is required for continuity and success.

I observed a dramatic example of this in the late 1990s when I was consulting for Cable & Wireless, PLC. The sense of personal commitment to the company and its different operating divisions varied widely around the world. There was a striking relationship between the strength of the local economy (and the resulting tight employment market for technical talent) and company performance and commitment. Strong economies in the United States and Germany contributed to low levels of Commitment there, and weaker economies in the Caribbean and Australia were associated with higher levels of Commitment. The low scores were associated with higher levels of turnover and lower levels of bottom-line performance. When management took steps to increase the Commitment dimension of climate, turnover decreased and the bottom line improved.

Strategy

In 1986 I co-authored (with Joel Uchenick) a book about business strategy. In *Strategy Traps and How to Avoid Them* we talked about different kinds of strategies, how strategies should be developed, and all of the strategy mistakes Joel and I had observed in our consulting careers. One of our observations was that implementing a winning strategy was a bigger problem than formulating a winning strategy. The reason we cited for this was the importance and difficulty of matching strategy with organizational climate. A company's performance depends on a close link between what it is trying to do (strategy), the energy that employees have to perform the work that is required by the strategy (motivation), and the environmental determinants of that level of energy (organizational climate). How does this link work? What do we know about the relationship between strategy and climate?

My experience tells me that different business strategies cause different patterns of organizational climate. Much of the influence of strategy on climate is indirect:

- Leadership practices will vary depending on the strategy the leaders are trying to implement.

- Organizational arrangements will be developed in order to reinforce different strategies.
- Over time, long-standing business strategies will have a noticeable impact on the historical forces that determine the climate of the organization.

In some cases, strategy can have a more direct influence on climate. To the extent that strategy defines what is important to the organization, what results are valued, and what behaviors are most likely to achieve the explicit goals of the strategy, then strategy directly determines the most salient Es and Is that surround the members of the organization. For example, Solomon Smith Barney's climate is characterized by high levels of Responsibility and Recognition and relatively low levels of Support and Commitment. In part, I think this can be attributed to a strategy that deemphasizes institutional collaboration and stresses an "individual meritocracy" approach to growth. It works!

Rather than debate this distinction between direct and indirect causation, it is more useful to describe the real-world linkages I have observed between strategy and climate, especially those linkages that seem to work so well in high-performing organizations. Samples of the linkages between strategy and climate are outlined in Exhibit 5.4.

There are many ways to classify and define business strategies. For example, Michael Porter has it boiled down to three "generic strategies." More recently, Adrian Slywotsky and David Morrison, senior consultants with Mercer Management Consulting, a partner company of MDC, defined 30 distinct patterns that they believe describe the various success formulas utilized by high-performing organizations. At Mercer Delta, we split the difference. We use a much shorter and simpler list of strategies than Slywotsky and Morrison but longer than Porter. I prefer simplicity even at the risk of oversimplifying. Exhibit 5.4 should be examined with this caveat in mind. Of course, there are more than seven types of business strategy. Of course, there are cases where "off-profile" climate patterns are associated with high performance. And, of course, there are many other factors that might account for the linkages and relationships I have cited. Nevertheless, as Joel Uchenick and I discovered when we wrote *Strategy Traps,* a lot of time, money, and heartache could be avoided if business leaders paid more attention to the implications of Exhibit 5.4.

Exhibit 5.4
The Links Between Strategy and Climate in High-Performing Organizations

STRATEGIES	EXAMPLES	KEY CLIMATE DIMENSIONS	COMMENTS	REPRESENTATIVE PROFILES
1. Low-cost producer	Costco Southwest Airlines	Higher structure, standards, and commitment Lower responsibility	• Everyone must be on the same page.	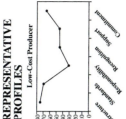
2. Differentiate on service	Dell Computer Nordstrom's	Higher standards, recognition, and support Lower structure	• Cynical employees deliver poor service. • Caring for people pays dividends.	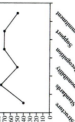
3. Differentiate on speed	McDonald's	Higher structure and support	• Have clear roles and goals, then be there when they need support.	
4. Differentiate on new-product innovation	Nokia 3M	Higher responsibility, recognition, and commitment	• Entrepreneurial spirit drives innovation. • Continuity keeps the new products flowing.	
5. Differentiate on marketing	P&G General Mills	Higher standards and commitment	• Constant pressure to innovate. • Sharp focus on leveraging the brand's budget.	
6. Differentiate based on technology	CMGI Cisco Systems	Higher responsibility and commitment Lower structure	• Encourage experiments. • Avoid rigidity and tight constraints.	
7. High reliance on distribution partners	Hain Celestial PepsiCo	Higher standards, recognition, and support	• Clear rules are important, but the real key is the quality of the relationships.	

Let me give one example—and it is a negative one—in which the lack of congruence between strategy and climate contributed to poor organizational performance. In the early 1980s Citibank (as it was then called) operated a large indirect lending business out of St. Louis. It was decided that the success formula for this business was to be the low-cost provider of auto, RV, and mobile home loans. Now, Citibank was and still is a world-class organization. If it decides to focus on cost management, it's going to focus on cost management. The problem was that this represented a big change for Citibank, and our climate surveys revealed that its organizational climate was all wrong for the low-cost–provider approach. Up until then, the bank had relied on its independent regional loan businesses to drive growth. Systems and procedures were flexible. Entrepreneurial initiative was encouraged. Even in St. Louis, Citibank had a New York attitude. The organization was staffed with free spirits. Structure was relatively low, Responsibility was high, and Support was low. Not surprisingly, Citibank's new low-cost strategy was a disaster. It was only when the indirect loan businesses went back to a strategy that differentiated the bank based on service and product innovation that performance improved. This was the historic strategy that had helped to create the St. Louis climate in the first place.

Organizational Arrangements

Other than leadership practices, the determinant I call organizational arrangements has the strongest impact on climate. I have borrowed the term from Nadler (see Nadler, 1998, p. 34) and I realize that there are hundreds of possible variables we could lump under this heading. George Litwin, John Bray, and Kathleen Lusk Brooke, in their 1996 *Mobilizing the Organization,* stress the importance of including informal or emergent arrangements along with those that have been memorialized in a policy or procedure manual. With this in mind, Exhibit 5.5 provides a list of the most important organizational arrangements when it comes to arousing motivation and their influence on the dimensions of climate.

Many secondary public schools provide good examples of how organizational arrangements determine climate. Strong teachers' unions often exercise control over the reward system in which pay raises result from levels of graduate education and years of experience rather than performance on the job, and in which there is virtually no

Exhibit 5.5

How Organizational Arrangements Are Linked to Climate

ORGANIZATIONAL ARRANGEMENT	CLIMATE DIMENSION MOST IMPACTED	OTHER CLIMATE DIMENSIONS AFFECTED
1. Formal Organizational Design and Reporting Relationships	Structure	Responsibility
2. Job Descriptions/ Accountability Statements	Structure	Responsibility, Support
3. Goal Setting/ Planning Systems	Commitment	Structure, Standards
4. Performance Measurement Systems	Standards	Commitment, Recognition
5. Appraisal System	Standards	Recognition, Support
6. Reward System	Recognition	Commitment
7. Training and Development Systems	Support	Recognition
8. New Policies and Procedures	Structure	Responsibility, Support
9. Career Management Systems	Responsibility	Recognition, Commitment
10. Other People Flow Systems (i.e. recruitment, placement, termination)	Responsibility	Recognition, Structure, Standards
11. Formal Committees/ Meetings	Structure	Support
12. Informal or Emerging Organizational Arrangements	Support	Responsibility

way to be "promoted" except out of the teaching profession and into administration. What's more, tenure policies protect teachers from being fired except for the most egregious behavior. Because of these organizational arrangements, it is very difficult to discourage mediocre teaching and encourage excellence and innovation. Teachers typically generate these on their own.

Sometimes with enthusiasm but often out of frustration, school administrators respond to the union's power by managing the schools through emphasizing policies and procedures that teachers consider irrelevant to the heart and soul of education. Examine the handbook of your local public school to see how many pages are devoted to the attendance policy, the discipline policy, the dress code, and the school calendar, in comparison with pages devoted to teaching and learning, which are seen as the province of the individual classroom teacher. Administrators are in charge of the halls and the cafeteria. They leave the classroom to the teachers except when they intrude through announcements on the public address system.

Because school administrators are so busy dealing with these policies and procedures, they are seriously pressed for time to make meaningful evaluations of their teachers. Some administrators effectively "coach" the teachers they evaluate, but others just go through the motions in order to see each teacher once every three or four years as the contract requires. Evaluation is often seen as just another policy hurdle to get over rather than a way to exert educational leadership.

The result is often a pattern of climate characterized by very high Responsibility (the teachers feel they are "all alone in their classrooms") with low Recognition, Support, and Commitment, although the latter may be strong when "school spirit," often expressed through support of athletic teams, arouses nAff.

In too many public schools, the other internal climate determinants, especially leadership practices and strategy, seem to be overwhelmed by the power of organizational arrangements. The Board of Education may conduct a retreat to devise a strategy, but it is difficult for that strategy to filter through all the organizational arrangements and find expression in the classroom. What passes for strategy in many cases are mission statements, complete with appropriate catch phrases, posted on classroom walls and ignored.

I'll discuss organizational climate in the schools more fully in Chapter 9. Although I conclude that the problems in the schools ultimately come down to failures of leadership, the way leaders are often handcuffed by organizational arrangements makes a difficult task even more difficult.

Historical Forces

The fourth determinant of organizational climate is history. In our original climate research study at Harvard, this determinant was completely absent. None of our three experimental organizations had any history whatsoever. They had no past. They had no traditions, no customs, no old-timers who could tell you how things "should be done around here." There was no institutional memory. There were no stories or myths or legends or precedents. But that was only an experimental situation.

In the real world, organizations have rich traditions and strong memories, and these factors shape people's expectations and have an impact on the organization's climate. We label this influence historical forces. Ed Schein calls it "culture." Whatever we call it, I have always found it hard to define. Joel Uchenick and I took a stab at a definition in *Strategy Traps.* We talked about five aspects of an organization's history and culture:

1. *Historical Values*—the ways in which employees assess certain traits, qualities, activities, or behaviors as good or bad, productive, or wasteful.
2. *Beliefs*—people's understanding of the way the organization works and the probable consequences of the actions they take.
3. *Myths*—the stories or legends that persist about an organization and its leaders, reinforcing the core values and beliefs.
4. *Traditions*—repetitive significant events in an organization that reinforce and perpetuate cultural values.
5. *Norms*—the informal rules that exist in organizations regarding dress, work habits, work hours, and implicit codes of interpersonal behavior.

The climate dimensions that seem to be most affected by these historical forces are Standards, Responsibility, Support, and Commitment. Let me cite examples from my experience:

- EDS in the 1980s had a climate profile that included incredibly high Standards. This sense that "perfection was possible" stemmed in large part from Ross Perot's personal value system and the sense of discipline and excellence he and his top team constantly reinforced at EDS. Striving to constantly improve performance was part of the EDS ethos in the 1980s, and it has remained part of its climate long after Perot's departure.

- When I worked with Merrill Lynch's Fixed Income Group, it had a climate characterized by very high levels of Responsibility. Most employees believed that the way to succeed was by taking risks, sticking their necks out and asking for forgiveness, not permission. As a matter of fact, senior management had retained me to help *reduce* the sense of freewheeling entrepreneurship. They wanted to see more teamwork and a bit less individualism. It was a tough assignment. The historical forces were so strong and the beliefs and myths reinforcing the importance of individual initiative were so pervasive that it took us a long time to moderate the Responsibility dimension. Even after three years of hard work, most of the old-timers were still considered to be too independent. You certainly can't change years of history in weeks or months.

- St. Francis Hospital in Roslyn, New York, provides an example of how historical forces can cause high levels of Support and Commitment, even when other factors are acting to decrease these dimensions. St. Francis is one of the highest-performing cardiovascular surgery centers in the United States, and it has an excellent reputation for caring and responsive patient care. It has always had a climate noted for its high levels of Recognition, Support, and Commitment. Competitive pressure led St. Francis to modify the incentive system for its nurses. The new system was aimed at having nurses pay greater attention to the costs involved in delivering high-quality patient care. It was feared that one of the consequences of this new system would be a lessening of the historical sense of Commitment and Support, but the benefits were thought to be worth this negative climate impact. In spite of the new plan, a follow-up survey showed no significant drop-off in the scores for these climate dimensions. Further investigation revealed that St. Francis's nursing managers had simply ignored the new system. Their habitual leadership style subordinated cost concerns to personal "high-touch" nursing practices. Therefore, they didn't reinforce the new cost-driven incentive system and the climate barely changed. Most nurses and nurse managers obviously failed to find much motivational attraction in cost control. I know of few organizations that have a higher level of Commitment than St. Francis Hospital. Loyalty to St. Francis is part of its history. In this case management's change in organizational arrangements could not overcome a pattern of powerful historical forces.

Leadership

Maria, the new president of Eagle Exports, is right in focusing her attention on her leadership practices. She is doing so, however, mainly by "working hard," which to her means putting in long hours and being an example to her employees of a good work ethic. She sees this as an alternative to her father's more charismatic leadership style.

There is obviously more to leadership than charisma and hard work. What Maria needs is a more systematic way to understand leadership practices. All of the other determinants of organizational climate—strategy, organizational arrangements, and even the perceptions of historical forces and the external environment—are filtered through the day-to-day practices of the leaders of the organization. For this reason, the single most important determinant of organizational climate is leadership. Because my laboratory research and my consulting experience have found leadership practices to be so important in arousing motivation and performance, I am devoting a separate chapter to the subject. For Maria, and for others in leadership positions who sense "something is wrong" with the organization or, better yet, want to avoid that "something is wrong" feeling, read on.

6

Leadership

Maria left home at 5:30 A.M. so she would be sure to beat the traffic that slowed her trip home the night before. She was able to unlock the doors at Eagle Exports by 6:00, a full two hours before the first shift was due to arrive. Time to get caught up on paperwork. And time to think.

Leadership. She knew from browsing at Amazon and at Borders that leadership was supposed to be important. She also knew that she was working her tail off, trying to set an example of high energy and conscientiousness. Isn't that the best way to lead—by your actions? And what about the nuts and bolts side of leadership? Like having a plan and budgets and holding people accountable for results. She'd read that this was called "management" in the books and articles—not "leadership," but all of her instincts told her these were important. She knew she was not as inspirational in running the business as her father had been, and she also knew that as a woman she could never achieve that macho buddy-buddy relationship with the guys at the shop. It had certainly appeared to smooth over a lot of rough edges for her father. And she could never be General Patton or what's-his-name, Vincent Gombardo, that football coach—not that she wanted to be!

She brewed a pot of coffee and poured herself a cup to help her through the budget figures and the stack of bids she was preparing for new jobs. Soon it was 8:00, and the crew began to drift in. Maria noticed that about half of them were late and no one was in a hurry. They took their time hanging up their coats, talking about last night's ball game, hanging out by the coffee. Ed, who was supposed to be supervising the workers on the floor, showed up in the office at 8:30—but at least he looked guilty as he avoided Maria's eyes. The newly appointed shop steward arrived at 8:40 and made a show of checking on each of the workers.

Maria sighed. There must be something more I can do, she said to herself. I've been here for over two hours, but it doesn't seem to make any difference. Should I go out on the floor and chew them out? Get another shop steward? Start watching football so I can be "one of the guys"? Maybe some people are born leaders, but I'm not one of them. I'm an organized person, and I always have been. What I need is a systematic way for me to *learn* what I can *do* to turn around the attitudes at Eagle Exports.

———

Maria is absolutely right in looking to leadership as a way "to turn around the attitudes," or improve the climate, at Eagle Exports. The glut of books and articles dealing with leadership that I mentioned in the Introduction to this book shows that everyone knows how important it is. But the same glut of books and articles suggests that the subject has proven to be very elusive. In much the same way, all the books on improving relationships have done little to stem the tide of divorces, and all the best-selling diet books have not caused a discernible slimming of America. In the case of leadership, and it may be similar with marriage and diet as well, the problem is not in coming up with a definition of what leadership really is. The problem is to come up with a way to understand leadership that enables people to make the kinds of changes that impact organizational performance. Nutritional advice doesn't do any good unless its embedded in a diet that people are motivated to follow.

———

Leadership and Climate

The approach to leadership I am taking in this book, and more specifically in this chapter, is one that is based on a chain of cause and effect. What the boss of a work group does is the most important determinant of climate. The boss's behavior drives climate, which arouses motivation. And aroused motivation is a major driver of bottom-line performance. Although many of the books on management or leadership can point to improvements in performance that are associated with "good leadership," they are less clear about *how* that happens. And, more importantly, they are not very specific in presenting that *how* in terms of practices that managers and leaders at all levels of an organization can follow. Bush and Gore may both have been guilty of "fuzzy math" during the 2000 U.S. presidential campaign and, similarly, many experts use "fuzzy logic" in connecting leadership with performance.

Let me put it another way. Many books on management and leadership present this:

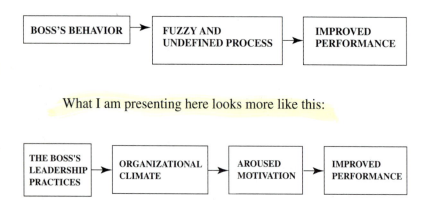

What I am presenting here looks more like this:

The research that I summarized in earlier chapters, combined with my real-world experience as a consultant, has given me insights into the "how" of effective leadership. I am not claiming to have the ultimate definition of leadership that will answer all questions and put this matter to rest. My claim is more modest: specific things that real leaders can learn to do that will improve the climate and, thus, the aroused motivation and, thus, the performance.

Let me repeat: A boss's behavior—his or her day-to-day leadership practices—is the most important determinant of climate. I say this for three reasons:

1. Leadership pervades an organization. The various other determinants of climate, factors such as organizational arrangements and strategy that I discussed in Chapter 5, are communicated to the members of the organization through the words and deeds of the manager or boss of the work group. They are presented as an expression of what I call leadership.

2. Research has shown that leadership has the greatest impact on climate.

3. Leadership is the climate determinant that is easiest to change, or at least work on, and so changes in climate and, thus, performance are most readily achieved by changing leadership practices.

Of course, I am not simply referring to the practices of the CEO or to the person at the top. As we will see, it more often is the leader of a work group, someone who is relatively low on the food chain of an organization. But it's leadership nevertheless.

One reason for the importance of leadership is so obvious that it might be overlooked. The development of a new strategy and its announcement and implementation are all carried out by those in leadership positions at various levels. Similarly, the organizational arrangements, especially when the reward system is involved or when the arrangements change, are defined to employees through the management hierarchy. And so, to a lesser extent, are the descriptions and, thus, the perceptions of both historical forces and the external environment, although co-workers largely communicate the former and media outside the organization communicate the latter. The influence of leadership on climate is pervasive.

The way a boss's leadership practices pervade an organization may explain a significant finding from numerous research studies: At least 50% of the variance in work group climates can be attributed to variance in the day-to-day practices of those who manage the work groups. George Litwin, my former research colleague at Harvard recently did a statistical regression analysis of our climate database. We found that we could predict up to 67% of the variance in climate by looking at a relatively small number of leadership practices. For the technically oriented reader, this is a correlation of .82, which is almost unheard of in the behavioral sciences. Even when we looked at the effect of leadership practices on climate two years later, we can still predict 50% of the variance in total climate scores by focusing only on leadership practices in a regression study. For more on this, see Chapter 7.

Real-world leaders have known this for a long time. So have academics and authors. Both researchers and practitioners in the real world simply have a lot of evidence and experience indicating that leadership matters. The day-to-day practices of the boss have a powerful and lasting impact on climate, and they contribute significantly to organizational performance—both good and bad.

Although the *direct impact* of leadership is relatively easy to demonstrate and understand, our climate research has demonstrated that the *indirect impact* of leadership is even more powerful and lasting. Leadership literally creates motive energy. Therefore, it persists in the organization even after the leader leaves the scene. This is what I referred to as "the cloud chamber effect" in the Introduction to this book, and this is what makes the study of the specific aspects of leadership and climate so important.

Maria is asking the right questions. To restate what she is asking: What aspects or kinds of boss behavior or leadership make the most difference? Maria is looking to learn what she can *do*. She is looking to learn about specific practices—something more concrete than "Be like Jack Welch" or "Develop a vision" or "Communicate effectively" or "Lead by example" or "Inspire your people" or "Make good decisions."

But here is where the research begins to become our enemy, not our friend. Because it turns out that *all* kinds of leadership or management behavior can matter. There are so many studies, examples, testimonials, and theories that it is almost impossible to draw any absolute conclusions about what makes for effective leadership. The information can be overwhelming. How is it possible to sort through all the various theories and studies? How is it possible to determine which of them can apply to Maria's business—or yours?

Leadership Practices

The first part of the answer to the preceding question is to focus on what people *do*—not who they are, what their personal character is like, or what they value. In other words, I believe you should focus on what I call practices rather than styles, skills, competencies, or even habits. I have found as a consultant dealing with over a hundred different organizations that this emphasis on practices has two benefits. First, it is the best way to explain leadership in terms that can be *demonstrated*. And, second, it leads to a practical way to *learn* leadership. I think this is what Maria is looking for. She is aware that some "nuts and bolts" practices (as she calls management) are important, but she knows that she was not born with her father's charismatic personality. She wants to reenergize her employees, and she has discovered that hard work alone is not the same as leadership. She is eager to learn about specific practices that she can implement at Eagle Exports.

What, exactly, do I mean by demonstrating and learning a leadership practice? Before I get to the list of practices that my colleagues found most effective in improving bottom-line performance in Chapter 7, let me give a few examples here.

In the early 1990s I was involved with the Pepsi-Cola organization and was working with one of Pepsi's top human resources (HR) executives. This executive—let's call him Bill—had recruited a top-notch staff, but he was disturbed because many of them expressed a desire to "move on." As a matter of fact, it was when several of his HR professionals transferred to other departments at Pepsi that I was asked to conduct a climate survey to find out what was going on. The survey revealed that Bill's climate was low in Commitment, and Bill scored relatively low in two leadership practices: "communicating excitement and enthusiasm about our work" and "encouraging me to participate in making important decisions." According to Bill's staff, he was too cerebral. His vision for the department was quite sophisticated, and his employees were not up to his speed when it came to this vision. Therefore, they felt they were being left out of important decisions. Armed with this feedback and a bit of personal coaching, Bill modified his approach to decision making and started to spend much more time explaining and discussing the HR priorities and projects with which his group was involved.

I wish I could say that the turnover in Bill's HR department stopped. It didn't. But it turned into *planned* movement. Bill's group had always been a feeder group for HR talent at Pepsi, but now Bill was better able to manage the turnover. And Bill saw his climate scores for Commitment and his leadership practices scores improve significantly.

My work with Auckland Healthcare provides another example of our approach to leadership development in which the amount of learning was mixed. Auckland Healthcare (AH) is the largest health services organization in New Zealand. For many years it operated as an extension of the government. In the mid-1990s, New Zealand moved to privatize its health care system, and a new management team was brought in to run AH. Sherbrooke Associates was asked to train a new generation of leaders and managers. As part of our involvement, we surveyed the subordinates of the top 150 executives and fed the data back to these executives in three-day leadership workshops.

Two of the practices in which AH leaders consistently scored the lowest had to do with creating a sense of clarity about strategy and goals, and creating a sense of challenge—what we call Structure and

Standards in our climate profile. These two practices were: "communicating a clear vision and strategy for our organization" and "establishing high performance goals and standards for people." Both of these practices represented critical components of AH's new business and management strategy, so we worked hard to educate AH leaders how to set clear and challenging goals.

It turned out that clarity and structure were much easier to create than high standards. AH executives were able to improve the sense of purpose and communicate the new AH strategy. They were also able to include much more concrete and specific goals as part of a new performance appraisal process. But getting them to really challenge their employees with tougher and higher performance standards was another matter. This practice is largely aimed at arousing achievement motivation, and that might explain what happened. There are strong cultural barriers to being a demanding boss in New Zealand, and historical forces operating in the hospital system, such as the belief that working at AH was a "noble calling" and managers had no right to put pressure on employees for more work, mitigated against our desire to change this leadership practice and people's willingness to go along with the change. In general, hospitals are more oriented toward affiliation than achievement, and AH was even more so.

In the end, I think we succeeded in making high standards a visible and important issue, and that alone raised the climate dimension of Standards. However, I'm not sure how much we changed the specific leadership practice that was so low. A few executives, usually those with some commercial experience, were able to "raise the bar" with their employees. But a resurvey of leadership practices revealed only a modest improvement in the overall scores for that practice. More work is needed if they really want to change that aspect of leadership and create a high-achieving climate.

Leadership Versus Management

The second part of the answer to the question of what model or theory of leadership will really work for Maria, and for the average manager, involves addressing the distinction between management and leadership. From time to time this issue arose in my work at Auckland Healthcare. (I always find Kiwi managers to be very well read.) I must admit that I have always been fascinated by the debate over leadership versus management. The debate suggests correctly that there is something missing or unsatisfactory in management alone. I believe that something is the motive arousal effect of certain leadership practices.

For my money, John Kotter does the best job of summarizing leadership versus management and offers the best explanation of the differences. Kotter explains that guiding organizations requires the people at the top (whom I usually call "bosses") to deal with two big issues: complexity and change. Most organizations are complicated. There are thousands of moving parts, all sorts of different technologies, and a myriad of different work processes. Handling all of the complexity of organizational life is what management does. But unless the external environment is static, effective organizational guidance also requires people who can deal with change. Rather than coping with complexity by creating systems and "managing" the work and people, coping with change involves "leading" the organization. That is Kotter's basic premise.

Kotter goes on to say that leaders and managers have to do similar kinds of work. They both have to set agendas for the organization. They both have to figure out how to organize tasks, activities, and people. And they both have to get the members of the organization to perform. Kotter and others point out that, although the work may be similar for managers and leaders, how they perform the work is quite different. Exhibit 6.1 illustrates how Kotter describes these differences.

Exhibit 6.1

The Difference Between Management and Leadership

Management

WHAT IT IS . . .	WHAT IT PRODUCES . . .
• Deals with complexity.	• Clear job definitions.
• Seeks to create order and discipline.	• Authority commensurate with responsibility.
• Is all about doing things right.	• Careful integration of plans and effort.
	• An emphasis on formal structures and systems.

Leadership

WHAT IT IS . . .	WHAT IT PRODUCES . . .
• Deals with change.	• Flexible job definitions.
• Seeks to create new approaches, "breaks with the normal, stimulates innovation.	• Constant adaptation and accommodation to shifts in roles.
• Is more about "doing the right things."	• Reliance on open dialogue and mutual trust to resolve conflicts.
	• An emphasis on informal networks.

As Exhibit 6.1 shows, Kotter captures what most people see as the real difference between management and leadership—the inspirational, visionary, or motivational component of being a boss. Somehow, leaders are successful motivators who get people going. Somehow they inspire people, and somehow they energize organizations. I believe we know how. Leaders manipulate the environmental determinants of aroused motivation, particularly the three powerful motives nAch, nAff, and nPow. In other words, leaders create climate, and they do this partly by means of their day-to-day behaviors that we call leadership practices.

Kotter emphasizes that both leadership and management are necessary if organizations are to succeed. Most organized activity involves managing complexity *and* leading change. This is more than just an interesting theoretical distinction. When I work with executives who want to improve their organization's performance, they know they need both. They want their managers to be more effective in practicing the functions of management—to set better goals, be more organized, and have good control systems. And they want them to practice a greater degree of leadership—to be more motivational or inspirational. Usually, because of the way complexity and change permeate today's organizations, they want the same people to do both.

The Forum Corporation and Citibank conducted one of the most interesting and thorough studies of leadership practices and organizational performance in the late 1970s. Citibank wanted to create a personalized management practices feedback system as part of a worldwide training program called "Managing People." The bank identified a matched sample of high- and moderate-performing managers and administered the same comprehensive practices questionnaire to subordinates of both samples. Exhibit 6.2 lists the practices that statistically distinguished the higher-performing Citibank managers.

George Litwin, then a consulting colleague at Forum, supervised the research for Forum. Under his guidance, the wording of the Citibank practices was intentionally oriented more toward what I call motivational leadership practices than toward functional managerial practices. For example, nowhere in the vocabulary of management will you find a great deal of attention paid to "going to bat" for subordinates. At Citibank and with most of my other clients, that turns out to be a critical aspect of building Support. You can see from Exhibit 6.2 that, although the Citibank practices included the managerially

Exhibit 6.2

Partial List of Citibank's Managing People Practices

1. You communicate high personal standards informally in conversation, personal appearances, etc.	8. You communicate your views honestly and directly during discussions of staff members' performance.	16. You make sure there is a frank and open exchange of ideas in work group meetings.
2. You demonstrate strong personal commitment to, and persistence in, achieving your unit's goals.	9. You consider all relevant information when appraising staff members' performance.	17. You periodically try to get a feel for work group morale.
3. Your staff members have a chance to influence the performance goals and standards that are set for their jobs.	10. You work with staff members to reach mutual agreement on their performance appraisals.	18. You emphasize cooperation as opposed to competitiveness among members of your group.
4. You establish clear, specific performance goals and standards for staff members' jobs.	11. You use recognition and praise (aside from pay) to reward excellent performance.	19. When conflicts arise in your work group, you make an effort to work them out with the individuals involved.
5. You build warm, friendly relationships with the people in your work group rather than remaining cool and impersonal.	12. You are more likely to recognize staff members for good performance than to criticize them for performance problems.	20. You establish departmental or work group goals.
6. You try to make the best use of staff members' skills and abilities when making assignments.	13. You provide staff members with the information they need regarding pay and other compensation policies.	21. The work group meetings you hold are well organized and thought out.
7. If you feel your staff members are right, you will definitely go to bat for them with your superiors.	14. You make every effort to be fair with staff members regarding their pay.	22. Your staff members have a clear understanding of what was decided at the end of work group meetings that you hold.
	15. The work group meetings you conduct serve to increase trust and mutual respect among work group members.	

focused behavior of "setting clear goals" (practice 4), it placed far more emphasis on practices that describe how to generate commitment to goals (e.g., practices 2, 3, and 10). In my opinion, these are leadership practices. Citibank supported this orientation, and the resulting "Managing People" practices list was used successfully at Citibank well into the 1990s.

Some clients, however, do not readily accept a shift in emphasis from management to leadership. After leaving The Forum Corporation, I supervised a study of managerial practices for Harbridge House, Inc. Like Citibank, we were interested in identifying practices that drove high levels of organizational performance. Unlike Citibank, Harbridge House wanted to create a more generic management practices model that could be used as part of its Advanced Management Program training workshop. We included over a dozen client organizations in our study. In a number of cases, we were asked to change the wording of our research practices because they were deemed to be too personal or too vague or lacked a clear connection to one of the traditional functions of management. In other words, practices that smacked too much of leadership tended to be weeded out even before we were allowed to administer research surveys.

For example, I wanted to see if the two practices that were the best predictors of high performance at Citibank were also predictors in our Harbridge House sample. These two were "communicating high personal standards informally" and "building warm, friendly relationships with the people in your work group." Clients rejected both of these—the first because it was deemed to be overly intrusive and personal and the second because it seemed to be so far removed from the stereotype of the high-achieving executive. These practices did not end up in our research questionnaire. Unfortunately, I had neither the insight nor the courage of my convictions to insist on a climate approach, which I now believe would have highlighted the importance of such nonmanagerial practices.

Not surprisingly, as you can see from Exhibit 6.3, the Harbridge House model of 25 "advanced management practices" turned out to be a blend of management and leadership behaviors. We organized them according to the functions of management and ended up putting a cluster of practices we called "leadership and motivation" in the middle of the placemat.

One of the lessons I learned from working with this model at Harbridge House in the 1980s was that management was easier to teach than leadership. Even when my workshop participants had personal practices feedback from their direct reports, it was much easier

Exhibit 6.3

Harbridge House's Advanced Management Practices Placemat

Management Practices

I. PLANNING AND ORGANIZING	II. MONITORING AND CONTROLLING	III. LEADERSHIP AND MOTIVATION	IV. TEAM BUILDING AND COMMUNICATION	V. PROBLEM SOLVING AND DECISION MAKING
1. Establishing and communicating goals for the group as a whole.	6. Using your time effectively.	11. Demonstrating personal commitment to achieving goals.	17. Being open and candid in your dealings with the group rather than being reserved and cautious.	22. Making clear-cut decisions when they are needed.
2. Establishing challenging objectives for subordinates.	7. Following up on important issues and actions.	12. Demanding that subordinates achieve a high level of performance.	18. "Leveling" with individuals and describing how you feel about their performance.	23. Getting to the heart of problems rather than dealing with less important issues.
3. Defining specific performance standards expected from subordinates in their work.	8. Meeting regularly with subordinates to review their performance.	13. Using recognition, praise, and other similar methods to reward subordinates for excellent performance.	19. Encouraging subordinates and others to express their feelings and positions, including disagreement.	24. Involving subordinates and others as appropriate in generating ideas, suggestions, and alternatives to complex problems.
4. Clarifying who is responsible for what within the group.	9. Discussing performance difficulties with subordinates and soliciting suggestions for overcoming them.	14. Recognizing subordinates for good performance more often than criticizing them for poor performance.	20. Making an effort to work out conflicts that arise within the work group.	25. Understanding the financial implications of your decisions.
5. Involving subordinates in establishing the goals and standards that are set for their jobs	10. Encouraging subordinates to discuss problems and complaints as they encounter them.	15. Encouraging subordinates to be original and innovative in their thinking.	21. Conducting team meetings in a way that builds trust and mutual respect.	
		16. Being supportive and helpful to subordinates in their day-to-day activities.		

109

for me to feel successful as a coach and teacher of the more managerial practices (e.g., practice 3 "defining specific performance standards expected from subordinates in their work" or practice 8 "meeting regularly with your subordinates to review their performance"). Not only could I describe how to do these practices effectively, but I could also cite any number of specific models, examples, rules, and guidelines that my students could apply and use in their jobs. The practices that were closer to Kotter's model of leadership, and my model of climate, proved much harder for me to teach (e.g., practice 11 "demonstrating personal commitment to achieving goals" and practice 12 "demanding that subordinates achieve a high level of performance"). My workshop participants understood and endorsed these aspects of leadership. I was pretty good at explaining them, but it was more difficult for me to structure specific behavioral guidelines or classroom experiences that captured what people had to do differently. There weren't as many crutches or tools to fall back on. Therefore, I never had the confidence that I had really helped my students learn as much.

Maria might want to begin her examination of her leadership by thinking about the areas in which Eagle Exports needs improved management and where it needs improved leadership. And if it's as much of the latter as it appears to be, then she must be willing to learn practices that are beyond the traditional scope of management.

Measuring What Bosses Do

If you are going to focus on specific boss behaviors or practices, as opposed to more general constructs such as leadership styles, habits, or managerial competencies, it is important to define each practice precisely. Not only must you identify practices that are associated with healthy climates and high performance, but you must also develop a questionnaire with items that are actionable, and that have strong face validity. And, furthermore, the assessment process as a whole needs to be administratively convenient. Otherwise, real-world clients will not let you work in their organizations. This means creating a measurement instrument for leadership practices that meets the same practical standards as the instrument created to measure climate.

Actionable Practices

In deciding which leadership practices to study, I had a consultant's bias. I chose to focus on those aspects of leadership that are "actionable" or "teachable" or "fixable." This means that the person who is being assessed can take action to change the practice and the consultant who is doing the assessment can help teach the person how to change. This point has always been the most challenging and controversial. As I noted before, almost all aspects of leadership seem to have some influence on organizational performance. I was primarily interested in those aspects that could be changed or developed. For example, a study might uncover a positive relationship between high performance and leaders who have blue eyes. The only way to take action on that data is to replace brown-eyed managers with blue-eyed ones. For my purposes, that's not a "fix." Even if blue eyes—or physical height, or a Harvard education—were an important aspect of leadership effectiveness, I would rather not measure it.

As the examples of my work with Auckland Healthcare and Pepsi both indicate, the emphasis on actionable practices leads to the kinds of improved climate and performance that clients are looking for. Because our leadership practices are actionable, a leader who scores low can have some hope of improving. As a matter of fact, we have developed a series of action items for each practice. These are reproduced in Appendix V on pages 261–284. In the business world, pragmatism is often an overriding value.

Practices with Face Validity

A pragmatic orientation means that face validity is an important part of any assessment of leadership practices. By *face validity* I mean more than making a good first impression in order to sell our assessment to a client, although I won't deny that is a necessary step. But, more importantly, we need to have a list of practices that makes sense to people who work daily with organizations and who are very capable of weighing a list of practices against their firsthand experience, their understanding of what managers actually do, and the goals of their organization. They are—and rightfully so—suspicious of "far-out" definitions of leadership that seem to have questionable relevance to their situation and needs. And they are equally suspicious—or should be—of vague but glittering generalities about leadership, especially those that involve highly subjective descriptions of qualities or personality traits that simply can't be taught, learned, or fixed. They want and deserve a list of practices that makes sense.

One of the reasons I was so comfortable working with the Harbridge House model, even though it was not as directly or highly correlated to high levels of organizational climate, was the ease with which clients understood and accepted the practices as "good things to do." I believe this was a result of two things. First, as I explained already, I felt as though I was able to help managers improve their scores on the practices. They were "fixable" behaviors, and I learned how to teach people to do them better and more often. Second, the practices and the way they were organized reflected traditional managerial behaviors. These made sense to the managers who attended our training programs.

Administrative Convenience

It is one thing to know that a particular behavior or series of behaviors leads to high levels of a climate dimension or bottom-line performance. It is another to put that knowledge into a usable and administratively convenient form. As we learned with climate, real-world organizations insist that your consulting tools be efficient. Managers and employees are busy. They have little tolerance or time for lengthy questionnaires, surveys, research studies, or fishing expeditions. They are often nervous about the whole idea of assessment. This means that the best assessment of leadership practices, like the best assessment of climate, is short and sweet.

From the beginning, I had to fight my desire to create long questionnaires. I knew that people would resist completing a survey that took longer than 15 or 20 minutes. So, I had to compromise. I couldn't possibly include all of the leadership practices that were associated with healthy climates, aroused motivation, or high performance. If I wanted to make measuring leadership a part of my climate improvement process, I had to have a very focused assessment tool, and it needed to be focused on the practices that really matter.

How Do You Change Leadership Practices?

Measuring leadership practices is one thing. Actually changing them in real organizations is quite another. Let me cite a brief example of how I use the climate survey to change leadership practices. Additional case studies that provide greater context and detail can be found in Chapter 8 of this book, but this example will illustrate my assumptions about and approach to leadership development.

The company is Rockwell International, specifically the Rocketdyne Division of Rockwell. These are the folks that build the rocket engines for the space shuttle. I worked with them several years ago as part of an overall effort to improve the company's performance, especially its space shuttle contract performance. Because of the expense and visibility of the shuttle program, the National

Aeronautics and Space Administration (NASA) was constantly monitoring all aspects of Rocketdyne's operations. The basic challenge for
Rocketdyne was to turn out highly complex rocket engines and support services that were absolutely flawless, and to do this month in
and month out under the pressure of very tight and demanding schedules. There was a never-ending battle between quality and timeliness,
and both of these aspects of performance were deemed critical.

NASA and Rockwell identified leadership, employee morale,
and people management as being important issues to address. Then,
as now, the Rocketdyne organization was loaded with scientists, engineers, and lots of other smart people, so it was not surprising that they
decided to do a scientific audit of their climate and management practices. They chose to use Sherbrooke's climate and practices survey,
and I ended up spending a good deal of time in southern California.

We designed a survey that included our standard climate measures, our 18 leadership practices, and a number of customized items,
some of them from previous surveys Rocketdyne had used in the past.
We also included several open-ended questions to allow respondents
to make suggestions about improving leadership at Rocketdyne.

Exhibit 6.4 shows the climate profiles we generated for the overall organization. As you can see, there was a significant difference
between what we called the "manager climate" (the views of those people with management responsibilities) and the "employee climate" (the
views of people who reported to first-level supervisors). The most significant issue at the top of the Rocketdyne organization turned out to be
Responsibility, whereas lower-level employees felt unrecognized and
believed that pressure to meet contract deadlines actually reduced performance standards, which were largely defined in terms of quality.

Armed with these results, we began a series of survey-feedback
meetings with groups of Rocketdyne executives and managers. As part
of the process, each manager has access to his or her own department's
climate profile and leadership practices scores. The purpose of these
meetings was to explain the overall Rocketdyne results, review the
departmental results, identify the most important issues, and develop
preliminary action plans to fix the issues that could be fixed. This is
where the leadership practices data becomes so important.

Let me take the case of Charlie Black (not his real name).
Charlie was a long serving engineer in charge of a major part of the
Propulsion Systems Group. Like most of the other Rocketdyne man-
agers, Charlie's climate was low on Responsibility, and he learned
that his direct reports saw him as over-controlling. Exhibit 6.5 shows
Charlie's list of high and low leadership practices scores.

Exhibit 6.4
Rocketdyne's Climate Profile

Exhibit 6.5
Charlie's Strengths & Weaknesses

STRENGTHS	WEAKNESSES
5 Demonstrating personal commitment to goals.	14 Going to bat for your subordinates.
11 Using recognition and praise to reward excellent performance.	8 Expecting subordinates to find their own errors.
16 Communicating excitement and enthusiasm.	3 Clearly and thoroughly explaining tasks.
15 Conducting team meetings that build trust.	7 Encouraging subordinates to initiate tasks they think are important.
	9 Encouraging innovation and risk taking.

Charlie shared his strengths and weakness with his staff and asked for their help. He was obviously upset, but he was also determined to address his weaknesses. During the initial meeting which I personally facilitated, none of Charlie's direct reports said much. There was a lot of posturing, head scratching, and denial. Several people spoke up with comments such as "Gee, Charlie, I gave you pretty good marks. I don't know why you would score low." After about an hour of this, we decided to adjourn the meeting and schedule a different session for the next morning. This one would not include Charlie.

Mary White, a member of Rocketdyne's human resources staff, had been present at the first meeting, and she proved to be an invaluable resource to me and to Charlie. At the second meeting, we were quickly able to identify and isolate the four or five "bad habits" Charlie had when it came to assigning work and following up on assignments. Just as his data indicated, his subordinates now were quite vocal in describing how Charlie generally overmanaged them. We invited Charlie to join the meeting, and (coached by Mary) he listened as I relayed the messages from the group.

Charlie defended many of his leadership practices as being necessary or called for according to the terms of Rocketdyne's contract with NASA. He claimed he trusted his people but couldn't have them straying too far from what the government expected when it came to propulsion system project management. The more we talked, the clearer it became to both Charlie and his team that (1) it was a real problem that was really frustrating people, (2) Charlie had more freedom to modify his practices than he initially thought he did, and (3) his direct reports were partially contributing to the problem by insisting on what Charlie considered to be excessive independence on certain matters. Then the hard work began.

Encouraging high levels of individual responsibility requires both management and leadership. Charlie and his team were able to agree without much argument on a better process for setting goals and explaining assignments. Getting Charlie to "let go" was a bit more difficult to fix. It involved building a new level of trust between Charlie and several of his key people. And that turned out to involve solving a few performance problems one level further down in the propulsion systems organization. Charlie finally admitted that he was hesitant to let go, not because he didn't trust his direct reports, but because he didn't trust *their* direct reports. This was at the heart of Charlie's leadership dilemma and his low score in the "expecting subordinates to find their own errors" and the "encouraging innovation and risk-taking" practices.

Although we brainstormed a few ideas during that second meeting, none of them proved very helpful. I soon flew back to Boston and Mary took over the job of helping Charlie develop a new set of leadership behaviors. Six months later, she reported that he had made significant progress. Mary used three techniques to get Charlie to change. First, she continued to give Charlie feedback on his delegation and responsibility-building practices. Each month for four months she met with his direct reports and fed back their comments. She gave Charlie positive as well as negative feedback. Second, she gave the team courage to "push back" at Charlie when he started to overmanage them. By selectively participating in propulsion systems staff meetings, Mary was able to insert herself at critical times. Charlie became less intimidating.

Finally, Mary was able to negotiate a number of very specific guidelines for Charlie's project leadership. This proved difficult, but after six months a leadership practices resurvey showed that there was less double-checking and nit-picking in Charlie's group.

What does this example tell us about how to change leadership practices? It told me the following:

- *Leaders won't change unless they see the need for change.* Charlie had a vague notion that morale was low and contract performance could be improved. But he never connected his own leadership practices to the problem. As a matter of fact, his tendency was to double- and triple-check things when performance slipped, which was just the opposite of what was needed.

- *Collecting credible, objective, hard data helps leaders see the need for change.* The more the data involve causes (leadership practices) *and* effects (climate plus group performance), the easier it is to create momentum for change.

- *Leadership practices aren't a "good–bad" issue; they are more a matter of "effective–less effective."* Charlie and all leaders will more readily accept negative feedback if that feedback is put in a nonevaluative framework. Double-checking doesn't mean Charlie is bad. It simply inhibits his effectiveness and the effectiveness of his people.

- *Leaders will change their practices when they feel they have real options.* This means generating specific alternative behaviors for them to consider. It means trying out various options, maybe on a trial basis. And it means paying close attention to results, not just the practices themselves. When Charlie saw that his climate scores for Responsibility actually improved after six months, he stuck with the guidelines that he, Mary, and his direct reports had devised.

• *Leadership skills can be learned.* But they are harder to acquire than management skills. Mary and I worked much harder and longer to help Charlie change his two low responsibility-building scores than we did to change his ineffective delegation score ("clearly and thoroughly explaining tasks").

Implications for Maria

So, what does all of this mean for Maria? First of all, she should realize that what she does counts. She isn't "stuck" with a low-morale, low-performing organization. She can change things. Second, she should realize that what she does is just as important as who she is. Maria is the founder's daughter and most Eagle Exports employees have "motivational memories" of her father. But more importantly, Maria's day-to-day practices coupled with active management of the other factors that create climate will impact the *E*s and *I*s of her employees that we referred to in Chapter 2. Maria is now the boss and she now controls many of the determinants of the climate at Eagle Exports.

Third, if Maria is going to work on the organizational climate and her day-to-day leadership practices, she should begin by sizing up her current situation. She takes pride in being an organized person. She knows things have to change. Why not do a quick assessment to take stock of the situation at Eagle Exports, and then work out an action plan based on what she learns?

7

A "Hit List" of Leadership Practices

Bird Brain is in deep trouble. In the 11 years since Cassandra Washington founded the company—named after the series of sculptural bronze lawn sprinklers that got the company off the ground and remains its signature product—she has taken it from a small family business operating out of a restored carriage house to a $26 million a year business with 230 people working out of a brand-new office complex (still referred to affectionately as "the carriage house"). Two years ago Cassandra agreed to sell the company to Acme Industries, and Bird Brain is now one of Acme's fastest-growing divisions. The company has manufacturing plants in Mexico and China, and its products are designed by a number of leading artists in the Midwest and California. Just last month, a Bird Brain sprinkler was featured on the cover of the new Smith and Hawken catalog. Good news, it appears—but Cassandra knows better.

She glances out the window of the China-bound 747, but all she can see is her own reflection. "Maybe," she thinks, "I'm better at running a small company than a medium-sized enterprise or, even worse, a business 'unit' of some big company." She senses that the magic of her enterprise is slipping away. Even in the early days as the company grew, Cassandra first had to hire managers to run Sales, Design, Production, and Finance—operations she and her husband used to run by themselves. Then she had to adjust to a round of venture capital investment. Then to moving her manufacturing offshore. And, finally, to the sale to Acme. Over the past several months, she has gradually come to realize that something isn't working. She can feel it in the office. People are just going through the motions, too often relying on memos and reports rather than on the spontaneous communications and excited collaboration that characterized the original Bird Brain.

"It's more than just being bigger," Cassandra muses, "although that's clearly part of the problem. And it isn't complacency, really, or incompetence. But whatever it is, the consequences are starting to show." The facts are clear, not only to Cassandra but also to anyone who looks at the Bird Brain numbers. Production schedules are not being met, people in the carriage house seem to resent the teams in both Mexico and China, and Sales is making promises that neither Design nor Production can meet. Even though the commitment to funky design, product quality, and fun that marked Bird Brain's corporate culture surfaces on occasion, it's largely gone now. Everyone seems bewildered, including Cassandra. As she feels the plane lower its landing gear, she realizes with a thud that the Smith and Hawken cover is becoming more of a mocking threat than a golden opportunity.

What Cassandra *doesn't* realize is what the actual climate profile of Bird Brain looks like. With virtually no formal business training—a fact of which she's proud—Cassandra is certainly not about to hire a consultant to come in and do an expensive number on her company (although Acme's personnel manager has mentioned that as a possibility). If she were to do a climate survey, however, she would learn that Bird Brain scores poorly when compared with the hundreds of companies that have used the same survey instrument. Bird Brain's climate profile would look like Exhibit 7.1.

What Cassandra *does* realize is that everything relating to Bird Brain's business environment needs work. And it's up to her, as president of the company, to exert effective leadership. And she needs to do it quickly or her beloved Bird Brain will go under. "What I need," she says, trying to stare through her reflection into the lights of Beijing coming into focus, "is a 'hit list' of leadership of actions that I can jump on right away to turn this place around."

What Practices Really Matter?

The more I studied leadership, the more I realized there was no perfect list of practices that defines effectiveness. In fact, through my reading of research and my consulting career, I have identified over 350 specific leadership practices that, at one time or another, have been correlated to high performance and high levels of employee motivation, commitment, and goal-directed behavior. It turns out

Exhibit 7.1

Bird Brain's Climate Profile

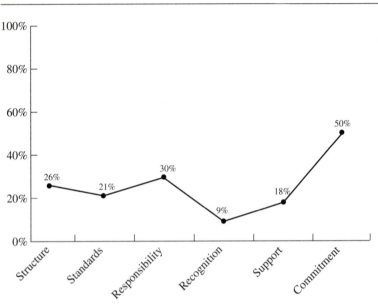

that the definition of *effectiveness* changes rather dramatically from situation to situation and organization to organization. So what I have had to do is to find a way to focus on a more manageable, useful list of leadership practices that can be broadly applied across situations and organizations. This is the kind of list that Cassandra is looking for.

In order to do so, I decided to organize the practices according to the six dimensions of organizational climate, and I tried to include practices that covered the basic functions of management. Going all the way back to my laboratory research with George Litwin, I had become convinced that the cause-and-effect relationship between leadership and performance looked like this:

We knew how to measure climate, and now I thought I knew how to measure leadership. Just as I had cut corners and streamlined the climate items and questions in my climate questionnaire, I realized I was going to have to do the same for leadership practices. Most importantly, I knew I wanted to include *both* climate and leadership in the same instrument. Measurement was key. Unless my clients could "see" what their climate looked like and unless they could "see" how others experienced their leadership, then they would never be able to change either one. Self-perceptions and guesswork would be the only reality, and it would take me forever to discover which practices mattered most and then to coach bosses to modify these specific behaviors.

The Leadership Questionnaire

There are 18 leadership practices we currently use as part of the climate survey. They are divided according to the climate dimensions they seem to be most clearly related to and logically impact. Neither the climate phenomena nor leadership practices can be neatly organized or categorized, so I realize that subdividing the practices into six dimensions is always going to be problematic. But it is helpful. It gives me (and my clients) a focus. I want a tool my clients can immediately use to guide them toward short-term, as well as more permanent, performance improvements. I don't want a tool that ends up with the same remedy, no matter what the climate and performance issues prove to be.

I believe the list of three target practices for each climate dimension includes relatively obvious and sensible things that bosses can emphasize if and when they learn that the particular dimension is lower than it should be. The inclusion of a number of more managerial leadership practices is a practical necessity for me. It increases the face validity of the approach I am taking and provides both consultants and clients with more actionable things to think about and work on. And, of course, as anyone in business knows, management practices are important to the overall success of an organization. In order to understand the relationship I am building between climate and leadership, I list the climate items that make up each dimension and provide a brief summary of the logic behind the inclusion of each of the three practices per dimension.

The basic issue with the Structure dimension of climate is clarity—clarity of roles, responsibilities, accountabilities, authority

Structure

CLIMATE ITEMS	TARGET PRACTICES
• The jobs in this organization are clearly defined and logically structured.	1. Establishing clear, specific performance goals.
• In this organization, it is sometimes unclear who has the formal authority to make a decision.	2. Clarifying who is responsible for what within the group.
• In some of the projects I've been on, I haven't been sure exactly who my boss was.	3. Making sure tasks and projects are clearly and thoroughly explained and understood when they are assigned.
• Our productivity sometimes suffers from a lack of organization and planning.	

levels, and expectations. Creating a sense of Structure is not really a leadership issue. As a matter of fact, John Kotter's model leaders care little about it. As he says, leaders care about the vision, the sense of purpose, and the overall alignment of the members of the organization with that purpose. And, as I emphasized earlier, leaders care about arousing the motivation of people within the organization. Structure, though obviously important to the success of an organization, is a bit more mundane, perhaps more mechanical. I consider it more of a managerial issue.

This is why the three practices I targeted to help leaders improve Structure are more practical than inspirational. Bosses who set clear, specific goals tend to create climates with higher Structure. Performance goals are the heart of a performance plan—a very managerial device! And it's not good enough to set the goals once or twice a year. Every assignment, every project, and every task need to be clarified so that performance expectations and work group roles are understood and accepted. The use of leadership practices that focus on the structure of both tasks and relationships refers back to our original thinking about Structure (see Chapter 3).

Despite the importance of the appropriate amount of Structure in an effective organization, a sense of structural clarity is often less a result of leadership than it is a result of other determinants of climate, especially organizational arrangements. But as I indicated earlier, the boss of a work group is usually involved in the way organizational arrangements are communicated throughout the organization.

Standards

CLIMATE ITEMS	TARGET PRACTICES
• In this organization, we set very high standards for performance.	4. Setting challenging performance goals and standards.
• In this organization, people don't seem to take much pride in their performance.	5. Demonstrating personal commitment to achieving goals.
• Around here there is a feeling of pressure to continually improve our personal and group performance.	6. Giving your subordinates feedback on how they are doing on their jobs.
• Our management believes that no job is so well done that it couldn't be done better.	

Standards is not a pleasant climate dimension. It is all about pressure and stretch and high expectations. That's why high standards arouse the need for achievement (nAch). And that's why the first practice bosses need to engage in to create a high Standards climate is setting challenging goals and standards. High achievers compete against their own internal standards of excellence, but bosses who constantly challenge their subordinates are more likely to stimulate nAch than those who don't. The interesting thing about our research on this practice is the frequency with which bosses discover that their own standards are less challenging than they thought they were. More often than not, bosses score themselves much higher on this practice than their subordinates do.

Target practice 5 is an important determinant of a high Standards climate. When the boss doesn't care, everyone knows it. Leaders who set the bar high and then reinforce and personally model their commitment are the leaders who bring out the best in their followers. For many years I used a practice that read "demonstrating personal commitment to and persistence in achieving goals." Ten years ago I dropped the phrase "and persistence in" because my clients insisted that persistence equals stubbornness, and that is not an admirable leadership behavior. I capitulated, even though our research showed that *both* commitment and persistence are important climate-molding leadership practices. In our next-generation questionnaire I plan to place greater emphasis on the stubbornness of effective leadership and to measure how vital it is to *sustain* personal commitment to achieving goals.

Target practice 6, "giving subordinates feedback on how they are doing on their jobs," describes another fundamental activity that must be engaged in by bosses who strive to create high Standards and high-performing climates. In my years of consulting, no aspect of leadership has been more closely associated with performance pressure and achievement motivation arousal than providing feedback. Whether the boss is the deliverer of the feedback, the validator of the feedback, or the architect of a system that communicates the feedback—whatever role the boss plays helps build a high Standards organizational climate.

But practice 6 isn't enough. In fact, the real test of high achievement/high standards leadership also includes the Recognition dimension and at least two of the three leadership practices targeted there. It turns out that *how* the feedback is communicated to a person has a lot to do with its motivational impact. Dynamic leaders who wrap enthusiastic praise and sincere use of all kinds of rewards around their feedback stimulate high levels of aroused motivation—nAch, nAff, and nPow. Leaders whose feedback is perceived to be impersonal or overly negative have the opposite affect.

Although the impact of personalized feedback can be profound, the "cloud chamber effect" of feedback on an organization's climate should not be ignored. The best leaders set up systems that automatically deliver performance feedback, even when they aren't around to add the personal touch. I'll never forget walking through a high-performing General Mills plant in Cedar Rapids, Iowa, and observing all of the productivity and safety and performance charts prominently displayed throughout the facility. It must have been impossible for employees not to know how the plant was doing every minute of the day!

Feedback motivates, and as you will see later in the chapter, feedback is equally important in improving the leadership of bosses themselves.

The Responsibility dimension of climate describes those aspects of the environment that define who "owns" the results that are attained. High achievers and those motivated by power want success (or failure) to be their own. In order to create a high Responsibility climate managers must delegate and leaders must encourage people to "just do it." Practices 7 and 8 focus more on leadership than management because both of them stress the inspirational role of the boss. High scores on these two practices are related to bosses who genuinely feel that their subordinates can be trusted to do the right thing. "Go ahead, do what you think needs to be done," is the core message of these practices.

It is interesting to note that bosses who score high in these two practices tend to create climates that are not only high in Responsibility but are also high in Commitment and Standards. I think this is so

Responsibility

CLIMATE ITEMS	TARGET PRACTICES
● We don't rely too heavily on individual judgment in this organization; almost everything is double-checked. ● Management resents your checking everything with them; if I think I've got the right approach I just go ahead. ● You won't get ahead in this organization unless you stick your neck out and try things on your own. ● Our philosophy emphasizes that people should solve their problems by themselves.	7. Encouraging people to initiate tasks or projects they think are important. 8. Expecting your subordinates to find and correct their own errors rather than doing this for them. 9. Encouraging innovation and calculated risk taking in others.

because bosses who don't meddle and who send out high responsibility messages of trust and empowerment are bosses whom subordinates respect and to whom they respond. They generate high levels of personal loyalty that are transferred to the organization and, if the climate has the right amount of Structure, their willingness to "let go" comes with the high expectation message of "OK, now don't screw it up."

"Sticking your neck out" in most organizations means taking a risk. It often means going it alone, and it always means being willing to rock the boat. Over the years, I used a number of practices to describe a boss's acceptance of and willingness to support "sticking your neck out" behaviors. The one that seems to be the easiest for my clients to relate to is practice 9. The practice includes the words *innovation* and *calculated* risk taking. Although these words tend to broaden the practice, I think they add interesting options to a boss's repertoire of responsibility-enhancing actions. *Innovation* suggests that you stick your neck out to implement something that will be adopted by the organization, and *calculated* suggests that the risk taking is not reckless but thoughtful. Both words emphasize responsibility.

A word of caution here. As we will discuss later in this chapter, the Responsibility dimension of our climate model is less driven by leadership practices than most of the other dimensions. It is often more of a function of organizational arrangements and historical forces than leadership. My feeling is that, for almost all of my clients, having bosses who score high in encouraging innovation is going to

Recognition

CLIMATE ITEMS	TARGET PRACTICES
• In this organization the rewards and encouragements you get usually outweigh the threats and the criticisms.	10. Recognizing subordinates for good performance more often than criticizing them for poor performance.
• There is not enough reward and recognition given in this organization for doing good work.	11. Using recognition, praise, and other similar methods to reward people for excellent performance.
• We have a promotion system here that helps the best person rise to the top.	12. Relating the total reward system (compensation, recognition, promotion) to the excellence of job performance rather than to other factors such as seniority, personal relationships, and so on.
• In this organization people are rewarded in proportion to the excellence of their job performance.	

be a good thing, even if it isn't always highly correlated to building a high Responsibility climate.

The Recognition dimension of our climate construct is a key determinant of both achievement and affiliation motivation. Need for achievement requires that rewards be linked to performance, whereas need for affiliation requires a more general emphasis on approval versus disapproval. In either case, bosses must stress the positive in order to create a high Recognition climate, which means being perceived as more rewarding than punishing.

It has always fascinated me how unaware bosses are of their tendency to be viewed as more negative than positive. Why is that? First, subordinates tend to "hear" negative feedback much more often than positive feedback. Most employees believe they do a decent job. Therefore, they expect some sort of positive reinforcement or recognition from the boss. Unless the recognition is *really* positive, it is likely not to be heard or viewed as significant. "Neutral" recognition does not arouse motivation. Second, many leaders fear giving praise or recognition that might be perceived as gratuitous or unwarranted. They think it signals that they have low standards or that they are soft. "Charlie did a pretty good job, but I won't say anything about it because he could have done better and, if I am too enthusiastic in my praise, Charlie will think less of me." The best leaders know better. They know that communicating high standards is different from withholding praise. And they know that frequent, personal, no-strings-attached recognition is a great motivator.

The challenge, then, is for leaders to significantly dial up the amount of positive recognition they provide. Practices 10 and 11 describe two important ways to do this. These are the two practices I was referring to when I talked about how bosses create a high Standards climate. Rather than *reducing* standards, emphasizing these two recognition practices actually *increases* standards. Why is this so? I think that when bosses express their genuine pleasure and gratitude for work well done by a subordinate, it reinforces the boss's expectations while, at the same time, affirms the subordinate's commitment to doing good work. High achievers don't require blubbery, cheerleading bosses, but they do respond to bosses who know good performance when they see it and aren't afraid to say so.

In most situations, both effort and results need to be rewarded if the climate is going to arouse nAch and nAff. The emphasis on meritocracy and a pay-for-performance climate, which is so central to achievement motivation, has led me to add practice 12 to the list. Measuring how a boss *uses* the company's reward system might sound like an overly managerial practice. Nevertheless, over the years my clients have found it to be an extremely helpful activity to focus on. Time and again I have observed that two supervisors, managing side by side in the same organization, subject to the exact same appraisal and compensation policies, can receive totally different scores from their employees on practice 12. Obviously, one of them is taking a passive, less involved stance and the other is leveraging the reward system to reinforce a high recognition/high achievement climate. The *system* is a management tool. How the system is *used* is a leadership practice.

Let me give an example from my consulting experience. I was engaged by the Stride Rite Corporation to help implement a new appraisal and performance management system. We implemented it in all of Stride Rite's divisions but discovered after six months that we were getting mixed results. It turned out that the deciding factor was the way the boss conducted the performance appraisals, not the system itself. More to the point, we found that the highest-performing work groups had bosses who coupled an active and aggressive use of the new system with constant informal recognition and feedback. Both formal and informal recognition is important to high Recognition climates. However, the ability to translate and actively interpret the formal reward system so that it arouses task-related motivation is the mark of an effective boss.

Support

CLIMATE ITEMS	TARGET PRACTICES
● You don't get much sympathy from higher-ups around here if you make a mistake.	13. Being supportive and helpful to subordinates in their day-to-day activities.
● When I am on a difficult assignment, I can usually count on getting assistance from my boss and co-workers.	14. Going to bat for subordinates with your supervisors when you feel they are right.
● People in this organization don't really trust each other enough.	15. Conducting team meetings in a way that builds trust and mutual respect.
● I feel that I am a member of a well-functioning team.	

Support is, perhaps, the most complicated dimension in our climate system. It describes teamwork, trust, and a sense of interpersonal warmth, as well as a general feeling that mistakes aren't the end of the world. Given these complex factors, it is hard to isolate three practices that will build a high Support climate. Practice 13 is a remarkably consistent predictor of nAff arousal and a mark of coaching prowess. It doesn't measure intent; it measures affect. The key here is that an act is defined as "helpful" *only* in the eyes of the boss's subordinate. What one person may see as helpful another may see as intrusive or even abrasive. In order to score high in practice 13 and in order to build a high Support climate bosses must be sensitive to the kind of coaching that is considered helpful to each of their employees. Ask them.

"Going to bat" is a practice that may look overly narrow. It is the act of challenging or pushing the chain of command on behalf of your employees. Therefore, it is a practice that communicates trust, assistance, and genuine team membership. It puts the boss on the subordinate's team, not on the side of "the higher-ups." I have found that practice 14 captures the essence of support in most large organizations, especially in the midlevels of the hierarchy.

One of the most visible arenas in which to demonstrate leadership is a team meeting. That is why I wanted to include a practice that speaks directly to the boss's behavior in meetings. Practice 15 goes back to our work at Citibank and The Forum Corporation. It is less specific than most of the other practices—a criticism I have heard many times. Yet despite its vagueness, I have found that managers know what the practice means and they know it contributes to a high Support climate. For more about types of meetings, agenda setting, facilitation, and closure, see the Practices Resource Guide section of the ToolKit.

Commitment

CLIMATE ITEMS	TARGET PRACTICES
• Generally, I am highly committed to the goals of the organization.	16. Communicating excitement and enthusiasm about the work.
• People take pride in belonging to this organization.	17. Involving people in setting goals.
• I don't really care what happens to this organization.	18. Encouraging subordinates to participate in making important decisions.
• As far as I can see, there isn't much personal loyalty to the organization.	

The Commitment dimension of our climate model captures people's thoughts and feelings of loyalty and their identification with the organization's basic mission. Sometimes a high level of Commitment can make up for a generally demotivating climate. In other situations, Commitment is the result of the other five climate dimensions. A person's sense of pride and caring is often the result of his or her sense of belonging, of being valued, rewarded, challenged and trusted. That is one reason why I have chosen to put it as the sixth and last dimension.

How does the boss generate a greater sense of personal commitment to the organization's goals? That is not an easy task. Most of us realize that commitment is not a fleeting thing. Pride and the sense of connection to an organization can be stimulated over a short period of time, but it will fade fast. Like the Structure and Responsibility dimensions, long-term Commitment is probably not as susceptible to change by leadership practices. It is more a function of the other determinants of climate. For this reason, I think of the practices that influence Commitment as an ending point to high-performance leadership rather than the place to begin.

I have worked with three practices that are closely related to healthy overall climates and drive higher levels of loyalty and commitment. Two involve increasing the sense of connection through participation. Practice 17 focuses on the all-important goal-setting process, and practice 18 relates to decision making. My experience is that the more you include people in these processes, the greater is their sense of belonging. Even if the goals or decisions are different from those an employee would make on his or her own, being involved forces a person to respect the process and improves his or her sense of commitment *to the organization*—if not to the goal or the decision.

In some ways, practice 16 is to Commitment what practice 5 is to Standards. It is what powerful leaders do. They signal to people that the mission, the jobs, and the work are worth doing. They role model. They get excited. And in so doing, they arouse all three motives. The problem, however, is in sustaining the kind of commitment that the boss's excitement and enthusiasm can arouse—especially if the enthusiasm takes the form of short-term or periodic cheerleading. Long-term Commitment, then, depends on all of the other practices and the level of all of the other climate dimensions.

How Well Do Leadership Practices Predict Climate?

Our list of 18 leadership practices has proven to be a practical and usable list. It isn't magic (i.e., do these and in a week you will lose 20 pounds, improve your love life, and double your profits). And it isn't meant to be definitive (i.e., a concise statement that captures The Essence of Leadership, or even a list of what constitutes The Complete Leader). But they are aspects of leadership that can be "seen" by direct reports. Because they can be seen they can be measured by means of a questionnaire. Once measured, managers can receive feedback on the extent to which they engage in these practices. Armed with this feedback, they can begin to attack those climate dimensions that need improvement.

The scientific question remains: How well do leadership practices predict climate? I have argued that leadership practices such as I have described are the primary cause of organizational climate—the primary cause and the single best predictor. But what is the evidence for this claim?

George Litwin and I recently completed a series of studies using a statistical method called multiple regression to select the practices that, in combination, best predict each climate dimension. Exhibit 7.2 shows the results from two of these studies. One involved a large, multiple-division organization, labeled "Big," and the other, labeled "Diverse," involved a sample of four companies in different industries and countries. From this exhibit, you can see how well leadership practices predict each climate dimension.

Here is how to read Exhibit 7.2. For each climate dimension, I have shown the percent of climate variance accounted for by combining the top five to seven practices. The regression studies produce a correlation coefficient (R). Technically, you then have to square this correlation to get the variance accounted for (R^2). For example, the correlation of practices with Structure is .696. If you were to square

Exhibit 7.2

How Leadership Predicts Climate

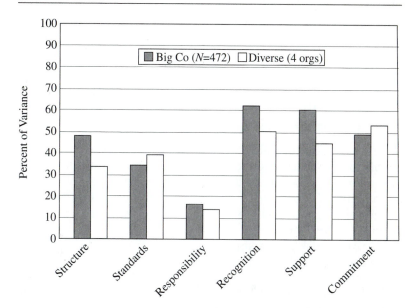

this number, you would be able to say that these seven practices account for approximately half (48.5%) of the variation in Structure.

Clearly, we are a little better at predicting climate in a single large organization where we hold constant some of the other variables that might influence climate. Nevertheless, the statistical evidence shows a very strong predictive link to climate. Even in the Diverse study, where the technology, strategy, and organizational arrangements vary, the statistical prediction of climate is quite remarkable. In fact, for Standards and Commitment it is slightly higher than for Big Co.

Exhibit 7.2 raises a number of interesting research questions and a couple of practical issues. First, as the correlation coefficients indicate, Responsibility is the climate dimension least influenced by leadership in our study. Less than 20% of the variance in Responsibility can be explained by the leadership practices we used. And two of our Structure practices were negatively correlated to Responsibility. This negative correlation makes intuitive sense. High Structure often means there is less room for individual initiative.

Second, none of the three practices we targeted at Support seem to correlate with high levels of that climate dimension, although "conducting team meetings that build trust" is an important predictor of overall climate. Why is this? One hypothesis is that, although "being supportive" and "going to bat" are obviously supportive behaviors, our Support dimension's emphasis on teamwork and trust is more about involvement and empowerment. Good support-oriented coaching is always going to be a highly valued leadership skill, but it is not always going to arouse motivation.

Our "Hit List" of the Most Powerful Leadership Practices

George and I kept digging into our data and we found that six of the 18 Sherbrooke practices have a disproportionate impact on organizational climate on all six of the climate dimensions. As you can see from Exhibit 7.3, our "Hit List" of practices that count the most turns out to describe leadership that is *high involvement, high trust, challenging, and committed.*

At the risk of oversimplifying both our research and reality, can we identify lessons of leadership buried in our short "Hit List" of six practices? I think so. These practices are not Lone Ranger or John Wayne practices—they don't describe a larger than life, individualistic, heroic leader. Effective leadership of today's organizations is more of a team leadership, where the leader is in a stimulating but interdependent relationship with other members of the organization. Not surprisingly, it stimulates achievement, affiliation, and power motivation, with perhaps an emphasis on nAch. The leader clarifies how things will work, invites the team to sign up, and keeps the lines of communication open so that the organization remains responsive to new ideas. These practices create climates that are demanding, even stressful, but they are not heartless. The leader believes that the demands and challenges are part of what motivates people, and he or she rounds out the motivational environment with a healthy dose of participation and involvement.

How the "Hit List" Predicts Total Climate

Just how important are these six practices in creating the kinds of climates that arouse motivation? Exhibit 7.4 shows how the six "Hit List" practices predict Total Climate—the sum of all the climate dimensions. Exhibit 7.4 also shows how much of the variance in climate stems from the "Hit List" as opposed to the full complement of 18 practices used in our climate survey.

Exhibit 7.3
A "Hit List" of Leadership Practices

Demonstrates Personal Commitment to Achieving Goals

Our single best predictor of total climate, and a "top 3" predictor of Commitment, Standards, Structure, and Recognition. Leaders must be role models, showing their people what is expected by actions, not just words.

Encourages Innovation and Calculated Risk Taking

Our second best predictor of total climate and an important predictor of Commitment, Standards, Support, Responsibility, and Recognition. Leaders motivate high achievers; believing in them and their ideas has a strong and pervasive effect on climate and motivation.

Clarifies Who Is Responsible for What

A "top 6" predictor of Structure, Responsibility, Support, and Commitment. Leaders motivate by defining the areas of possible achievement or power.

Sets Challenging Goals

Our best predictor of Standards and a support predictor of Commitment (top 7). It is up to the leader to "raise the bar," to ask more of people, to raise their aspirations.

Conducts Team Meetings That Build Trust

A "top 3" predictor of Commitment and Recognition (and a negative predictor of Responsibility). Leaders understand a basic function of team meetings that needs to be emphasized in the hurly-burly of everyday management.

Encourages Participation in Decisions

A "top 6" predictor of both Support and Commitment. Effective leadership makes people feel they are important and that what they do counts.

Our regression analysis demonstrated that the first three practices of Exhibit 7.4 account for most of the variance in Total Climate. The implication is that you can create a healthy, high-performing, overall climate if you:

- demonstrate personal commitment to the organization's goals
- encourage innovation and risk taking

Exhibit 7.4
How the "Hit List" Predicts Climate

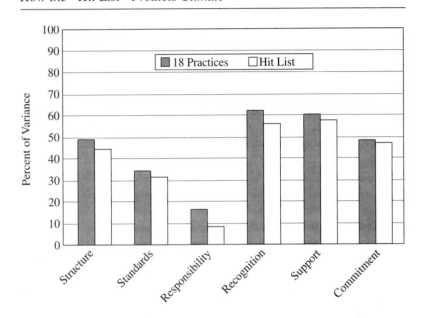

- clarify people's roles and responsibilities (say who is responsible for what)

You continue to enhance the motivational potential of the climate when you:

- encourage people to participate in decisions
- set high standards
- conduct team meetings that build mutual trust

Although the second three practices may not account for as much of the variation in Total Climate as the first three, they turn out to be very important predictors of dimensions such as Standards, Recognition, and Support.

Not a bad success formula for Cassandra to adopt at Bird Brain. Of course, a survey of organizational climate and leadership practices would target more specific fixes for her. Fortunately, even without that diagnosis, our research suggests some immediate actions that can lead to immediate results.

Part III

How Can We Use Climate

The real value of organizational climate as a concept lies in the ways that actual organizations use it to improve their performance. In order to see how this is done we must move away from theory and research and hear "real-life" leadership and climate management stories.

In this section, we examine a series of case studies. In Chapter 8 we look at ways that business leaders have used climate surveys to improve performance and develop more effective personal leadership strategies. The results indicate that our climate management tools really work. Climate and leadership practices data get attention and focus energies on stuff that matters. Consultants can teach managers how to use the tools. It doesn't take years to see positive results. Of course, given the inherent messiness and complexity of changing work environments, the process of improving performance is not a simple one. That's why we need to tell stories rather than just presenting a recipe or an all-purpose solution.

Schools and hospitals have not, typically, been receptive to the kinds of management intervention that business organizations have been using for years. These types of organizations have a distinctive set of problems. However, we are learning how to apply our climate management tools to schools and hospitals, and the initial results are encouraging. Chapter 9 describes how climate surveys can be used in public high schools, and Chapter 10 illustrates how to apply our approach in health care systems to improve health care performance and the overall quality of patient care. Both cases highlight the value of applying organizational climate concepts as well as the need for further research in how best to do so.

Chapter 11 explores how climate and leadership will develop in the future. The concept of organizational climate will help us understand and manage the motivational experiences of, not only those who "live" there, but also those who *visit* our organizations—the customers, suppliers, patients, and students who often make or break an organization's success. Chapter 11 also includes a discussion of how our climate concept might apply to the world of the Internet—how you can create meaningful, measurable cyber-climates. I conclude with my thoughts about leadership in the future, the emotional challenges leaders will face, the rising importance of facilitation skills, and the significance of having more women in leadership positions.

135

8

Using Climate as a
Performance Management Tool

The Organizational Climate Survey works, but *how* does it work?

We know, especially because it is founded on a well-researched theory of human motivation, that it measures stuff that counts. The survey can reveal the profile of an organization's climate, indicating the thoughts and feelings of the people who work there. We know how climate can arouse or fail to arouse three important sources of motivation—need for achievement, need for affiliation, and need for power. We know what causes climate and that leadership practices are the most important determinant of different climate profiles. We know how to describe and assess those practices, and we know how they are linked to the six climate dimensions. We even know which few practices have a disproportionate impact on overall climates. We know all this because our survey has a solid intellectual foundation based on solid research and experience.

Equally importantly, we know that in the survey we have a tool that people will actually use. It doesn't take an inordinate amount of time to administer. The questions are clear and user friendly, and they don't generate a lot of resistance. It meets the test of intuitive face value. Simply put, it makes sense to people who use it. And the administration process, including data collection, analysis, and data feedback, is straightforward and streamlined. The process fits well with the pragmatic needs of business organizations. It has rigor and discipline but also flexibility. Different organizations and managers can add special items to the survey and adjust parts of the process to suit their needs. (See the ToolKit section of this book for a more detailed description of the climate survey-feedback process and the tools used as part of the process.)

What's more, the feedback reports are also user friendly. They are easy to read and understand, they make constructive use of graphics but aren't overengineered, and the results are displayed using normative data so that people can assess how their results stack up against others. (A sample of one of our feedback reports is included in the ToolKit.)

But how does it all work? Gathering data, no matter how convenient, valid, and well presented in the written reports, is only a means to an end. The end is improving organizational performance. The real value of a climate survey is the extent to which it leads to constructive changes in the organization being surveyed. We have learned that this means that along with the feedback reports, which include our analysis of the data, we need to supply the right amount of context, coaching, and support. Without consulting assistance, the climate survey-feedback process will almost always be underleveraged, and the information will never be converted into constructive action. When done right, the entire process becomes a powerful tool for performance management.

I can't say that the process always works, but I would like to share a few success stories to give you a sense of how and why it often does. The key here is in the data and the way we present the data, using six climate dimensions and a short list of 18 leadership practices, with results always fed back against a large, stable international norm base. Our system gives people a common language with which to see, understand, and address organizational problems. The numbers that our surveys generate, along with the reliability of our research and track record with the numbers, present a hard reality that can overcome personal defenses and a general disinclination to face facts.

In Chapter 6 I described one example of how we used our climate survey data to manage performance—the case of Charlie at Rocketdyne. In the next few pages I will describe four other cases that illustrate how organizations have successfully used climate surveys to improve performance. Although I have changed the names to protect the innocent, the essential facts and features are real.

Educational Books Corporation: Managing Creativity

Sometimes those who lead successful organizations know little about leadership and even less about management. Sometimes all they are good at is creating or selling a great product. The better the product, the quicker this lack of leadership and management catches up to them and the people they lead. Their organizations grow too large and too complex to handle without greater discipline, without more process, and without an appreciation for "people management." I've found that the climate survey gives leaders who have never focused on the art or science of leadership a valuable perspective. It provides leaders who are newly curious about the work of people management with a language to help them think through problems and a way to talk about what's going on in the organization. As the following case shows, this perspective and this language can be a framework for performance management.

When Edna called me she was very low. She was one of my favorite clients—bright, successful, ambitious, intuitive, and kind of crazy-creative—but she sounded awful. A perfect executive for Educational Books Corporation (EBC), one of the largest book publishers in the United States, she was one of EBC's most effective executives. Edna ran the Children's Book Group, and this group accounted for 55% of EBC's revenues and almost 75% of its profits. She was acknowledged to be a genius when it came to children's publishing. She was trusted, admired, loved, and feared, all at the same time by almost all who worked for her. And Edna's boss, Rob Johnstone, EBC's father figure and CEO, knew he couldn't live without her.

So, why was Edna so worried? The problem this time was in the Picture Book division, which was the smallest of Edna's three divisions. The largest division by far was Reading Groups. Imitating the highly successful Scholastic Book Clubs, employees in this division set up reading groups in thousands of classrooms around the country and sold millions of books to kids of all ages. Employees in the Science Book division organized science clubs and events at these same schools, selling millions more books, tapes, posters, and computer programs. Then there was the Picture Book division.

Picture Books at EBC had historically been a lower priority. Selling children's illustrative books at Barnes & Noble, Kmart, and Molly's Corner Bookstore was not a very profitable business. EBC's schools were the mother lode, and everyone in Edna's Children's Book Group knew it. Oh, they realized that EBC had to have a division that sold books through retail channels because you couldn't attract authors or titles without it, but Picture Books seldom got much top-management attention. That began to change with *Mugwumps.* And then came *Pooh II,* an update of the children's classic whose copyright was owned by EBC. These two blockbuster children's book properties were so popular that Edna had to expand distribution well beyond the Reading Groups and Science Book division. In 1996, Picture Book revenues were $62 million. By 2000, they were $221 million. Thank you, *Mugwumps,* and bless you, *Pooh II.*

That's why Edna called me. Instead of jumping for joy with high-fives all around EBC's corporate headquarters, people in Picture Books were "totally stressed out" and "totally pissed off." According to Edna, "This should be the best of times for us, but it's the worst. I think our success with *Pooh II* is overshadowing a big morale, motivation, and productivity problem. And you have to come back and fix it."

Fixing it turned out to be at least an eight-month project. It's not over yet, but I believe Edna and her managers have a grip on the problems. Here's what I found and what I did.

EBC is a major player in the children's publishing business. Publishing is as much an art as it is a science and as much a calling as a business. And the world of children's publishing is even more values driven than adult publishing. So Edna's part of EBC attracts people who have a mission. I discovered 10 years earlier, when I first met Edna and did my first assignment at EBC, that values-driven people with a mission are hard to manage. I found the EBC Children's Book Group to be filled with very creative, very intuitive, very high-powered women. I found a few men, but most of the talent is female. On top of this, few employees and even fewer executives at EBC know much or care much about management. They care about books and children, about education, and about reading and science. They care about making money—many of them own EBC stock or have options—but "management" to most of the people in the Children's Book Group means acquiring good titles and getting them sold and delivered. The people side of running the business is simply not something they focus on.

Because of this, Edna and most other managers in the Children's Book Group have developed highly personalized leadership styles. So you have an environment that is exciting, verbal, creative, spontaneous, and always on the verge of being out of control, especially when people are pressed to respond to the explosive popularity of one of their products—in this case, *Pooh II.*

The first thing I did was talk to people. I interviewed Edna, and she admitted that she didn't know if the head of Picture Books, a 10-year publishing executive who had joined EBC 20 months earlier, was going to make it. "Rick hasn't earned the respect of some people. He's not a leader. He's too cautious," she said. Then I interviewed all of her direct reports. I talked to Rick and all of his direct reports. I talked to Joan Daniels, the brilliant and outspoken head of EBC's editorial department ("the mother of *Mugwumps*"). And I talked to the people in other EBC functions who had to support Edna and the Picture Books division.

I got an earful. Edna was right—people were unhappy and confused. They didn't think that Rick was capable of running his division, and they thought he had a weak team of managers under him. They complained about the work, the customers, the company, the way the place was organized, and Edna. And they had absolutely no idea how to fix things.

When I gave my initial report to Edna, she was discouraged. We had both hoped for a simple problem with a simple solution. "Can't we just reorganize," she asked, "or bring in someone else or change a few people?" Instead, I recommended we do a climate survey. I explained how the process worked and what Rick and his team would (hopefully) learn from the survey. I was convinced that, unless Edna and the Picture Book executives had hard data that defined their situation in nonintuitive, non-publishing-industry language, they would not be able to act. They would continue to duck responsibility and "blame out," a term I use to describe when a person feels it's everything except her that is the cause of her problems. I explained to Edna that the survey results would be confidential (e.i., I would not reveal anyone's personal results to anyone else), but that I would give her a general summary of the overall Picture Book climate profile.

At first, Edna hesitated. Three months went by. Edna sat on my proposal and I buried myself in other projects. The second in the *Pooh II* series hit the market with more fanfare and hoopla than ever. There were a few bumps, but the launch was considered a success at EBC. Edna was relieved, if not happy. Surprisingly, Rick and the Picture Book team managed to cope with the increased pressure and workload. Nobody quit, but the complaints continued. One of the realities of EBC's organic, informal, personality-driven organization was that Edna heard everything, so she *knew* things were still broken in Picture Books. Once the *Pooh II* launch was over, she called and we did our survey.

Exhibit 8.1 is the climate profile in Picture Books. These data were revealed to Rick and his team in a half-day workshop.

Exhibit 8.1
EBC's Picture Book Climate Profile

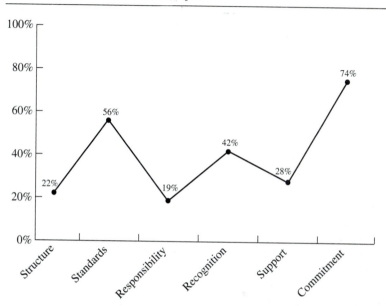

Low Structure and low Responsibility were not a surprise, but the team was embarrassed by just how low the numbers were. And they thought that Standards would be higher, given all the complaining about being "stressed out." The more we talked about it, the clearer it became that the people who filled out the questionnaires believed that things were so screwed up that deadlines and performance expectations were virtually meaningless. They served very little motivational purpose. The survey also revealed what was keeping the Picture Book division afloat. It was the sense of Commitment that people had—commitment to EBC, to Edna, and to Children's Books and its mission of helping children to read.

Although the team was initially hesitant, we generated five flip charts full of issues, opportunities, and action plans. Afterwards, Rick and each of his managers received personal feedback. I delivered the reports to each person and spent an hour discussing the results, identifying implications and possible fixes and coaching each person about how to best leverage the survey and follow-up with their own teams.

Three things happened as a result of the survey. Two were good and one wasn't. First, Rick realized he needed to reorganize his group.

He discovered that one of his direct reports—one who had been the most negative—had followed up the survey by criticizing her own team for giving her low scores on the leadership practices section. After an emotional discussion with me, he decided to terminate this manager. He also developed a plan to clarify the responsibilities of the two departments that were having the most conflict.

Second, the climate survey seemed to energize Rick's direct reports and provide them with an opportunity to "get on the table" a lot of the organizational issues that had heretofore been whispered about in private. The Picture Book group climate feedback meeting was cathartic. There was still a good deal of cynicism about Rick and some of his managers, but people said that they now saw "light at the end of the tunnel." They reported to me that they no longer had the feeling of being out of control. I attribute this to the fact that the climate survey process created a common language. It was a language of climate and leadership and management. These topics had not been widely discussed before and people were uncomfortable with them. The survey with its numbers, graphs, and climate management tools gave Rick and his team something to grab onto, a way of defining issues, and a road map to guide them toward solutions to their problems.

Unfortunately, the third consequence of the Picture Book climate survey was not positive. Rick failed to act on the results. Expectations were high after the feedback session. Almost all of Rick's managers knew that Rick planned to terminate the negative, troublesome manager, but he didn't. He procrastinated. Two months after the climate results were fed back, he still hadn't reorganized. And this proved to be a significant problem. As Edna said to me: "It's almost worse to have done the survey and highlighted the issues so clearly. Now, with Rick sitting on his hands, what am I to do?"

Edna's question frustrates me. Climate surveys help leaders frame problems. They provide focus. They point leaders toward solutions. They provide people with a common language and a common understanding of the cause-and-effect relationships that impact bottom-line performance. But they don't fix things. Surveys alone aren't going to improve organizational effectiveness. Surveys are a performance management tool, but they are only a tool. In the hands of leaders who want to lead, they can be a powerful tool for change. In the hands of leaders who don't want to act, they are a waste of money. And because of the need for confidentiality, I did not show Edna any of the personal climate survey results. Rick and I agreed that he would share his own results and the overall Picture Book climate profile with Edna and go over all of his organizational improvement plans, but he never did.

So, as a consultant, I am stymied at EBC. Edna continues to have a big problem with the performance of her Picture Book division, but all I seem to have done is provide her with a new language to describe the nature of the problem. As this case goes to press, I am advising her to terminate Rick: "If he doesn't have the courage to lead, given the data he has and the momentum for change the climate survey generated, he's got to be replaced."

Grand Traverse Cherries: Raising the Bar

It's easy to be an agent of change when everyone knows the organization is failing. But what about trying to stimulate change when things seem to be just fine? In this sense, some organizations are cursed by their own success. What can leaders do when they see the sky is falling, but nobody else does? How can leaders get the attention of their organization? I've found that the climate survey, especially when supplemented by questions dealing with the need for change, can be a stimulus to improved performance. Although the following case may lack the glamour and drama of some of the work we do, it's typical of the way the survey can be used by leaders who want to jump-start an organization that is only coasting along.

"What we need," said Grand Traverse Cherries' human resources manager, "is a good kick in the butt." Todd knew that Penny Baker was right.

Todd Spencer joined Grand Traverse Cherries (GTC) as the new CEO in April 2000. He'd been hired away from General Mills by Arthur Chatham, chairman of Chatham-Fitz, GTC's parent company. The company enjoyed a secure market position with its Cherry Juices commanding a 75% share of market and its Tropical Slam brand virtually alone at the top of its segment. GTC employees were mostly long serving, and turnover at all levels of the organization, except at the very top, was low. This was part of the reason they needed that kick in the butt.

The environment Todd inherited was affected by GTC's relationship with its parent company. Located in Detroit, GTC's executives were used to receiving a constant stream of requests, orders, and guidance from Chatham's headquarters in Birmingham. Financial controls were quite strong, and half of the members of Todd's senior team were either British or Canadian.

Todd was an American and so was Penny Baker. Shortly after Todd arrived, they created what they called an "internal PR campaign" to try and get the GTC organization moving at a faster clip. They called it "The Keystones of Excellence," and it included a revised mission statement, a set of five "values," and a series of company meetings in which groups of employees were introduced to these "keystones" and asked to identify ways they could help Grand Traverse Cherries improve its performance. It was a flop. "Everything we said was good stuff," Penny explained to me. "We just didn't *do* anything differently."

I got a call in October from Adam Port, an old consulting colleague and friend from our days of working together at The Forum Corporation. Adam had been working with Penny and GTC for years and thought that my Climate Survey might just be the tool Todd and Penny could use to "kick the GTC organization in the butt." I trusted Adam explicitly and armed him with copies of our survey, examples of how other clients had customized it, samples of feedback reports, resource guides, and other climate propaganda. (Most of what I gave Paul is the ToolKit in Part IV of this book.) Thirty days later Adam told me he had sold GTC on the Climate Survey.

Here's what he sold and what we did. We surveyed the entire GTC organization, including the hourly workers at its three manufacturing plants. The survey questionnaire consisted of our standard climate and leadership practices sections, a section of special questions about other aspects of the GTC work environment, plus two open-ended questions that asked people for their ideas about how to make GTC a better place to work. Questionnaires were distributed in late October and three weeks later Adam and I were scheduled to meet with Todd and his management board of eight senior executives to feed back the survey results.

Before this meeting, Penny and Adam wanted to review the data. They wanted to see how the climate varied level by level at GTC, so we ran three different "level reports." Exhibit 8.2 shows the climate profiles of the three levels of the GTC organization.

Penny was fascinated and Adam was pleased. The survey had confirmed exactly what they had sensed was going on at GTC, but it provided Penny with hard numbers that she knew would be much more compelling than the anecdotal data to which she and Todd had been referring up to now. And Adam was about to implement a training program that focused on performance feedback and coaching,

Exhibit 8.2
Levels of GTC Climate

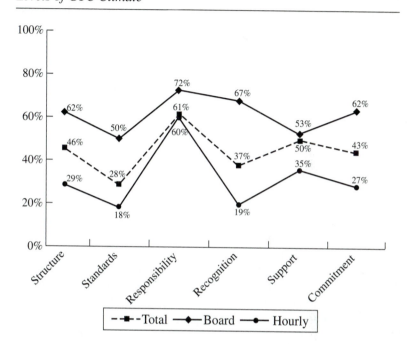

which were two of the leadership practice areas that the survey showed were most in need of work. Although they were excited by the survey results, the challenge was to package these results in a way that got the attention of the management board without stimulating management's defensiveness or resistance. Todd was an advocate for change, but Penny and Adam knew that there was a vocal minority of board members who were threatened by the whole process.

In addition to showing the board the overall results and the three levels, we decided to create group reports for each member of the board. In other words, the CFO would see a report that described the perceptions of all of her finance people, Penny would see a report of all of the HR staff, and so on. Todd would get a binder that included all of the various group reports. In addition, we produced individual feedback reports for each member of the board. We wanted each executive to appreciate how his or her personal leadership was impacting the climate at the top of his or her group and how the climate at the top impacted the overall group climate. It was going to be a lot of data for the board to absorb, so I agreed to prepare two additional GTC reports. One I called a "top-line summary" of all the results. It was simply my personal impressions of their survey data compared to other consumer products companies I had worked with. In two pages of bullet points, I emphasized that GTC employees were somewhat frustrated by the lack of performance-based rewards, the lack of openness and candor of GTC managers, and the relatively "laid-back" attitude of the entire GTC organization.

The second report I prepared compared GTC's manufacturing plant climates with those of several other beverage companies I had studied over the years. When Penny saw the results for the GTC plants, she was quite surprised at the low climate scores for most of the dimensions and the peak in the Responsibility score. I told her that this pattern was common in hourly level or highly unionized environments. The questions in our climate survey were created for managerial, or white-collar, populations. The language, particularly the wording we use for the items in the Responsibility dimension, is not always well suited to the realities of the shop floor as experienced by blue-collar workers. For example, the concept of "double checking," which may be anathema to a high achiever in middle management, is often taken for granted by an hourly employee working on a production line.

Exhibit 8.3 illustrates how similar the GTC's hourly employee climate was to the climates of two other groups of beverage company hourly employees. This comparison proved helpful and allowed Penny and her fellow board members to better understand the need to use the survey results differently in different parts of the organization.

We hoped that my "top-line" summary and supplemental analysis of the hourly climate data would stimulate and focus the board's attention and keep them from getting lost in all the numbers. We were right.

Todd started the meeting off with a review of his basic objective, which was to upgrade the performance of the entire GTC organization. "We've tried to shake the place up and are making some progress," he stated. "But the Keystones initiative has run out of gas. We are looking to this climate survey to identify where we need to focus." I then asked the board members what kind of organizational climate they felt was *required* in order for GTC to maximize its performance. This proved to be a highly interactive and somewhat contentious discussion. Different executives had quite different points

Exhibit 8.3
GTC's Hourly Climate Profile Compared to Others

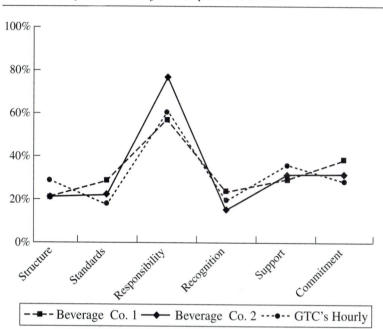

of view about what kind of climate would be most appealing to GTC employees and what kind of climate was called for in the various parts of the GTC's organization. It was obvious to me that there were two "camps" on the GTC board. One group was with Todd and believed that people at GTC were too comfortable and that much higher levels of performance could be achieved. The other wasn't so sure. Their objective seemed to be to deliver only the performance that Chatham expected, and this was the 5% to 6% growth that had been historically achieved. Todd's camp wanted to see lower Structure, higher Standards, higher Responsibility, and higher Support. The other camp focused more on having high levels of Recognition and Support. Everyone believed high Commitment was important.

Exhibit 8.4 outlines the "consensus" climate requirements that the GTC board came up with, along with the actual results. In the meeting we highlighted the two biggest gaps in the climate dimensions: Standard and Recognition.

Exhibit 8.4

Climate Gaps from the GTC Board's Analysis of Climate Requirements

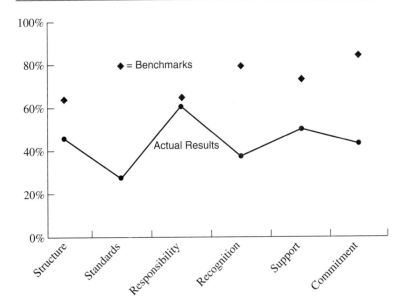

When I showed them the actual results, there was an immediate and emotional reaction. Todd smiled, glanced at Penny, and listened while the we-don't-have-to-change camp tried to explain why the gaps in the Standards and Recognition dimensions weren't meaningful. After a half an hour, these board members more or less ran out of steam. But I knew they weren't convinced. I then fed back the rest of the survey results, and these confirmed the fact that GTC employees weren't happy with the way things were going in the company and wanted to see changes made. One of the items in the customized part of the survey, for example, asked if the "pace of change was too fast" at GTC. The overwhelming response was "no." Penny pointed out that there were a number of written comments suggesting that GTC was not a challenging environment. Several went so far as to characterize GTC as a "country club."

These results got people's attention. Slowly but surely even the resisters realized that a bit of "butt kicking" was needed at GTC. It took two hours, but we ended the board meeting by generating a short list of actions that the top team should take to follow up on the survey. Each individual board member was to meet with me and go over his or her personal results. Each member was to conduct a feedback session with his or her direct reports and come up with action plans to improve the climate, focusing explicitly on ways to "raise the bar" and communicate a sense of higher Standards. Each was to report back to Todd regarding these plans.

We replaced the vague call to action embodied in the initial "Keystones of Excellence" initiative with a much more specific and actionable effort. The Climate Survey gave Todd and Penny their performance improvement platform. They decided to provide every participant in Adam's new training program with a personalized climate feedback report. The leadership practices section would allow each person to build an individual leadership improvement agenda. Every level, every department, and every manager at GTC could "see" what the opportunity was. The graphs and numbers were compelling and the message was clear.

GTC is getting the kick that it needs. But the reason it's working is not that a charismatic leader has come in to provide inspiration, and Adam and I were certainly not hired to be "motivational speakers" to deliver a one-time shot in the arm. What we did is use the Climate Survey to generate data. And we made sure these data were displayed in a way that highlighted "gaps" and benchmarked GTC as "below normal." We also provided GTC managers with tools to respond to the gaps. Armed with these data and tools, Todd could be a more effective change agent, and leaders at every level could self-administer the butt-kicking that the data revealed to be necessary.

Pita Plus: Firing Your Boss

It's a truism that the higher up you are in an organization, the less performance feedback you get. When I work at the senior levels of an organization, I frequently have to deal directly with the consequences of this lack of feedback. I've found that the climate survey gives me a way to objectify and depersonalize what can be difficult personnel decisions and very tough personal experiences. The following case was one of the most difficult consulting assignments I have ever had.

From the minute Dan called me, I knew I was in trouble. I did not think I could turn the assignment down without jeopardizing my relationship with NutriCo, and I didn't think I could do the assignment without jeopardizing that same relationship. Dan Nelson was the number-two human resources executive at Pita Plus, then a wholly owned subsidiary of NutriCo. What he asked me to do was get his boss, Roy Autry, fired.

In the early 1990s, Pita Plus was under tremendous pressure to grow and increase its profitability. Nutri's soft-drink business was flat and Wall Street looked to the restaurant division for growth. In addition to adding new outlets, the key top-line number everyone looks at in the fast-food industry is called "same store sales," and Pita Plus was always scrambling to increase this number. That meant adding new menu items, new advertising, and new marketing promotions, as well as adding new stores. On top of this, Nutri wanted Pita Plus to improve its margins. That meant squeezing costs out of the operations. And the biggest cost to squeeze was labor.

So human resources (HR) at Pita Plus was an important function. Both Dan and Roy were veteran Nutri HR professionals. Before coming to Pita Plus, Roy had been head of corporate Compensation and Benefits in NutriCo's New Jersey headquarters. While in that position, he had earned a well-deserved reputation for innovation and creativity. As head of Compensation, Roy was used to hobnobbing with all of Nutri's senior executives. Early in 1993 he decided to broaden his HR skills portfolio by running a big field HR function. With his close relationships to top Nutri executives, it didn't take him long to land the top job at Pita Plus. Roy was 46 years old.

Dan came to Pita Plus from the Nutri-Ade Company where he had been the head of HR for one of Nutri's regional businesses. Dan was ambitious, and he was one of my best clients. Over the years he had called on me to run numerous training programs, strategy sessions, team meetings, and climate surveys. Dan's ambition was obvious to all who knew him. His favorite topic was his own career. Dan was also very good at his job. At 29, he was the youngest HR director at Nutri, and at 35 he was the youngest divisional HR head. When he took the number-two job at Pita Plus, working for Roy, he told me he thought it would be a two-year assignment. "Then," he confided, "I want my own function."

Dan had been at Pita Plus eight months when he called me. He told me he was acting in the name of Joe Dolan, Pita Plus's longstanding and highly creative CEO. "Bob, we have a problem," Dan began. "You know that Joe is a great restaurant executive but a lousy leader. Well, he doesn't trust Roy and the situation has become impossible. Roy turned out to be a wild man and it's killing us—and hurting the entire HR function out here. Joe wants you to interview all of his team (Roy and his peers) and see if you can advise us what to do." Dan went on to explain that he and Joe had developed "a special relationship" over the past few months, due mainly to Joe's lack of trust in Roy because of Roy's "unpredictable leadership style."

"What does Roy know about all of this?"

"Well, he's all for it. He thinks you are coming out here to look at how Joe's team functions. And I've convinced him to conduct a climate survey in the HR department as part of your assignment. That will give you an excuse for giving Roy lots of feedback."

"Swell, Dan. Let me get this straight. You and Joe think Roy is terrible as the head of HR. Joe's too chicken to tell him that, so you want me to dig up a bunch of dirt on Roy from his colleagues and his direct reports. Then you want me to sit down with Roy and tell him nobody likes him. And then what?"

Dan didn't even pause to catch his breath. "Then Roy will know he's not cut out to be a line HR guy and he'll go somewhere and be a brilliant compensation and benefits guru."

I should never have agreed to do it, but I said OK.

I spent four days in Boston, interviewed the entire Pita Plus top-management team, handed out climate surveys to all 60 members of the human resources department, and learned that Roy was not held in high regard. There were two main reasons for this: (1) He had never been the head of a business HR department and was making what others thought to be bad judgments and decisions, and (2) he had so many friends in high places back at Nutri headquarters that nobody dared confide anything in him for fear it would find its way back to New Jersey. I also learned that Roy was presiding over an unhealthy organizational climate and that Dan's back-stabbing strategy was completely obvious to everyone except Dan.

Exhibit 8.5 is Pita Plus's HR climate profile. This profile reflected the thoughts and feelings of Roy's direct reports, as well as the responses of Roy's top team. Exhibit 8.6 is the profile of the climate at the top of the HR organization. This report was generated by only Roy's six direct reports. Exhibit 8.7 is a summary of how these same six people viewed Roy's leadership practices.

Here's what I did with the data. First, I told Dan that I wasn't going to show him any of my data until I had spoken to Joe. Second, I arranged a day to feed back climate and practices data to all members of Roy's team, meeting as a group in the morning to go over Exhibit 8.2 and meeting privately in the afternoon to hand back individual reports to Roy and each of his managers. I had wanted to debrief with Joe before I fed back the HR climate results, but (surprise, surprise) he was called out of town the day I was to meet with him.

Exhibit 8.5
Pita Plus HR Climate Profile

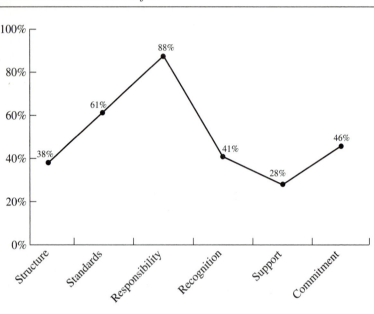

Exhibit 8.6
Roy's Climate Profile

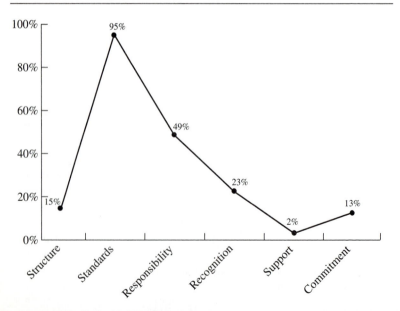

Exhibit 8.7
Roy's Leadership Practices

Part II: Management Practices

The following scores for the 18 management practices were derived from Part II of the questionnaire, which asked people to describe the practices of the manager to whom they report. The percentile score for each practice is based on the average of the responses of the people who completed questionnaires. the spread is an indication of the dispersion of the responses. The number in parentheses following each practice is the raw score at the 50th percentile of the norm base.

DIMENSION	PRACTICE	SCORE	SPREAD
Structure	1. Establishing clear, specific performance goals for your subordinate's jobs. (3.75)	7%	Narrow
	2. Clarifying who is responsible for what within the group. (3.75)	7%	Narrow
	3. Making sure tasks and projects are clearly and thoroughly explained and understood when they are assigned. (3.50)	9%	Narrow
Standards	4. Setting challenging performance goals and standards for subordinates. (4.00)	47%	Narrow
	5. Demonstrating personal commitment to achieving goals. (4.17)	7%	Narrow
	6. Giving your subordinates feedback on how they are doing on their jobs. (3.67)	12%	Medium
Responsibility	7. Encouraging your subordinates to initiate tasks or projects they think are important. (4.00)	3%	Medium
	8. Expecting your subordinates to find and correct their own errors rather than doing this for them. (4.00)	49%	Narrow

continued

DIMENSION	PRACTICE	SCORE	SPREAD
	9. Encouraging innovation and calculated risk taking in others. (3.67)	9%	Medium
Recognition	10. Recognizing subordinates for good performance more often than criticizing them for poor performance. (4.00)	5%	Medium
	11. Using recognition, praise, and similar methods to reward subordinates for excellent performance. (3.75)	4%	Medium
	12. Relating the reward system (compensation) recognition, promotion) to performance rather than to other factors such as seniority, personal relationships, and so on. (3.67)	8%	Narrow
Support	13. Being supportive and helpful to subordinates in their day-to-day activities. (3.88)	2%	Medium
	14. Going to bat for your subordinates with your supervisors when you feel your subordinates are right. (4.00)	4%	Medium
	15. Conducting team meetings in a way that builds trust and mutual respect. (3.60)	3%	Narrow
Commitment	16. Communicating excitement and enthusiasm about the work. (4.00)	3%	Medium
	17. Involving people in setting goals. (3.67)	2%	Narrow
	18. Encouraging subordinates to participate in making decisions. (4.00)	2%	Medium

However, we spoke by telephone. I reported how tenuous Roy's credibility was with the other members of the team and how ignorant Roy was of the situation. Joe asked me only one question: "What should we do with Roy?" I told him Roy was probably not "fixable" and that the situation was likely irreversible and, therefore, that he should be moved out of the top HR spot.

"But, he'll be labeled as 'damaged goods' here at Nutri and no one will take him," Joe said.

"Get Bruce McCoy (the head of Nutri's HR function) to take him back. He's always been a winner as a compensation and benefits expert. That's where he belongs, Joe. Everyone but Roy knows that."

"Well, you tell him." And Joe was gone.

So I did.

It was painful and profound. You have to know Nutri back in the early 1990s to realize how proud and how driven its HR professionals were. Nutri's human resources function was considered to be one of the best in the *world*. They attracted extremely high achievers. The function was also very powerful. So, in addition to high nAch, Nutri attracted people with extreme high nPow. That's what I was dealing with.

The climate survey saved me.

Using the survey results, mainly Exhibits 8.6 and 8.7, I met with Roy for three hours to discuss not so much his relationship with his peers (which is what both Dan and Joe wanted me to focus on) but his inability to lead a high-performing HR function at Pita Plus. At first, he rejected the data. "Dan has poisoned them against me," he said. "I ought to get rid of him tomorrow." Over and over again, I attempted to bring him back to the numbers.

"Roy, Dan didn't give you the 7% or the 12% or the 2%. All of your people are frustrated and demotivated. The spread for these practices scores is narrow." Slowly he began to accept the data. We started to examine some of the causes and to brainstorm possible actions he could take to address the underlying issues. We agreed that one of the first steps would be to open up to his team members and include them in the action planning. We decided that I would facilitate a meeting with all of his direct reports, and we scheduled it for the following week. In the meantime, he was going to remain calm and statesman-like while I spoke to all of his people to explain what we were doing.

The meeting was a disaster. Roy couldn't help himself and attacked the team for giving him low scores. Nobody spoke. Dan said nothing. I was useless. The meeting was over before it began.

Afterwards, I went to dinner with Roy and had one of those "come to Jesus" sessions every executive coach or counselor knows about. I told Roy what I thought about his leadership. I told him I thought he was better suited to run a smaller, higher-level staff group—that he needed more intellectual and fewer interpersonal challenges to be successful. I'm sure I raised my voice. He cried, and we both probably drank too much. Roy finally came to the conclusion that his days at Pita Plus were numbered.

Roy Autry is today one of the most highly respected executive compensation experts in the country. He's still with Nutri, and he's undoubtedly saved them millions of compensation and benefits dollars. Dan Nelson left NutriCo soon after my assignment. Too many people thought he was too ambitious. Today, he is a very successful HR executive at General Motors. Joe Dolan retired from Pita Plus without ever having told Roy Autry what he thought of him.

At Pita Plus the climate survey proved to be a tool that enabled a high-powered but out-of-place executive see the negative impact he was having on the overall organization. In a very real sense, it "depersonalized" what was happening. It helped Roy gain perspective. It allowed him and those around him to discuss and work on the situation as they would a marketing or operations or business problem. The survey feedback reports and materials I used gave them numbers, measures, benchmarks, and action alternatives.

By the way, I no longer do any consulting for the NutriCo HR function. I'll never know what they said about me or my work at Pita Plus. But the calls stopped coming in about five years ago.

Preston King: Rigging the Data

Over the years it has become clear to me that one of the powerful aspects of the concept of organizational climate is that it makes squishy things tangible. It puts numbers on phenomena that don't lend themselves to quantification, making the soft side of management hard. Enlightened leaders know that managing motivation is important and that holding executives accountable for the soft stuff is smart. And they often wonder if the climate surveys and tools we have developed could be used as a way to *directly* manage this aspect of managerial performance.

Preston King Beverages tried this. Here's what happened.

Preston King is the largest beverage company in Canada. It's mostly a beer company, but its portfolio also includes the MegaCola franchise as well as a wines and spirits business. Because of its relationship with MegaCola International, Preston attracted a top-flight senior management team that was 100% committed to developing people and aggressive performance management. I began working for Preston in the early 1990s, first developing a customized leadership program, then helping the company improve its strategic planning, and finally implementing a top-to-bottom climate and culture survey. It was this survey that led one of my clients, Henry Fisher, to consider using climate scores as part of his company's formal appraisal process.

Henry was the head of human resources for Maple Breweries (MB), one of Preston's most successful businesses. Located in Quebec City, MB brands had long been market leaders. A year earlier, Ed Zeller was appointed managing director of the brewery. Ed had spent 12 years in human resources and the MB position was his first line executive appointment. He and Henry were determined to take the MB organization to a new level of performance, and they viewed Preston's climate and culture survey as a unique opportunity.

"Look, Bob," Henry said to me. "We've already established a baseline with last year's survey. This year Ed and I are simply going to measure each of our managers' ability to move their scores higher. We'll reward those that are able to do this. It's simple."

"It's not simple, and you know it," I replied. "The minute people know that you are going to use the scores as part of your formal evaluation and compensation scheme, you're going to screw up the process. Respondents won't be candid. Managers will try to game the system. It makes me nervous, and it's not how we intended to use the survey."

"Well, Preston's corporate office has told us we can do whatever we want. And we're going to use it this year [1993] as a real performance management tool. Just the climate part, not all the other stuff. Will you help us?" Henry was adamant and I agreed to help. I figured they were going to do it anyway, so I might as well try to make the whole process as workable as possible.

Henry wanted two things from me. He wanted me to establish benchmarks for each climate dimension. We both agreed that the benchmarks should be slightly different for different parts of the MB organization. But because Henry wanted to keep things simple, we ended up with very similar profiles. The hourly employee climate benchmarks were the ones that were the most different. Exhibit 8.8 illustrates the initial (1992) climate profile for the overall organization, the general benchmarks we came up with for MB, and the coal face benchmarks.

Exhibit 8.8
Maple Brewery Climate Profile and Benchmarks

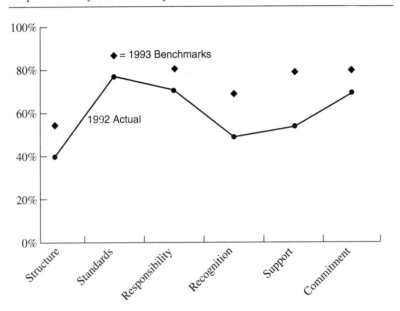

As you can see, Henry and Ed set the bar high. Each MB manager had his or her own personal target for each climate dimension, but it was expected that a minimum improvement of 10 percentile points in all six dimensions was to be achieved on the next climate survey, which would be conducted in 10 months. I suggested to Henry that he set different targets for each manager on each dimension, but he decided not to. "That's too many numbers to worry about. Let's keep it simple." You had to know Henry to realize how focused he was.

The second thing Henry asked me to create for him was a resource guide that MB leaders could use to help them affect each climate dimension. The guide I developed was similar to the resource guide reproduced in the ToolKit. The Preston King climate and culture survey did not use our 18 leadership practices. The company had its own customized set of leadership practices that was used in its leadership training programs, and it didn't want to confuse matters with a second set of practices. Therefore, I created an MB leadership guide that listed the climate survey items for each dimension and provided a number of "tips for managers." These tips included many of the same "ideas for action" found in the ToolKit, but I also tried to speak directly to the climate items. For example, I created a section of "to do's" on business planning

that were aimed at the Structure item "Our productivity sometimes suffers from a lack of organization and planning." And Henry and I put
together another section on Preston King recognition programs aimed at
the Recognition item "There is not enough reward and recognition given
in the organization for doing good work."

Preston conducted its second annual climate and culture survey
in late 1993. In Quebec City, everyone understood that the survey
results were going to be public. That is, Ed and Henry were going to
receive copies of every manager's climate profile and use the results
as part of each person's year-end appraisal. I predicted that the scores
would rise, and they did. Exhibit 8.9 shows the 1993 profile and com-
pares it to the one from 1992s.

What I didn't predict was MB's enthusiastic response to the
process. Not only Ed and Henry, but almost all the managers thought the
use of climate data to measure all-around managerial performance was
appropriate. I had expected to find cynicism, anxiety, and resistance.
Instead, there was an obvious, almost matter-of-fact, acceptance.
Henry told me that two or three managers had seen their numbers

Exhibit 8.9

Maple Brewery's 1992 and 1993 Climate Profiles

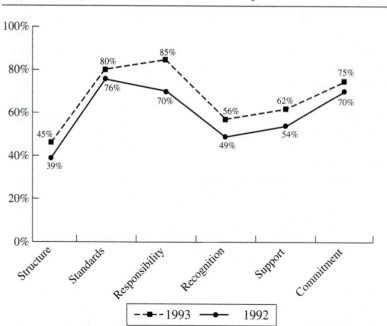

"slip" and Ed's response had been clear and evenhanded. Bonuses were smaller based on the lower climate scores. I am sure the fact that overall MB performance had markedly improved in 1993 helped cushion the anxiety. But I also gained a new appreciation for climate surveys as a performance management tool.

I found myself in Quebec a year later and stopped by to see Ed and Henry. Ed was preparing for a new assignment (this time running Preston's biggest brewery in Toronto) and Henry was in the middle of MB's third annual climate survey. He was his usual upbeat self: "We kept the same targets for 1994, a 10-point improvement in all climate dimensions that were below the benchmark. I talked about changing the targets, but our managers wanted to keep them the same."

Two months later, the 1994 results were in, and once again, MB's climate scores improved. When I called Henry, he explained that most managers were "hard at work" figuring out how to raise those dimensions that were below expectations. "Recognition is proving to be the toughest issue for us. And Support actually showed a two percentile-point dip," he said. "It sure does focus you. However, I'm not sure about next year. . . ."

For the first time, I sensed a note of caution in Henry's voice. Although I was very curious about what was happening in the brewery in Quebec City, four months went by before I next caught up with Henry. He had been transferred to Edmonton, Alberta, and was now running the sales function for Golden King, one of Preston's best-known beer companies. Over a couple of Goldens, here is what Henry told me about using the climate survey as part of Preston King's performance appraisal system:

> It works really well for two years. Then it wears thin. I am sure that managers "rig" the system. That is, right before survey time, they take out the resource guide and beaver away trying to fix those aspects of their climate that have the lowest scores. They sometimes try to tell their employees how to fill out the questionnaire. I know that goes on. But there are two beautiful aspects of the process. First, the games that they play trying to raise their climate scores are *exactly* what they should be doing. I mean, I don't care *why* a manager is delegating more and more effectively. I just care that he's doing it! So what if he's trying to "rig" the climate survey? And the second saving grace is that the individual responses on the survey are confidential, even though the reports aren't. Enough employees are honest so that managers can't really dictate the results. At least that's what I believe. The problem is that after three years of surveys the whole process loses its impact. The "low-hanging fruit" has already been picked or fixed and what's left are the bigger, less tractable, climate issues.

Personal climate data—and personal leadership practices data—are too effective as an individual development tool to be used for performance appraisals. You can "have your cake and eat it, too" for a year or so, but you're kidding yourself if you think that employees will be as honest and candid over the long haul once they see the data being used to stack rank individual managers.

Despite this qualified endorsement by Henry, as a consultant I remain skeptical. I'm pleased whenever a client can use the climate survey to improve performance—I'm pleased when my clients are pleased. But, as a researcher, I'm also aware of the care we took in developing the survey as a valid instrument and the uses we had in mind as we modified and perfected the instrument. And so I'm troubled by the "rigging" that Henry described, but I can live with it, as long as everyone knows how the game is being played.

A Two-Part System

Information, no matter how accurate and how well validated, is just information. People actively engaged in leading organizations must find a way to convert the information into constructive action. It's a two-part system: The data represent thoughts and feelings as more or less hard facts and present them in a language that helps explain organizational realities. The leader applies that information to improve the performance of a living organization. Neither of the two parts works very well without the other.

In the stories I've just told, Edna at EBC and Todd at Grand Traverse Cherries were both provided valuable data from climate surveys. Todd combined these data with skillful and tactful application in order to improve organizational performance. Edna may yet do this. Dan at Pita Plus and Henry at Preston King both used the climate surveys in more unorthodox ways but still succeeded through a bold and forceful application of data. The information gained through the climate survey can become a valuable tool for leaders to use in managing performance, if they have the wisdom to understand *how* it can be used. Although I obviously see the value of consultants in effecting the conversion, the process can work with in-house resources provided that those within the organization are trusted and have the perspective to understand the context of the information along with the knowledge and skills to provide needed coaching and support. As the next chapter illustrates, some organizations are, so far, unwilling to use this valuable leadership tool.

9

A Tale of Two Schools: "Irrelevant Leadership"

Ellen McGraw sits alone at her desk in her small office just beside the high school's chemistry lab. It's after 4 P.M., and the school is nearly empty. A stack of lab reports waits for her, but for a change she has not tried to get a start on them before heading home. Instead, she is considering her options.

It's been a rough day. Her classes went well enough, although she wonders how many more students they will try to cram in. The labs were constructed with stations for 24, and her numbers are currently over 30. But that isn't the main problem. It happened during her second-hour class, when she stepped into the hall to try to quiet down two students who were arguing loudly. She said to them, "Gentlemen, you should be in class now, not out here disturbing my class." They replied with a direct "F—— you, lady!" and sauntered down the hall, laughing. At the end of the period McGraw reported the incident to Dr. Atkinson, the principal. She did not know their names, but she gave a complete description of the two, and he seemed to know right away who they were. He promised quick action.

But then during sixth hour they were back again, obviously trying to lure her out into the hall. She ignored them for about 15 minutes until they went away. Obviously, nothing had happened to discourage them—or to encourage McGraw that she was getting any support from the school's administration.

She doesn't mind the fact that she never receives any help with her teaching. She's been teaching chemistry for 20 years, and for 10 of them she's taught Advanced Placement (AP). In fact, for the last five years she has been invited to Princeton to help grade the

AP tests. She knows what she's doing in the classroom, even though she has never received any recognition beyond the annual raise that everyone gets. And she doesn't mind that Dr. Atkinson was two years behind in evaluating her teaching, for his evaluations were always blandly positive, focusing mainly on *classroom management* and *student empowerment,* buzzwords in the district for the last few years. No, McGraw has been content to just shut her door and teach. That seems to work well until noise in the hall blasts in through her door.

Options. She thinks about transferring to the other high school in town, but she doubts the situation is any better there. Maybe it's time to take an early retirement and get a job at the big pharmaceutical company in town. She had looked into that a year ago, even meeting with its human relations director, and she knew she could make more money there. But the problem is that she enjoys teaching. It's just school that she doesn't enjoy.

———————

———————
Schools Are Different

Unlike businesses and health care systems, public schools typically are not competing for customers, although recently many critics of the schools argue that it's precisely the lack of competition that has allowed schools to remain mediocre. And schools are different because there is no "bottom line" as a way to measure their performance, although some have argued that student scores on standardized tests are a good way to measure the effectiveness of schools. With schools, the "products" that they hope to turn out—educated citizens, involved participants in the community and the economic system, fulfilled and happy individuals and family members who lead meaningful lives—do not lend themselves to easy measurement. It's difficult to evaluate schools.

Despite these difficulties, of course, people evaluate the schools all the time. It's done by the news media, by politicians across the spectrum, by employers of high school graduates, by university professors and admissions officers, and by parents based on their limited but intense firsthand experience with the schools. And, similarly, since 1983's *A Nation at Risk,* there has been a steady stream of books critical of our schools. The problem is that most of the criticism bypasses what is "fixable" in the schools. Critics can lament scores on standardized tests, the breakdown of the American family, and the ascendance of glitzy television, the Internet, and video games. They can attack the values and literacy of students and the education levels and commitment of teachers. But none of these attacks suggests a solution. It's more like finger-pointing.

What's needed is a systematic way for schools to focus attention on factors they can deal with to make a difference in the quality of education they offer. The public schools can't simply choose to deal with a better bunch of students, although private schools with restrictive admissions policies can do so. And public schools can't get rid of their teachers and get some better ones, for a teaching shortage is looming, especially in math and science. What is needed is a way for the schools to arouse the motivation of their teachers and other employees and to focus that aroused motivation on doing the kind of work that the communities define as important through the processes of school board elections and meetings, PTA meetings in specific schools, and other public forums. They need to find ways to make Ellen McGraw feel that her school is part of the solution rather than part of the problem.

In other words, I believe that it's important to analyze the organizational climate, leadership practices, and other determinants of climate in our schools and then to use those data to target the kinds of changes that will be most productive.

Schools are different from many businesses because of the kinds of people who typically work in them. George Litwin and I discovered in the late 1960s that elementary school teachers tend to be high in nAff, which is not surprising given the warmth and support that successful elementary school staff members tend to radiate. I suspect that the same high nAff would be found in the high schools, although there would probably also be a large number of people with high nPow. People who have a high need to organize and control others have ample opportunities to exercise that need with teenagers, and the simple two-level hierarchy of the classroom would also be to their liking.

Neither high schools nor elementary schools, nor middle schools for that matter, have much to attract people with high nAch or to arouse the nAch of those teachers who are working there. None of the things that turn on high nAch people are present in the typical school systems. Teachers tend not to be rewarded for high performance. In almost all contracts, pay raises come with years of experience, whether you had a good year or not, and there are no promotions except out of the classroom. A successful teacher might win "perks" such as favorable course assignments or a desirable classroom, but these tend to come more with experience than with excellent performance. In fact, high performance can sometimes lead to negative consequences with more students assigned to certain classes because of parental wishes, student word of mouth, or guidance counselors doing what they see to be in the best interests of their students. This is probably why teachers like Ellen McGraw have an additional "teaching load."

The kind of regular, concrete feedback that high nAch people require is missing in the typical school. Performance evaluations, usually required by union contract, occur every three or four years, but I found that in some schools this is a goal that is not always met by busy administrators who are putting out disciplinary brushfires or dealing with parents, superintendents, and boards of education. Two teachers I spoke with in a large high school had not been formally evaluated in eight years. And once teachers are granted tenure—most often after four years—it is very difficult to remove them except for the most egregious behavior, usually involving criminal or immoral acts, or in some cases persistent absenteeism. Ineffective teaching may be mentioned in the written evaluations that administrators make, but the consequences are few, largely because of the highly subjective nature of the evaluations. Although Ellen McGraw seems to accept her profession's lack of concrete feedback, there is nevertheless very little going on in her school district to arouse her performance through her nAch. Being invited to evaluate Advanced Placement Tests at Princeton—outside the district—has been her primary source of professional recognition.

Despite these differences, however, schools are organizations comprised of people who are supposed to be working toward common goals. The people have measurable subjective feelings about their work environment, so collectively that environment has an organizational climate. That climate may or may not arouse the motivation of the people who work there. And the degree to which the motivation of teachers is aroused directly impacts their performance—no matter how one measures that performance. Furthermore, that climate is caused by a number of identifiable determinants, the most important of which is leadership. Ellen McGraw would not be so discouraged, and her school would not be in danger of losing a valued teacher, if the climate of her school were better. That climate would be better if the leadership of the school were better.

A Case Study in Two Public High Schools

My work with schools centers on a project I conducted in 1997 for two comprehensive high schools in the Midwest. Although I do not have the broad database on school climate that I have for businesses and health care organizations, I believe that a close examination of climate and leadership in these two organizations suggests the nature of the problems and the solutions in many of our troubled public schools.

The two high schools, which I'll call Washington and Jefferson, each house about 2,000 students and about 120 professional staff consisting of teachers, guidance counselors, and administrators. Both schools are very successful by most objective measures. They boast extensive Advanced Placement Programs, and many of their students do well on the AP tests. Both schools have had recent Presidential Scholars and top scorers in statewide mathematics competitions. Both have award-winning groups in music, drama, and publications. Both send more than 70% of their graduates on to college, including Harvard, MIT, and Stanford. Both schools are successful in athletics, with many state championships through the years.

Despite these successes, however, both schools are plagued by an achievement gap between Caucasian and African American students despite frequent calls by the board of education, administration, and community members to solve this problem. Both schools are criticized for neglecting nonacademic students, and both suffer from overcrowding. There are minor problems with drugs, gangs, and weapons, but these are not nearly as severe as in other nearby urban schools. Both schools are racially diverse, with Jefferson 24% African American and 6% Asian American and Washington with 12% African American and 1% Asian American. Other ethnic groups, notably Arab American, also play significant roles.

In other words, the two schools I studied mirror the strengths and the weaknesses of many public high schools. Some students do very well, but the achievement gap is intractable, and many students are bored. Our research brought to the surface problems that suggest serious trouble ahead.

The faculties of the schools are not as racially diverse as the students, but the administrations of each school (principal, assistant principal, class principals) are disproportionately African American. The principal of Jefferson is African American; the principal of Washington when I worked there was Italian American. (The current principal is African American.) Both faculties are very well educated, with many master's degrees and a few Ph.D.'s in each building. Both buildings have veteran staffs with more than half of the teachers boasting more than 20 years' experience. In other words, many teachers like Ellen McGraw are working in the schools. Among them was Jeff Hall, chairperson of the social studies department at Jefferson, who assisted me in this project.

We made some slight modifications in a survey form that I have used frequently with clients in the corporate world. The survey had four sections: one designed to survey perceptions of the climate of the school, a second to evaluate the leadership practices of the principal, a third to evaluate the same practices of department chairpersons, and a fourth for open-ended written comments. We decided to evaluate leadership of principals and department chairpersons without including other administrators because we judged these to be the most important roles and because including all the administrators might lead to a confusion of data. We also expanded the list of 18 practices to 30 in order to study a broader range of behaviors that might affect school climate.

The results were tabulated and analyzed, and when I returned to the school district several months later, Hall reported that several colleagues at Jefferson had told him how the survey gave them a chance to "tell it like it is." Even so, a veteran German teacher had said that this would only result in business as usual, that is, a careful analysis with nothing being done about it. I met separately with each principal and groups of department chairpersons from each school to discuss the data and their implications.

Feedback Sessions

Only the principals of the two schools saw the evaluations of their leadership practices. The data on "Management Practices of Your Principal" were low in all 30 practices, with an average of 14th percentile. Neither principal was cheered by these numbers. The principal of Washington, the affable and gregarious son of Italian immigrants, had worked up through the ranks of the city schools, serving as head of the teachers' union before moving into administration. He swallowed hard as he saw the dismal figures describing his school and his leadership. Still, he struggled to put on a brave face and to search for constructive steps he could take, even when I explained, "The data don't suggest you are doing such a bad job. The teachers simply see you as irrelevant."

The principal at Jefferson, a personable man who had recently taken the position after years of job-hopping, was no less disturbed by what he saw and heard. But he tended to shrug off the results, saying,

"People like to complain," and pointing to the questionable truism that schools are really not like business organizations.

Only the department chairpersons saw how their department members evaluated their leadership, although they all saw the climate survey results for their school. We met with department chairs at Jefferson in a carpeted math classroom. About 20 people attended the session, including most of the chairs and a few others who had responded to the open invitation. After a few introductory remarks about organizational climate, I got straight to the point:

"Your organizational climate is lousy."

Laughter broke out in the room. Teachers exchanged knowing smiles, heads nodded. The mood was euphoric. Private intuitions about the climate and leadership of their school were clearly borne out in empirical data.

"Look, I don't know a lot about schools," I continued, "but in corporations I work with, places like Xerox and Citicorp, numbers like yours mean the organization is in deep trouble. I'm told this is a high-achieving school, but I predict very tough times ahead." I explained that the school was being carried by the extraordinary efforts of the teachers who work well despite the organizational climate rather than because of it.

Teachers agreed that the climate survey results were a clear call to decisive corrective actions, and many mentioned privately their eagerness to act on my recommendations.

The Results

The results of the climate surveys at Washington and Jefferson show that the two schools share remarkably similar organizational climates, so I've combined them in Exhibit 9.1.

During the debriefing sessions, I pointed out that the generally low scores should not be seen in the context of 99th percentile as ideal in schools for all six climate dimensions. For example, how high a score for Structure would be best for a school that values the autonomy and academic freedom of its teachers? Remember that the norms were derived from surveys taken at large corporations. However, this is not meant to suggest that scores under 12% are not a sign of serious problems.

The data on "Management Practices of Your Principal" were generally low in all 30 practices, ranging from 3rd percentile (practice 5: "Understands which decisions can be made alone and which

Exhibit 9.1

Organizational Climate at Washington and Jefferson High Schools

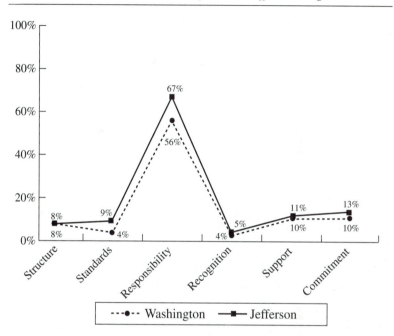

decisions need to involve others") to 30th (practice 26: "Communicates excitement and enthusiasm about our work"), with an average of 14th percentile. Exhibit 9.2 dramatically shows these low scores.

When I explained to them that the data generally indicated the irrelevance of the principals in establishing a constructive organizational climate rather than their poor performance, I was cushioning the blow. I reached my conclusion about the irrelevance of the principals in part from examining the data describing "Management Practices of Your Department Chairperson" as shown in Exhibit 9.3.

There the percentiles were clearly higher, ranging from 26th (practice 10: "Pushes me to constantly look for new and better ways of doing my job") to 73rd (practice 25: "Is open and candid with me rather than being vague and indirect"), with an average of 57th. An excitable history teacher, one of the most vocal critics of the school, exclaimed, "We kicked AT&T's butt." The implication here, I told

Exhibit 9.2

Management Practices of Your Principal (Washington and Jefferson)

Part II: Management Practices of Your Principal

The following scores for the 30 management practices were derived from Part II of the questionnaire, which asked people to describe the practices of your principal. The percentile score for each practice is based on the average of the responses of the people who completed questionnaires. The spread is an indication of the dispersion of the responses. The number in parentheses following each practice is the raw score at the 50th percentile of the norm base.

DIMENSION	PRACTICE	SCORE	SPREAD
Structure	1. Establishing clear, specific performance goals for me in my work. (3.75)	5%	Medium
	2. Clarifying who is responsible for what within our work group. (3.75)	9%	Medium
	3. Making sure tasks and projects are clearly and thoroughly explained and understood when they are assigned. (3.50)	7%	Medium
	4. Giving me a clear-cut decision when I need one. (3.83)	4%	Medium
	5. Understanding which decisions can be made alone and which decisions need to involve others. (4.00)	3%	Medium
Standards	6. Setting challenging performance goals and standards for me. (4.00)	5%	Medium
	7. Demonstrating personal commitment to achieving goals. (4.17)	11%	Medium
	8. Giving me feedback on how I am doing my job. (3.67)	6%	Medium
	9. Communicating high personal standards. (4.00)	18%	Medium

continued

DIMENSION	PRACTICE	SCORE	SPREAD
	10. Pushing me to constantly look for new and better ways of doing my job. (3.88)	8%	Medium
Responsibility	11. Encouraging me to initiate tasks or projects that I think are important. (4.00)	12%	Medium
	12. Expecting me to find and correct my own errors rather than doing this for me. (4.00)	25%	Narrow
	13. Encouraging innovation and calculated risk taking. (3.67)	20%	Medium
	14. Encouraging entrepreneurial behavior by avoiding excessive controls. (3.75)	22%	Medium
	15. Empowering people at all levels to make decisions. (3.83)	12%	Medium
Recognition	16. Recognizing me for good performance more often than criticizing me for poor performance. (3.90)	23%	Medium
	17. Utilizing recognition, praise, and similar methods to reward people for excellent performance. (3.75)	22%	Medium
	18. Relating recognition to the excellence of job performance rather than to other factors such as seniority, personal relationships, and so on. (3.67)	23%	Medium
	19. Noticing and showing appreciation when I have put in extra time and effort. (3.75)	10%	Medium

continued

DIMENSION	PRACTICE	SCORE	SPREAD
	20. Making every effort to be fair with people. (3.80)	27%	Medium
Support	21. Being supportive and helpful in my day-to-day activities. (3.86)	8%	Medium
	22. Going to bat for me with his or her superiors when he or she feels I am right. (4.00)	11%	Medium
	23. Conducting team meetings in a way that builds trust and mutual respect. (3.60)	13%	Medium
	24. Listening carefully to what I am saying. (4.00)	21%	Medium
	25. Being open and candid with me rather than being vague and indirect. (3.85)	9%	Medium
Commitment	26. Communicating excitement and enthusiasm about our work. (3.88)	30%	Medium
	27. Involving people in setting goals. (3.67)	22%	Medium
	28. Encouraging me to participate in making important decisions. (4.00)	4%	Medium
	29. Communicating an exciting vision of the future for our organization. (3.50)	29%	Medium
	30. Explaining how my job contributes to the overall success of the organization. (3.33)	9%	Medium

Exhibit 9.3
Management Practices of Your Department Chairperson (Combined)

Part III: Management Practices of Your Department Chairperson

The following scores for the 30 management practices were derived from Part III of the questionnaire, which asked people to describe the practices of your department chairperson. The percentile score for each practice is based on the average of the responses of the people who completed questionnaires. The spread is an indication of the dispersion of the responses. The number in parentheses following each practice is the raw score at the 50th percentile of the norm base.

DIMENSION	PRACTICE	SCORE	SPREAD
Structure	1. Establishing clear, specific performance goals for me in my work. (3.75)	35%	Medium
	2. Clarifying who is responsible for what within our work group. (3.75)	52%	Medium
	3. Making sure tasks and projects are clearly and thoroughly explained and understood when they are assigned. (3.50)	63%	Medium
	4. Giving me a clear-cut decision when I need one. (3.83)	58%	Medium
	5. Understanding which decisions can be made alone and which decisions need to involve others. (4.00)	43%	Medium
Standards	6. Setting challenging performance goals and standards for me. (4.00)	30%	Medium
	7. Demonstrating personal commitment to achieving goals. (4.17)	49%	Medium
	8. Giving me feedback on how I am doing my job. (3.67)	36%	Medium
	9. Communicating high personal standards. (4.00)	62%	Medium

continued

DIMENSION	PRACTICE	SCORE	SPREAD
	10. Pushing me to constantly look for new and better ways of doing my job. (3.88)	26%	Medium
Responsibility	11. Encouraging me to initiate tasks or projects that I think are important. (4.00)	56%	Medium
	12. Expecting me to find and correct my own errors rather than doing this for me. (4.00)	71%	Narrow
	13. Encouraging innovation and calculated risk taking. (3.67)	54%	Medium
	14. Encouraging entrepreneurial behavior by avoiding excessive controls. (3.75)	71%	Medium
	15. Empowering people at all levels to make decisions. (3.83)	59%	Medium
Recognition	16. Recognizing me for good performance more often than criticizing me for poor performance. (3.90)	67%	Medium
	17. Utilizing recognition, praise, and similar methods to reward people for excellent performance. (3.75)	48%	Medium
	18. Relating recognition to the excellence of job performance rather than to other factors such as seniority, personal relationships, and so on. (3.67)	53%	Medium
	19. Noticing and showing appreciation when I have put in extra time and effort. (3.75)	53%	Medium

continued

DIMENSION	PRACTICE	SCORE	SPREAD
	20. Making every effort to be fair with people. (3.80)	72%	Medium
Support	21. Being supportive and helpful in my day-to-day activities. (3.86)	72%	Medium
	22. Going to bat for me with his or her superiors when he or she feels I am right. (4.00)	62%	Medium
	23. Conducting team meetings in a way that builds trust and mutual respect. (3.60)	65%	Medium
	24. Listening carefully to what I am saying. (4.00)	61%	Medium
	25. Being open and candid with me rather than being vague and indirect. (3.85)	73%	Medium
Commitment	26. Communicating excitement and enthusiasm about our work. (3.88)	63%	Medium
	27. Involving people in setting goals. (3.67)	62%	Medium
	28. Encouraging me to participate in making important decisions. (4.00)	60%	Medium
	29. Communicating an exciting vision of the future for our organization. (3.50)	66%	Medium
	30. Explaining how my job contributes to the overall success of the organization. (3.33)	67%	Medium

them, is that department chairpersons are highly respected and impactful and, thus, they can be central to the efforts to improve the organizational climate of each school. "This also means," I added, "that you bear a great deal of responsibility for the dismal climate."

I concluded that neither of the high schools has the kind of organizational climate associated with high levels of performance. The high levels of Responsibility show that teachers carry the high performance in the two schools. Although individual responsibility is appropriate in a high school, the low scores in the other climate dimensions predict that it will be increasingly difficult to achieve high outcomes. The dismal scores for Standards and Recognition indicate that teachers feel the "powers that be" do not share the teachers' standards of quality. Thus, teachers feel little external incentive to improve performance. The example of Ellen McGraw in the case that opens this chapter illustrates how the leadership in the school does not arouse her motivation to excel in the classroom.

Teachers expressed a great deal of confusion and frustration because the roles and responsibilities of the principal and chairs are not clear. Unfortunately, the overly intrusive role of district-wide administrators will make it difficult to improve the sense of Structure in the school unless there is strong leadership within the buildings. A key function of building leadership is to block the intrusion of central administration into the operation of the building! Ellen McGraw and many other teachers at Jefferson and Washington see the Support dimension in terms of keeping a variety of interruptions out of their classrooms, such as disruptive students, announcements over the PA system, and district-mandated surveys and tests. And they are often frustrated at the relative lack of even that kind of support. It does not occur to them to seek support from the administration in terms of academic content or classroom teaching techniques.

Both principals and department chairs are to blame for the poor organizational climate. And both groups, I told them, should take aggressive action. Chairpersons in the two high schools are teachers, and they are trusted because they are close to the action. Principals can make life less frustrating or miserable, but they can't really make it more satisfying or stimulating. Principals in these schools are in charge of all of the negative aspects of educational leadership, for example, discipline, attendance, bell schedules, and the physical plant. The positive aspects, such as curriculum and the rewarding of outstanding teaching, are left to department chairs or are left undone. The television show *Boston Public* that debuted in 2000 shows, in somewhat exaggerated style, how much of the principal's job consists of dealing with personal and schoolwide brushfires and how little consists of educational leadership.

Department chairs should set more challenging goals and standards for their departments and help teachers find new and better ways to teach. They need training sessions to learn how to increase their influence over colleagues and the flow of new ideas into all classrooms. They also could be more active in giving candid feedback to teachers. By union contract, evaluation is a duty of the principal. Still, praise and recognition can be informal, private, or public. Schools can institute a peer review system for continuous feedback and coaching, along with training sessions focusing on interpersonal skills to help department chairs find ways to be more comfortable working with unsuccessful teachers.

Hall had mentioned to me a comment from an administrator as they prepared to debate in front of a parent group during a teachers' strike. He said that the single toughest issue for administration is what to do with the occasional poor teacher who is protected by tenure laws and the cumbersome processes of formal evaluation. I see it from a different angle. The single biggest blow to organizational morale is seeing how the system tolerates poor performance. My work with the high schools suggests ways to address this debilitating problem.

I predict that low morale and teacher frustration will make it more difficult to introduce innovation and change to these schools. Both high schools had been struggling with efforts to change for several years, most recently with the introduction of flexible "block" scheduling. After two years of research reports, subcommittees, and lengthy faculty meetings, Washington had dropped the innovation and Jefferson had decided to table it for another year of study. Hall reported that at Jefferson the most important factors preventing the change are cynicism, disillusionment, and factionalism: lousy organizational climate.

Two years after my work with these two high schools, momentum toward the changes I suggested has dissipated. In fact, many teachers indicated that this sort of thing is typical of the district: Despite a rich analysis of problems, there is little commitment to follow through with solutions. I did my work there *pro bono,* in part to gain research data on the schools, and I did not provide the kind of follow-through that I usually offer to paying clients, which involves working with them on strategy, goal setting, commitment, and evaluation. And as I indicated in Chapter 8, I often use the climate survey to work with my clients to solve specific performance management problems involving individuals and teams. But I did not personally push for this kind of follow-through, except by means of the urgency of my warnings and recommendations.

To emphasize this urgency, I described the climate profiles of two companies with whom I've worked: one a leading-edge business unit at the giant financial services company, then known as Citibank (Exhibit 9.4), the second a London-based major entertainment and publishing company, EMI–North America (Exhibit 9.5).

Exhibit 9.4
Citibank's WHCG Climate Profile

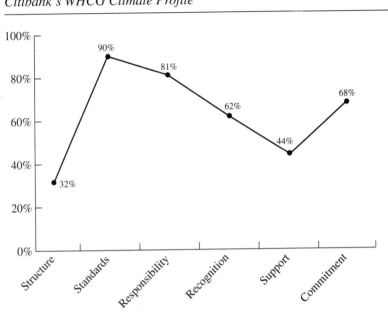

I commented about the first, "This is a very high-performing organization. The climate profile drives performance, even though the Structure and Support scores are lower than we'd like to see. In the Citibank environment the sense of urgency overwhelms everything else. And Citibankers have a New York attitude—they are macho and proud of it. But it works for them."

About EMI–North America, the entertainment company, I reported: "This is a disaster. The performance of this organization was so poor that within a year of the survey the boss was fired, and within two years the entire division was wiped out. Everything sucks."

Which of the two climates more closely resembles that of the high schools in Exhibit 9.1?

Hall did offer to conduct training sessions to help department chairs learn to deal with department members who were experiencing various kinds of problems, and I helped him design role-playing exercises with that goal in mind. But the principals, after some initial interest, declined the offer, saying that they were busy with other priorities.

Exhibit 9.5
Climate Profile of EMI–North America

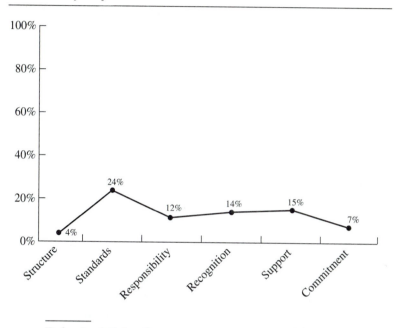

Principal Selection

Many of the reasons for poor climate in the schools are embedded in their climate determinants, as I describe later in the chapter. But Hall also tells a revealing story about the process that led to the selection of the principal at Jefferson. For two years Hall chaired the Principal Selection Committee, a group comprising 20+ people: teachers, students, parents, community representatives, and Jefferson administrators. The committee met regularly for a year to define criteria, do a "paper-screening" of applicants, interview the candidates, and make a selection. They made their recommendation to the district administrators, who offered the position to the candidate, a self-described "maverick." He declined the offer, reportedly turned off by the insistence that he "play ball" with the district rather than being able to run his own school. Hall reports that a strong-minded principal at Washington had recently resigned for the same reason. So Hall's Principal Selection Committee repeated the process during the next year with the same result. Both candidates took positions in nearby communities.

At that point, Hall says, the superintendent stepped in to suggest another candidate, a man who had applied for an opening in the district's alternative high school under the mistaken notion that it was a more traditional high school. The committee agreed to give the candidate a brief half-day tour and interview. Following this, they told the superintendent that they could not recommend him for the position at Jefferson. He was offered the job, accepted, and he has been there for five years.

I see a lesson in Hall's story. It confirms my impression of the overly intrusive role of district administration both in discouraging two strong candidates (if stories about their reasons for declining the position are true) and in demoralizing teachers and others on the committee by placing an apparently prechosen candidate as Jefferson's principal. Hall tells me that his principal is an experienced and caring man, but his leadership skills, when combined with the ongoing intrusions from the district, make for a climate that discourages innovation no matter how much he tries to push for it.

A number of principals who Hall interviewed in helping me prepare this chapter cited the inability to "run their own ship" as a discouraging aspect of being a principal. To some extent this is a result of the "public" part of public education. Because principals are answerable to the public through elected boards of education, they don't have the relatively free hand of a CEO in the private sector. All the more reason, then, to make the principal's job more attractive by helping to arouse his or her nAch and nPow wherever possible.

Implications

It's difficult for me to draw definitive conclusions about all public secondary schools after working with only two. But it's clear to me that these schools have organizational climates that have a powerful impact on the teachers who work there. Chapter 11 describes George Litwin's recent research showing how the climate experienced by teachers is also very consistent with the climate experienced by students of those teachers. And it's clear that this climate is to a large measure determined by the leadership practices—or lack of them—that are part of the daily experiences of teachers and students in their buildings. Groundbreaking research by former Washington teacher Ron Edmonds, who went on to a distinguished career at the Harvard Graduate School of Education and founded the Effective Schools Movement, confirms the overwhelming importance of leadership in the schools, especially by the principal. Edmonds (1981) argues "that five instructional organizational characteristics consistently were evident in the effective schools and were absent in whole or in part in the ineffective schools: the style of leadership in the building; the instructional emphasis in the building; the climate of the school; the implied expectations derived from the teacher's behavior in the classroom; and finally the presence, use, and response to standardized instruments for measuring pupil progress" (p. 58). His work went on to emphasize the role of the principal in creating a positive climate in the schools. Although Edmonds does not establish the kind of causal connections between leadership practices, school climate, and performance that our research has demonstrated, it is clear that we are addressing the same problems.

The other determinants of climate also play a very significant role in public schools.

- *External environment,* according to many teachers in the schools I worked with, was generally hostile, and this reinforced their bunker mentality. The governor was seen as hostile to public education. The board of education, in part because of sometimes acrimonious labor negotiations, was also seen as hostile. And although the teachers acknowledge the high levels of parental involvement in the schools, this is a mixed blessing, for many parents in this high-income city project a sense of superiority to the people who teach their children.

- *Strategy* is playing an increasingly important role in school systems around the country, but this strategy does not always filter down to the schools. In the district I studied, boards of education and central administrators occasionally go on "retreats" to set goals and priorities, but teachers are left to read about these in the newspaper. Although each school must compose a mission statement in order to gain accreditation, it usually ends up tacked to bulletin boards in the schools with little follow-through in the classroom.

- *History* is very important in determining the organizational climate of schools. Washington has a long history of success in athletics and academics, and the school appears to be well unified around these traditions. Jefferson, through its "River Rats" nickname and mascot, cultivates its underdog, "new-kid-on-the-block" spirit, even 30 years after it

split off from Washington. It is proud of its lack of central-
ized school spirit, although when I worked with the school,
the football team's playing for the state championship created a temporary exception. Washington is proud of its
decades of combined athletic and academic success, and it
cultivates its role as a "winner." In the schools, what I have
identified as history often takes the form of what Sara
Lawrence Lightfoot in *The Good High School* calls the
"ethos" of the school. It's the traditional way that people
behave there and the codes of behavior accepted by students and staff showing school spirit in ways that go
beyond cheering for athletic teams.

- *Organizational arrangements,* as I discussed in Chapter 5,
  play a substantial role in defining the organizational climate in the schools. As I noted earlier, promotion is virtually nonexistent, and financial rewards that are usually dictated by union contracts typically come automatically with
  experience or degrees earned regardless of the quality of
  teaching. Evaluation of teaching is often hampered by
  legitimate "due process" concerns, along with the difficulty of measuring good teaching. So there is virtually no
  reward or punishment system operating within the schools.
  This is an ironic twist, given the heavy system of rewards
  and punishments through grades that schools use to motivate students. And in many schools, concern with policies
  and procedures, such as attendance, discipline, and grade
  reporting, can be overwhelming. They may all be prerequi-
  sites for quality education, but in terms of organizational
  climate, they do little to arouse the motivation to excel.
  The formal structure within the high school may be weak,
  as is fitting for an institution that values academic freedom
  and the independence of its teachers. But when this lack of
  structure leads to confusion about roles and a lack of motivational leadership when such leadership would help
  teachers like Ellen McGraw, then it's a problem that needs
  to be addressed.

In other words, the public schools present numerous organizational barriers to improving the classroom performance of teachers
and students alike. These barriers will vary from community to community and from school to school. It makes sense to address the issue

directly. Rather than lamenting the decline of American youth culture or the preparation of our teachers, schools should invest in analyzing the factors that inhibit organizational effectiveness. Most importantly, they should invest in implementing proven measures to improve themselves. Our work on organizational climate can help them understand how organizational arrangements and strategy can be made more productive, although both of these may be difficult to change because of tradition and union contracts. Our approach can be especially helpful in identifying leadership practices that are most actionable in improving the climates, which in turn improves the motivation and, thus, the performance of the people in our schools.

10

Health Care Organizations: Generating a "Margin for Mission"

Marcus Pierce rereads the cover letter that accompanies the lengthy quarterly report from Margaret Houlihan, CFO of Angels of Mercy Health Care System (AMHCS). Nothing but bad news—losses in almost every branch of the huge 4,000-person organization. Houlihan's analysis identifies several causes of the system's poor performance. Most significant are the staggering losses from Medicare and Medicaid reimbursements, typically about 40 cents on the dollar. Pierce sighs. Nothing new there, and there's nothing he can do about those reimbursement levels.

Houlihan's recommendation to address the problems is "increased efficiencies," which Pierce knows to mean "treat more patients faster using the same or fewer staff." This makes sense because it seems to be the only option on the table. But how can he do it? How can they do it?

Angels of Mercy Hospital has a long-standing reputation as a high-quality tertiary hospital that provides care for threats to life, limb, or function, such as cancer, serious burns, pediatric cardiology, orthopedic surgery, and the like. Primary care doctors and community hospitals, which handle more routine childbirths, broken arms, and appendectomies, refer patients to Mercy for more sophisticated treatments. But as market conditions changed, medical technology and Mercy-trained physicians became available in clinics and local hospitals, and so fewer patients are being referred in to Mercy's sophisticated technology and physicians. In response, AMHCS was created. They purchased three community hospitals and formed alliances with three others. In addition, they bought more than 300 primary care practices, as well as establishing a hospice care center and a rehab facility. AMHCS is now a huge sprawling network. It's a mess. And it's losing money.

Many days Pierce feels overwhelmed by his job. Fifty years old and a pediatrician by training, he was recruited into administration five years ago. He still keeps some patient hours, although he doubts he can keep it up. It was tough enough managing organizational dynamics when Mercy was a single hospital with independent-minded physicians who were used to giving orders, not following them, and caregivers who looked at "business types" in administration as "suits." Now he has to navigate through the merging of different cultures and rules of engagement between institutions with historically different missions and identities, along with all the old problems compounded by greater size and complexity. He tries to remember if his medical school offered any classes in business administration and people management. If it did, he failed to take them.

As a physician himself, he has mixed feelings about Houlihan's idea of "increased efficiencies." He became a doctor largely because he wanted to care for people. And to him, that means taking the time to listen and giving them the kind of personal attention that is now labeled as "old-fashioned." He thought that as a hospital administrator he would be able to help doctors in the system continue to find time to answer family members' questions fully, and nurses to find time to get an extra pillow or adjust the TV set. But he knows that "increased efficiencies" mean that this kind of "quality of care," so long associated with Angels of Mercy, might have to be sacrificed.

He thumbs through Houlihan's report again, looking for a way out. "Nobody in his right mind," he says aloud, "would get into this business."

Dr. Pierce's conclusion might very well be that of anyone experienced in the business world who examines the distinctive set of pressures, restrictions, contradictions, and complexities of what is called these days, without a trace of irony, "the health care business." A health care organization is not U.S. Steel or General Motors. Yet in many ways it is forced to act like a business. At the same time, health care organizations are something more than businesses.

And when a single organization such as a hospital is combined with multiple hospitals, clinics, and practices such as AMHCS, they become big, complicated something-more-than-businesses. They become some cobbled together creation—a Frankenstein monster, or in the old joke, a camel as a horse created by a committee. A platypus. It's remarkable that today's multiunit health care systems function as well as they do. For Marcus Pierce and most health care enterprise leaders, the trick is to get them to work more effectively.

How do you define effectiveness and high performance in a health care organization? How should the leaders of something-more-than-businesses be judged? Once you define the right performance standards, what management tools might health care leaders use to improve the performance of their organizations?

Distinctive Problems

Health care systems have many of the same difficulties as other large organizations, but they also have a set of problems all their own.

Conflicting Missions

Organizations in the private sector often recognize that they need to be good members of the community in which they live, but when push comes to shove, their fundamental mission is to deliver shareholder value. Health care organizations function under an often conflicting dual mission:

1. To deliver high-quality health care. This is their fundamental mission and their reason for existence.

2. To earn enough money to keep the institution going. Although this may appear to be secondary, it is absolutely essential. Without it, hospitals can't deliver health care. Some go out of business entirely.

Academic health care systems have the additional functions of conducting medical research and teaching. This results in additional financial strain, because research grants and income from tuition typically do not match the costs of research and teaching. The extra income required to operate has to come from patients and their insurance providers. Thus, the title of this chapter is a slogan being heard more and more frequently in hospitals and not-for-profits. "Margin for Mission" states directly that health care systems need to make enough money to provide the care that it is their mission to provide.

The problem is that many people on the caregiving side, such as nurses, doctors, and others who have direct contact with patients, just don't get it. It's almost as if they see the businesspeople as the bad guys who are only interested in making money, while the good guys are the ones who actually help people! When this is the case, it is hard to enlist their commitment to the organization. The result is often conflict between the caregivers and the administrators, inefficiency, and a waste of precious time and organizational resources.

Lack of Control

Another distinctive problem of health care systems is how little control the members of a health care organization have over events that impact them directly. They are highly visible, and they are subject to the politics of public policy decisions. In many ways they are victims of their environment.

- The level and quality of service are essentially mandated by state, federal, and professional codes of conduct. Health care organizations cannot cut services without the threat of losing their license as well as their business to the competition. And then there's always the threat of litigation. To a large extent, the product-service "deliverables" of the organization are out of their control.

- The economics are also out of their control. Thanks to the Balanced Budget Amendment, reimbursements from Medicare and Medicaid are very strictly limited, and reimbursements from private insurance companies can be negotiated only under the threat of insurance companies' refusal to be involved with an entire health care system.

- The speed or pace of activities in a health care organization is also less controllable than in most businesses. For better or worse, speed in a hospital is dictated by medical necessity (how long high-quality treatment takes) and economics (how long insurance coverage will last).

We often tell our business clients that they will have to attack at least one of the key variables of quality, cost, or speed in order to increase profitability. Health care organizations do not have even that level of flexibility.

Role Diversity

People working in health care systems play drastically different roles that are more diverse than the roles typical in schools and businesses.

- Hospitals are hugely complex organizations involving physicians, nurses, technicians, support personnel, maintenance people, cafeteria staff, clerical help, and administrators at many levels. There are widely different pay scales among these groups. Some are unionized, some are not. Unlike most other organizations, these different populations are thrown together in close physical proximity. Where do you find the factory floor in a hospital and whom do you see there?

- Typically, most of the members of the organization are employees of the health care system, but often doctors are not. Instead, they are more in the role of customers whose business the health care organization is soliciting. It's almost like a business that has outsourced R&D, manufacturing, marketing, and sales. The expectant mother may choose her doctor for a variety of reasons, and then it is the job of the hospital to get the doctor and the mother-to-be to choose its facility for the delivery.

- The sense of hierarchy is unclear. Physicians have been trained to be aware of their high status, but in a sense they are "working for" a hospital administrator who is their "boss." At the same time, low-status nurses actually run many functions at a hospital, just as secretaries run many schools and businesses. This is no secret. And although nurses may assert an admirable level of ownership and commitment in claiming "my patient," the physician makes the same claim, as does the hospital itself.

- In many hospitals, specific functions are subcontracted to outside organizations, most typically emergency rooms, radiology, and pathology. This makes the sense of role and hierarchy even less clear.

High Touch

People who do business with a health care system as patients don't want to be there. With the exception of those delivering babies or receiving immunizations and check-ups, they come because they are sick or injured. They feel vulnerable, often exchanging their clothes for paper gowns and a familiar language in which they understand their lives for a bewildering technical vocabulary. In this condition they are subject to "high-touch" encounters, where doctors and nurses literally touch or invade their bodies while at the same time interacting with their intense emotional responses to everything involved in being a patient.

The emotional intensity puts a special kind of pressure on everyone working in a health care organization. If a high school teacher has a bad day, his students don't learn about how to use the apostrophe or the causes of the Civil War. If someone at L.L. Bean has a bad day, a lot of shirts get returned in the mail. If a surgeon has a bad day, a patient dies, and if a hospital administrator has a bad day, patients in the emergency room are stacked up in the halls waiting for eight hours to be seen. Hospital people know this, and so do patients and their attorneys.

By "high touch" I mean that caregivers are face-to-face with their clients, and hand to body, and emotion to emotion. There's a lot at stake.

Leadership Challenges

Given these complexities and the enormous difficulties confronting health care organizations, what is a leader to do?

The first step is to manage the manageable. It's true that health care systems have little control over the reimbursements from Medicare and Medicaid. They can lobby at the state and federal levels, they can issue press releases or write Op Ed pieces, but that's about it. In this way they resemble schools, which have little control over the amount of money they receive from the state or local taxing authorities. Rather than wringing their hands over their plight, health care leaders can focus their attention and energy on matters where they can have an impact on performance. As I argue throughout this book, this is through managing climate and the determinants of climate, especially their own leadership practices.

Many health care leaders are people like Marcus Pierce, doctors and nurses who have moved into administration because they wanted a change or saw an opportunity to advance their careers while continuing, less directly, to serve patients. Physicians, especially, are trained to confront a problem, do an analysis/diagnosis, write a prescription that they hand over with the expectation that it will be carried out, and then the matter is done. It would never occur to them that people might not carry out their instructions. As a doctor, *you* make the decisions. And many physician-leaders tend to manage that way, and the issue of *how* to manage may not occur to them. After all, these people have always been successful doing things their way. But as we know, that's not the best way to manage individuals, teams, or organizations.

Other health care leaders may be more grounded in business management, having moved into health care administration from positions in private industry. Whatever their career paths, they face enormous challenges.

We see these leadership challenges as twofold:

1. To reshape the complex and often messy amalgam of roles, hierarchies, processes, cultures, and systems that constitutes the typical health care organization into a coordinated team.
2. To sustain the mission-driven feelings that motivate the practices of many health care workers while helping them to make the tough decisions that will allow them to stay in business.

It's my belief, and it's been the experience of my colleagues, that accomplishing the first goal will go a long way toward accomplishing the second. Insight into the problem and guidance regarding possible solutions can come from the judicious use of a climate survey.

Don Leopold, a colleague at my former firm, utilized the organizational climate survey as part of his work with a large health care system not unlike the one that is stymieing Marcus Pierce at Angels of Mercy. I'll call the system "Unified Health Care System" (UHCS), revolving around the highly regarded "U-Hospital." Don worked with the CEO, let's call him Doug, and Doug's problem was quickly defined as one of overall organizational effectiveness, that is, how to get the entire network of health care institutions to perform better.

UHCS's Integrated Delivery Network

Under Doug's leadership, U-Hospital had implemented an expansion strategy as a way to steer more physician referrals, which meant more opportunities for teaching and research as well as more income, into the system. The theory was that having a large number of physician practices and smaller primary and secondary care facilities as part of an integrated system would bring in more business. But, in fact, this was not happening. Doug was hoping that 50% of the physician referrals would go to U-Hospital, but the number was closer to 20%, which was not much better than before the expansion strategy was implemented.

Not only did the new health care system model fail to increase revenues, but it also added a level of complexity to an already complicated situation. It also forced all of the administrators at UHCS to deal with people who were fairly independent. The physicians had their own private practices, and they were used to doing things their own way.

Furthermore, many of the community hospitals were formerly independent entities, each tied to its local community and immersed in its own culture and practices. Neither the physicians nor the community hospital administrators were eager to adapt to the requirements of a remote organization. Doug had hoped that U-Hospital would be the "gold standard" for UHCS. Instead it was "the enemy."

When Don was invited into UHCS by Doug's vice president of human resources, he was told that "Doug is brilliant at strategy, but not at operations, and he doesn't always realize it. . . ." Don saw that although Doug's brilliance lay in his ability to create complex and ambitious expansion plans, his colleagues, many of them physicians like Doug, sometimes found it hard to work with him on a day-to-day basis. How he wanted his creations to operate was not always clear.

The Climate Survey

After extensive interviews with all members of the UHCS senior team and groups of employees at all levels in the various hospitals, departments, clinics, and practices, Don understood how widespread and serious the confusion and mistrust were. He concluded that Doug and his leadership team needed a common perspective, a common language, and a forum and framework for problem solving. There were simply too many organizational effectiveness issues to tackle without what he called a "road map." And he knew that the highly educated and skeptical physicians and health care professionals would insist on using a proven, research-based process. He believed the climate survey would be the key to solving the problems at UHCS.

In the summer of 1999 questionnaires were administered to 150 of the most senior employees of UHCS. We analyzed the results and created reports that described the climate profiles of the different groups within the system. Before feeding back any of the results, Don and I met with Doug to discuss our ideas for using the data as a road map. We also asked him what kind of climate was required if UHCS were going to be the high-performing system he envisioned when he created the expansion strategy.

This exercise is best done with all the senior managers in a group setting. Such a setting provides the entire top team with an excellent forum to discuss their motivational desires and frustrations. It also allows people to communicate directly to the boss, with the help of the facilitator, where they want to take the organization. And they indirectly communicate what they think of the boss's leadership. Doug decided against a group meeting. He wanted to set the climate profile benchmarks and review the survey results by himself. Exhibit 10.1 shows the profile that emerged from our required climate exercise, together with the actual climate profile for the entire UHCS organization (all 150 responses).

The numbers we collected at UHCS not only tell a story of the impact of Doug, his expansion strategy, and his organizational effectiveness challenges, but they also tell a story of the leadership challenges facing all health care organizations today. It's not a happy story.

Structure

Structure is the key. In most businesses, the best-performing organizations generally score in the range of the 40th to 60th percentiles. For a large and complex health care system with all the challenges described earlier, it's essential that they score at least in the mid-70s. Don believes that UHCS's 14th percentile explains most of its problems.

The complex and varied roles, the lack of clear hierarchy, and the balkanization of so many health care networks cry out for a high sense of structure. People need to be crystal clear about who is accountable for what. Otherwise, someone will drop the hand-off as a patient moves from specialist to specialist through a system, and a patient will be "lost." Records misplaced or unread, steps in a complex procedure skipped or duplicated, calls unreturned, or vital information not recorded so that the patient can't be properly billed. Nurses especially, Don has found, appreciate having clear and direct instructions. They have little tolerance of ambiguity, which is an attitude that serves the system well if it is functioning properly.

In a health care organization, especially when multiple organizations are expected to function as an integrated network, each entity's role needs to be clear. What's expected of me? What's my

Exhibit 10.1

Climate Profile at UHCS and Doug's Required Climate

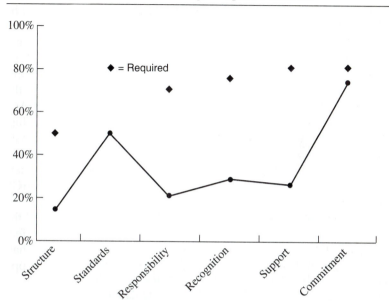

unit's role? And what's the priority of the system as a whole? Are we trying to make money? Are we trying to maximize in-house referrals? Are we trying to implement the high standards and expectations for care that are associated with the health care system's "brand name"? At UHCS the conflicting loyalties and multiple institutional identities were preventing people from having such clarity of purpose.

Although an overall sense of purpose must be established, it's important for health care leaders to understand that even within a single and "unified" health care system, different entities can and should have different priorities. We've found that the less sick a patient is, the more important are such things as the quality of the personal interactions and the ease of access. How convenient is the parking? How many rings does it take before the phone is answered, and can you get a friendly human being to answer it? Is the waiting room family friendly? How courteous and unthreatening is the processing of paperwork? How much time do people give you?

But at a larger, tertiary care hospital like U-Hospital, serving people who are suffering from cancer, heart disease, and life-threatening traumas, convenience and courtesy are not so important.

Of course, they need to do a base level of these things, and they can't be horrible, but when push comes to shove, patients with serious diseases or injuries are seeking the physicians with outstanding reputations and hospitals with the most advanced technology and the latest treatment options.

This kind of hospital should not be managed the same way as the primary or secondary care facility described earlier. It has a different competitive advantage, and its leadership should manage its climate in order to leverage that competitive advantage. No single hospital can offer the best of everything and be viable economically. Some may choose to pay its "star" physicians more, or invest in the newest PET-Scan technology. Others may choose to hire an extra secretary to answer the telephones and greet incoming patients and their families. A clear sense of structure helps everyone within a unit of the health care system understand just what its role is. This was missing at UHCS, and the more Don and Doug talked about it, the more Don came to feel that fixing the low Structure score was the big fix for this organization.

Clear structure also means that the decision-making process is clear. When there are medical or administrative disagreements, is there a process in place to hear the arguments and make a decision that everyone can live with? Without such a process, or with ad hoc or improvised processes, trust in the organization declines, resulting in the kinds of lack of coordination, dropped hand-offs, and miscommunication that characterize far too many health care systems. Doug often found himself simultaneously juggling the interests of an individual physician, a hospital, and a network of health care entities.

Standards

The Standards dimension of organizational climate generally means two things:

1. How high is the bar?
2. How much pressure is there to keep raising the bar?

Don feels strongly that standards must necessarily be high for high-performing health care organizations, but he does not see the need to keep raising them. Many of the standards are set for you by government agencies, and most are set at appropriate levels, presenting enough of a challenge. Applying constant pressure to raise standards can make people feel that it's impossible for them to do a good job, and this is an especially acute problem in a hospital.

Consider the situation many nurses are in. They find themselves with more and more to do every day—increased patient load, more records to keep, more meds to keep track of, more questions from informed or misinformed patients, and a sicker population because uninsured people wait longer to seek help. And they can't just enter their notes on a patient's chart at the foot of the bed, but they have to go down the hall to type them into the computer—if it's working properly. Pressed for time, many find themselves unable to deliver the standard of care that drew them into nursing in the first place. They don't have time to reassure a frightened child who is awaiting surgery the next morning, or to get an extra pillow for an elderly man whose back is hurting. And backrubs, which always used to earn her a very gratifying thank-you, are now a thing of the past. No time! It's no wonder that nurses are discouraged, and many of them are leaving the profession. Raising the sense of standards by putting more pressure on nurses, in this case, would be counterproductive. Individual nurses can't do everything, and it makes no sense to ask them to do it better.

Standards at UHCS were not low, but they were lower than Doug wanted them to be. And this played into the CEO's uncompromising leadership style. Don had to work hard to convince Doug that the solution to problems with Standards was largely the same as the solution to low Structure. Yelling louder and demanding more would not fix things. An organization with high Structure is one where people see their roles as clear and possible. It may be that it's not the best use of nurses' training and experience that they get the extra pillow or give the backrub. Perhaps a nurse's aide could do these, and perhaps a volunteer could provide the sometimes necessary hand-holding and reassurance. Only when the roles and responsibilities are clear does it make sense to challenge people to fulfill those roles and responsibilities at a high level.

Responsibility

Responsibility is a problematic dimension of organizational climate when we're talking about health care organizations. Environments where decisions are double-checked earn low Responsibility scores, but with hospital personnel, as with air traffic controllers, high performance often requires that there be a lot of double checking. At Sherbrooke we are constantly debating what the required level of Responsibility in health care organizations should be. At UHCS, Don found most leaders wanted their score here to be in the 50th to 60th percentile range, although Doug benchmarked Responsibility at 70%.

it, "I want the double checking balanced by a climate that ~~es~~ independent thinking."

~~Jo~~ matter where you set the benchmark, the Responsibility ~~rating~~ of 21st percentile for the overall UHCS organization was viewed to be inadequate. Don was convinced that, in the context of the entire climate profile, it indicated that people were abdicating their responsibilities. They were saying, "I give up." We want people, when they see a problem, to be motivated to fix it and have the authority to fix it. This is as true for people giving care as it is for people working with administrative and financial matters. The double checking can and probably should follow in a predictable and clearly structured way.

The problem at UHCS may again go back to the very low Structure score. People who are not clear about their jobs may feel overwhelmed. The high score in Commitment shows that they care about what they are doing, but applying that sense of Commitment in a poorly defined Structure is very discouraging.

Although the gap between the required and actual level of Responsibility was as large as any at UHCS, Don and I were hesitant to push Responsibility to the top of Doug's or his team's "to do" list. First, because we believed UHCS's low Structure was at fault. And, second, we hesitated because of our experiences with other hospitals. The best example of what we call the Responsibility Dilemma is St. Francis Hospital. In Chapter 5 I referred to St. Francis as one of America's highest-performing cardiac care hospitals. It makes money. Its historical occupancy rate is well over 100%. Its reputation in the New York area for quality care is unequaled. But take a look at its climate profile.

By our measures of climate, St. Francis is a low Responsibility environment. Yet it is a high-performing organization. It appears that some of our questionnaire items do not define Responsibility in a way that fits health care organizations. For example, a lab technician or nurse may feel they are being strongly encouraged to take responsibility, and the insistence on double checking does not undermine that feeling. The important point here refers back to the discussion of the perfect climate in Chapter 4. "Healthy" climate scores vary with the nature and the purpose of the organization and the expectations of its members.

Recognition

Although there is no such thing as a perfect climate in gereral, each organization or type of organization may have its own "perfect cli-

Exhibit 10.2
St. Francis Climate Profile

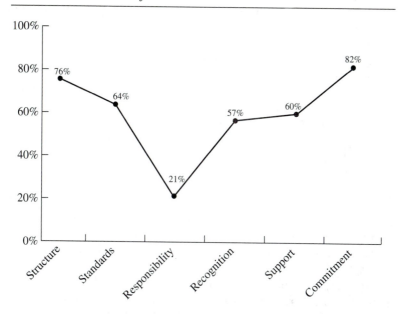

mate." Don explained to Doug that a high-performing organization should have a Recognition score of the 60th percentile or above. In spite of his direct and often underrecognizing style, Doug was well aware of this. He and Don both agreed that UHCS's 29th percentile score for Recognition was clearly a problem. Caregivers typically receive recognition from patients and their families, much the way successful teachers receive it from students and their parents. And in both professions, people with a sense of mission about what they do receive inherent satisfaction, a kind of recognition, from the work they do. But none of this suggests that the leaders of health care organizations are not responsible for recognizing and rewarding good performance. This is especially true for performance by those who do not earn the kinds of recognition caregivers earn.

At UHCS and most health care organizations, leaders do not have access to pots of money, perquisites, or lavish nonmonetary rewards. Budgets are tight and getting tighter. Under such circumstances and given the increased demands placed on these organizations, how do you create a high Recognition climate for people? Don and I have come to the conclusion that, even more than business leaders, health care leaders must focus on arousing intrinsic motivation. This means looking at nAch, nAff, and nPow. Physicians we have studied have strong nAch and nPow. Not surprisingly, nurses have strong nAff. Therefore, the climate should arouse all three of these motives.

Intrinsic motivation may be the only game in town for most health care organizations because there just aren't enough extrinsic rewards to play with. This means engaging people, it means giving them influence, it means having goals and letting people participate in decision making. Doug and other health care leaders might take a look at the "hit list" of leadership practices we developed in Chapter 7. They work in business entities and they are especially relevant in health care organizations.

Support

Teamwork is important to the success of business organizations, and it's even more important to the success of hospitals and health care systems. If there is a lapse of teamwork at General Mills, the launch of a new kind of Honey-Nut Cheerios is delayed, or the editing of an ad is not fine-tuned before the Big Game on Saturday. If there's a lapse of teamwork at UHCS, a biopsy report is lost or delayed, or the surgeon's notes from the mastectomy are not passed along to the oncologist who is conferring with the patient about whether or not to begin chemotherapy.

Teamwork is also crucial in health care because of the extremely diverse and specialized functions that are involved. Quality of care, especially in tertiary hospitals, requires collaboration among experts. Although the family doctor may be all-knowing enough to have the answers to the health problems that he or she sees every day, in big hospitals this is seldom the case. It's not a caregiver, alone, giving care. This kind of teamwork doesn't just happen. When the organization is complex, the roles are diverse, and the health problems are increasingly multifaceted, the leadership of the organization needs to step up to the plate and provide a climate of Support that motivates people to collaborate. Allow the emergency room team to meet twice a day to coordinate their procedures and standards. Encourage patient care teams, for example, nurses working with nurse's aides and perhaps residents and physical therapists, to meet together to coordinate their efforts at the beginning of each shift.

We want caregivers to feel, "I'm a part of a well-functioning team." At first, Doug was not convinced that UHCS could overcome its legacy of independent entities and factions to achieve his bench-mark Support score of 60%. Don, however, kept emphasizing that people's feelings of being supported and part of a team derive from a clearer sense of Structure where their roles, responsibilities, and UHCS procedures are clearly defined and understood. Don also pointed out that, in health care organizations, Support is related to Standards where you know that everyone on the team feels that others can be trusted to work at levels of high professional quality.

At UHCS, it's probably too much to ask that individuals extend this feeling of "We're a team" to the whole health care system. It's too big. What is important is that leaders encourage cross-functional teams. With the highly diversified roles I've been describing, there is a natural tendency for nurses to bond together, physicians to do the same, and corporate people the same—often with one group set against another. This kind of fragmentation needs to be countered by deliberate and visible efforts. This takes time and money to allow and encourage meetings to plan, monitor, and adjust the quality of support and teamwork.

Commitment

Commitment is an elusive quality, but in a limited sense it's a very important one. It's important because of all the difficulties in health care described earlier in the chapter of increasing demands combined with economic constraints. Many people in health care feel as if they are under siege, and the organization needs to encourage them to do the extra stuff that makes the difference between a satisfied patient and a delighted one. This "extra stuff" often involves working beyond the eight-hour day, but it may also involve extra effort and attention during the day. A visiting nurse may pick up some fast food for a patient on the way to his home. Someone in pathology may do a hurry-up for a physician who he trusts really needs it when she asks. A director of HR may schedule a half-day "doing rounds" in the hospitals in the system so she can meet people and see their jobs first-hand, even though this means important paperwork will have to be done after hours.

For caregivers it's important that they feel commitment to the health care organization, or the system as a whole, but mainly we want commitment to their patients and to the team they work with. This kind of commitment, when combined with the inner drives of professionalism and sense of mission, will arouse the motivation to "go the extra mile."

For administrators, it's more important to arouse their commitment to the organization and its goals. Administrators hold the organization together and facilitate its functioning. This would be impossible without high levels of Commitment (and hard enough with it!). With resources constrained, administrators frequently have multiple roles requiring an additional commitment of time and energy. Also, given the difficulties of health care administration, it's important to retain people whose experience has given them valuable skills and knowledge.

Sometimes Commitment seems to be built into the professionalism of the staff. If you examine the climate profile at UHCS in Exhibit 10.1 alongside that of Washington and Jefferson High Schools in Exhibit 9.1, you see that both indicate high levels of Commitment where the other five scores are relatively low. In these cases, it's extremely unlikely that the high Commitment and resulting performance levels have anything to do with what the organization (i.e., its leadership) is doing. In fact, the high Commitment probably comes *despite* the other dimensions of organizational climate. Following Ed Deci's conclusion as discussed in Chapter 2, we might conclude that the very failure of schools and health care organizations to provide extrinsic rewards has accidentally encouraged intrinsic motivation. Teachers, like health care professionals, often have a set of professional standards that are powerful intrinsic motivators. They combine this with a sense of mission that they are doing important and good work for others to generate their sense of Commitment. But it is not always commitment to the organization and its goals, except coincidentally. A high Commitment score is no cause for health care leadership to rest easy. High Commitment alone suggests a "bunker mentality" (i.e., me, or sometimes us, against the world). If a person feels that "nobody cares about me," which UHCS's low Support and Recognition scores indicate, then it won't be long until that person will cease to care for others.

High Commitment unaccompanied by high Support and Recognition also predicts problems in reaching out to others in the team and organization. People will stop asking for and offering assistance (it's not encouraged or rewarded), and the bunker mentality predicts that people will protect their current practices rather than growing professionally and changing with the organization and its goals.

It was this last point that really got Doug's attention. His expansion strategy depended on people adjusting to a new way of working. It required that people willingly let go of old habits and adopt new ones. He knew that some members of his senior staff were simply "digging in" to their formerly successful ways of thinking about and going about their jobs. Some of them might have to be let go, for the good of UHCS.

After three hours of explaining, discussing, and coaching, Don and I were at last able to see a few "light bulbs" click on in Doug's head. We had walked him through lots of numbers, lots of war stories, and lots of anecdotal data about the climate of UHCS and why it needed to be improved if the system was going to achieve higher levels of performance. Maybe we could have gotten there without the survey and the benchmarks and without the physical report and the graphs. Don and I don't think so. We were able to coach and cajole and convince because we knew what we were talking about. The climate profile proved it. And Doug couldn't ignore what he was seeing and hearing.

Now, as Don reminded me, comes the hard part—helping Doug to change his emphasis from strategy to operations. Doug needed to do something constructive to "fix" the climate.

Intervention

Don and Doug together devised a seven-step plan to address the problems identified by the climate survey.

1. Doug was encouraged to let everyone in the organization know that "I feel your pain" and that he understood the difficulties expressed through the climate survey. He expressed this understanding through speeches and written communications.

2. Doug also clarified the existing strategy and priorities of UHCS. The focus was on the role of each entity within the system and the decision-making process. For example, he clarified whether a certain type of decision was to be made by the department head or the president of the hospital and also what the appeal process was if the final decision appeared unreasonable.

3. Doug put together a design team. Leaders of the various entities within UHCS together with functional leaders met to redesign the entire organization. The goals:

   - Provide clarity to the organization. (Structure)

- Establish benchmarks. (Standards)
- Identify who is responsible for what. (Structure)

4. Consultants coached senior executives, including Doug, in the performance of their new roles.

5. Members of the senior team who could not adjust to the new way of doing things were fired.

6. As an extension of these changes, we used the climate survey as part of the ongoing institutional training program to provide feedback for people at the managerial and supervisory levels. This process helped people become more familiar with their new or newly clarified roles and priorities. And it helped them understand how the organization wanted them to do business and to evaluate how well they were doing it. For example, once the organization clarified the system's "brand standard" in customer service, we created a "People First Program" to train and motivate staff to perform up to that standard when, say, dealing with the public on the telephone. And we evaluated how well supervisors managed a climate that would motivate performance that met the UHCS brand standard.

7. We implemented an initiative called "Workout," a highly focused reengineering of problematic work processes that an organization is experiencing. Let's say you have a problem with the time it takes to get results back from radiology, or you are only bringing in 50 cents for each dollar billed, largely because of failure to capture information about patients and their insurance as they enter the system. In solving each of these problems, Workout clarifies or redefines the roles, responsibilities, and processes. You are also addressing deficiencies in the Structure dimension of organizational climate, thus arousing motivation. Although Workout was not the central feature of our intervention with UHCS, it has enormous potential for solving many of the problems common to health care organizations.

Prognosis

Don Leopold reports that UHCS had mixed results in implementing his suggestions. "The operation was a success," he says with some exaggeration, "but the patient's prognosis is guarded." The structure and processes became dramatically better from the interventions, but there was a fundamental mismatch between the Doug's creative expansionist strategy and the more routine management skills required to foster a climate where the strategy could be executed. (Refer back to what I said in Chapter 5 about the links between Strategy and Climate in high-performing organizations.) Doug's original vision of a totally integrated network was abandoned and several parts to the system were spun off. By mutual agreement, Doug left UHCS before all of the seven interventions bore fruit. As is the case with most organizations, improving organizational effectiveness at UHCS must always be labeled as work in progress.

It's hard to predict the future of health care systems. Large networks like UCHS may very well prove to be a winning performance improvement strategy, especially in urban settings with a university hospital presence. Or it may be that the breakup of UHCS is prophetic, and that the difficulties of managing such a complex organization will prove insurmountable. I don't think the latter is the case provided that health care leaders are willing to learn and apply lessons learned by large organizations in the private sector.

Think back to the point I made in the Introduction to this book with what I called "the cloud chamber effect." Leadership works indirectly, not just through the charismatic and hands-on presence of the leader, but through the way the leader manages organizational climate. The larger the organization, the truer this is, because size alone means much of the leadership will necessarily be indirect. Leadership practices create climate, for better or for worse, and effective leaders of elaborate health care systems and stand-alone hospitals would do well to use the tools of climate management deliberately and wisely. Hospitals are not reluctant to use diagnostic and therapeutic tools such as CT scans and radiation therapy to accomplish their primary mission: to heal. Now it's time to use the available management tools, especially those focusing on the climate dimension of Structure, to accomplish the second crucial branch of their mission: economic survival. Physician, heal thyself!

11

The Future of Leadership and Organizational Climate

i.

You walk into the service department at the VW dealership. A man in a white lab coat, with a name tag that says "Ed Penn" greets you with a smile, says, "I'll be with you in a moment, sir." He takes a minute to finish typing something on the computer behind the counter. "Now, how can I help you?" You explain that you only have a brief period of time and that you understand if they can't do the work now, but the left brake light is not working and the car is still under warrantee. Can they fix it? He says he'll check with the guys in the back and returns promptly to say, "No problem. Where are the keys?" He explains briefly that if it is the bulb, it's not covered under warrantee, but in any case it won't cost more than $25. As you thumb through magazines in the waiting room, you help yourself to some coffee and return a greeting from the salesperson who sold you the car 15 months ago. You notice that people are walking briskly—salespeople to the lot with customers, technicians to the front desk and back to the shop. Others are busy on the telephone. You are not surprised that your car is ready in 15 minutes, but you are surprised when he tells you that the repair is, in fact, covered under warrantee because it was the holder, not the bulb. He also tells you that since you are in a hurry he will mail you the paperwork along with the Customer Satisfaction Survey.

ii.

You listen in disbelief as Mrs. Green explains how your eleventh grade American History project on the causes of the Civil War will work. She says that you are to work in groups, and at the end you will receive a "group grade," which will be the same for all of you. That grade will be based "a lot" on how well your group "works together." You wonder how she is going to measure that! And you suspect she'll probably stick you in a group with three bozos who will expect you to do all the work. And if you do it all, you may end up getting marked down for not working together. And then as a final touch, Mrs. Green mentions that for extra credit, you may all write an essay about what you learned about your fellow group members "as people" from doing the assignment together. What a bunch of crap! You can hardly wait to get to college where you will really get a chance to show your stuff.

iii.

You are still in shock from the first phone call when the second one hits. This time it's Dr. Porcine's nurse, and she is in tears. You are not yet able to comprehend what Dr. Porcine told you so abruptly—that the biopsy shows the lump in your breast is cancer of an especially invasive kind. When you asked him if you should come in to see him, he said, "I don't know. Check with my nurse." And then he hung up. Tara, the nurse, apologizes for the way the doctor talked to you. She says that he has no right to give you such news on the telephone, and that she tried to talk him out of it. She also apologizes for his tone of voice, saying, "That's just the way he is. Besides, he's extremely busy with a lot of other patients to see." You ask if you should come in to the hospital. Tara says you should, this afternoon if possible, and she will try to arrange for you to see another doctor instead of Dr. Porcine. Tara adds that it will be difficult because there are no notes on the chart describing last week's lumpectomy, and the office only heard the lab results read over the telephone. Tara apologizes again and says she will do what she can.

The Future of Climate: Visitor Climates

For more than 25 years we have thought about climate as the internal weather of an organization. And it is. But just like the weather in a city or a region, organizational climate affects not only the permanent residents but the visitors as well. In fact, some cities and regions build a whole industry of tourism and conventions on the quality of their visitor climates. Think of Vail without any snow or Hawaii with sleet.

Although all businesses have permanent residents or employees, for some businesses, schools, and health care organizations, visitors can be the most important people impacted by the climate of the organization.

When I leave Boston in November it is usually cold, damp, and awful. When I arrive in Sarasota for my golfing vacation, the weather is usually sunny and warm. I may have a memory of icy roads and cold wind and my shoes may still be wet from the slush at Logan, but my immediate environment now arouses a different set of motive states. I smile and think about golf, and as I walk from the airport, I check my knees to be sure the cartilage will hold up for tonight's run on the beach and tomorrow's 18 holes. My behavior is more a function of what I experience in Sarasota than what I experienced where I came from, although the contrast sharpens my appreciation.

In fact, even when I fly through a city, its weather can change my expectancies and incentive values. Looking out the huge windows of Dullus Airport in Washington, DC, on my way from Florida to London for a meeting can change my mood. Gray skies and rain can snap me out of my Sunshine State in a hurry, and I open my laptop to ready myself for hard, serious work.

If you think about the visits to the kinds of organizations we all make in the course of a year, such as car dealerships, our children's schools, medical and dental offices, and favorite coffee shops, you can see how important it is that the climate of the organization have a favorable impact. The "visitors" to a school are the students, and it should come as no surprise that the climate of the classrooms, as well as the halls and the cafeteria, play a huge role in motivating (or demotivating) them to perform. They come every school day for several years, and as young people they are deeply influenced by their immediate environment. In the same way, we can see that the visitors to a hospital are its patients. They may come only once, or they may be repeat visitors. The climate that they encounter, as expressed in the physical surroundings, the attitudes and evident priorities of employees, and even the amount of "wait time" required when they telephone and want to speak with a human being, impacts not only their health but also their willingness to return to that hospital. And, likewise, visitors to a store or an auto dealership as potential customers or as suppliers are responding to the climate and making conscious or unconscious decisions about whether they want to do their business there. The three examples I used to open this chapter—all of them true stories, by the way—suggest how powerful an impact climate can have.

This may sound persuasive, but do we have any evidence that we can expand the climate concept from a description of the *internal* qualities of an organization that arouse different kinds of motivation to a description of how those qualities arouse the motivation of *external* visitors to the organization?

Exhibit 11.1 illustrates the relationships among leadership, organizational climate, and what we might call external or visitor climate.

Students, customers, suppliers, and patients "pass through" the organizational climate. They don't live there, but they become aware, at both conscious and unconscious levels, of the same climate factors that impact the motivation of the organization's more permanent residents. In a research study of the climate reported by teachers in the Bethesda–Chevy Chase School System, George Litwin found that teacher perceptions of the school climate were correlated with student perceptions of the classroom climate. If teachers reported that the school had high standards, the students in their classrooms tended to perceive the classroom standards as high. Likewise, when the teacher reported a climate of low recognition and high criticism, the students tended to perceive the classroom as having "more criticism than positive recognition." This finding is not altogether surprising because students, like staff members, spend more than a thousand hours per year exposed to the climate of the school. The climate experienced by

Exhibit 11.1
The Diffusion of Climate

teachers, largely from the leadership of principals and other administrators, is also experienced by students, although in a less direct form. Students typically do not attend faculty meetings or read the Principal's Bulletin. But they experience the climate of the classroom under the leadership of the teacher, and that teacher passes along the motivational cues absorbed from the various climate determinants.

What happens in schools also happens in hospitals, hotels, car dealerships, department stores, and airlines. Think of your own personal examples where you have encountered an organizational climate and, as a result, found yourself motivated to act in a certain way. The most obvious example is a restaurant, where there is an overt effort to create a climate. Recall the elegance and sophistication of a fine French restaurant. How did the organization motivate you to go there and then to spend a little more on dinner and wine? The Cracker Barrel chain has its own distinctive climate of hearty "down home" food and old-fashioned, folksy charm. The same kind of thing is true, although perhaps more subtly, in our dealings with banks, department stores, or home and building megastores. Home Depot wants you to feel like you are in a warehouse, getting stuff more cheaply because you don't have to go to a, you know, store. And the guys stocking the shelves have been trained to drop whatever they are doing to answer your questions and help you out. It makes you feel like an insider.

Of course, there are so many other influences on the motivation and behavior of any "visitors" that it is hard to isolate and measure the influence of the climate they visit. After all, they are only visitors. So do we know if it makes sense to talk about or measure visitor climate, or if it even matters in terms of the goals of the organizations?

Just because the influence of climate is limited and hard to measure doesn't mean it should be ignored. Each visitor's awareness of and response to climate is critical.

- Students must be aroused to learn, and classroom climate might spell the difference between a good or a great learning environment in an educational institution seeking to connect with its student body. Think of the way the climate that Mrs. Green is creating discourages students with high nAch.
- Customer climate might have a profound impact on the relationship between buyer and seller. The combination of efficiency and consideration in the chapter-opening example will create repeat customers for this VW dealership.

- Patient climate might be the deciding factor for some people seeking an ongoing quality relationship with a health care provider. The telephone calls described in the chapter-opening example along with similar examples of coldness and confusion drove this patient to seek her treatment at the other major health care facility in the city, even though her insurance coverage made the switch difficult.

Fortunately, we have some numbers to illustrate just how important these encounters can be.

The Value of Visitor Loyalty

Tom Cates, a partner at my old firm, Sherbrooke Associates, is interested in how to create client or customer loyalty, and his work relates directly to the importance of visitor climates. He makes an important distinction between loyalty and simple retention. Cable companies, he notes, have historically enjoyed very high retention rates even as they were regularly derided for poor service. Loyalty, on the other hand, is a matter of emotional attachment that results from consistently exceeding client-defined standards over time. In other words, you don't just satisfy your customers—you delight them. Retention is simply keeping a customer as a customer from one purchase decision to the next. Loyalty involves the customer's giving you benefit of the doubt when performance is substandard, for example, when the car repair takes longer than promised, or the wait in the emergency room is a matter of hours. Loyal client "visitors" look for excuses to do business with you and even become vocal advocates for you, referring others in to deal with your organization.

Why and when do you delight them? Delight is a function of the amount of *value* the client believes he or she is getting. Cates answers the question of when visitors are delighted by borrowing the term *moments of truth*. An organization needs to create a relationship with its clients—those who I've been calling visitors. The nature of this relationship is created through a series of critical encounters between the client, as the student in the classroom, the patient waiting to see the doctor, or the customer dealing with the service department, and the organization. Every year companies face hundreds, perhaps thousands, of opportunities to create (or destroy) value for their customers—service calls, telephone conversations, time spent on hold or navigating an automated system in search of a human voice, pricing decisions, face-to-face encounters with receptionists or salespeople, doctors or nurses, teachers or school secretaries. The point is that these moments of truth do not only occur when the customer drives away in a new Beetle or the patient awakens to learn that the bypass surgery was successful. They may occur during smaller moments, perceived over time. And it's the visitor who decides which moments are important, although the successful organization must learn what its visitor clients value.

What does this all have to do with organizational climate? Everything. Think back to the weather analogy. When you are in Louisiana, the distinctive humidity and the weight of the air influence how you feel and, indirectly, how you behave. The same is true for the smell of the sea in the air of Cape Cod. In a sense, these are moments of truth. In organizations, the moments when visitors experience the climate of an organization almost always involve their encountering people, often in the physical surroundings of the workplace but sometimes on the telephone, who reflect the organization's priorities and values. Or perhaps it is the ease of movement in response to a visitor's question or problem, often through interaction with a person but increasingly represented by the links of a Web site. These all reflect the organization's climate. The same climate that is arousing employee motivation is indirectly arousing the motivation of whomever these employees encounter. Litwin's work with Maryland schools shows that this "climate diffusion," as he calls it, passes from leaders to employees to clients. It passes during sustained encounters in the schools, during critical moments in hospitals, and it passes during significant moments of truth in auto showrooms, hardware stores, restaurants, and banks.

Recall our earlier discussion of the dimensions of climate: Structure, Standards, Responsibility, Recognition, Support, and Commitment.

- Mrs. Green's American History assignment sent a clear and uninspiring message about Standards.
- Dr. Porcine and his nurse projected a lack of Commitment and Support.
- Ed Penn at the VW dealership demonstrated a very different kind of Commitment, Standards, Support, and Responsibility.

In each case the visitor had only a brief glimpse of the organizational climate, although for students that climate saturates day after day in classrooms and throughout the school, but the impact is powerful. If you were Mrs. Green's student, you might respond grudgingly to the school assignment but you would be even more motivated by the change of soon getting out of that environment. However, if you encountered Ed Penn, you'd return to his car dealership. And if you had to deal with Dr. Porcine, you, too, would change hospitals.

How important is external climate? Cates's research on health care systems reveals that reducing defections by 5% boosts profits from 25% to 85%. He estimates that a defecting hospital patient costs the organization $14,200, whereas creating a loyal patient is worth $10,500. What this means is that turning a single potential defector into a loyal patient is worth about $25,000.

And, of course, it is not just health care organizations where this happens. Organizations frequently spend a lot of time and money up front on their clients. It takes a lot more work to create a new account, which involves soliciting the business, processing the initial paperwork, cultivating the relationship, and so on, than it does to sustain one. Again, think back to the opening examples. Encounters such as these create loyal VW customers and cause hospital patients to take their business and their insurance money elsewhere. Schools used to be a bit different, with students in the public school system as a captive audience. But that environment is changing, for public schools are in competition with private schools, and the proliferation of charter schools has caused all schools to actively compete for students. In the case of colleges, competition for incoming freshmen can be substantial. Even if they don't compete, schools have an obligation to create a constructive climate for their students.

These are not just random encounters, a matter of the visitor running into the wrong person on the wrong day. Mrs. Green probably always teaches and evaluates that way, and her principal lets her. Dr. Porcine's nurse knows that his telephone rudeness was no anomaly, and the hospital tolerates it. And I'll bet there is something in the VW dealership, if not the corporation, that helps create the kind of climate that Ed Penn expresses to his customers. As I have shown in earlier chapters in this book, these climates are measurable, they are manageable, and they make a big difference to residents and visitors alike.

What is fascinating is that you can only get at external climate through the internal door. Ben Schneider, David Nadler, and George Litwin have all documented that there is a match between the internal climate experienced by members of an organization and the external climate experienced by visitors. For example, studies of retail neighborhood banks show that tellers treat customers exactly the way the manager treats the tellers.

We will find a way to conveniently measure visitor climate. Companies are hard at work on this, whether they use the term *climate* or not. But then we must ask the next question: What do we know about managing it, not for the purpose of arousing the nAch, nAff, or nPow of the organization's members, but for the purpose of arousing the motivation of its visitors?

Managing Visitor Climate

How do you manage climate to support your external objectives? The same five factors that determine internal organizational climate— external environment, historical forces, organizational arrangements, strategy, and most importantly, leadership—also determine the external climate experienced by visitors. But the important difference is that visitors perceive only what is most visible—the weather for the days they are there rather than the patterns of climate that persist over decades. Because of this, management needs to focus on the most visible.

Don't get me wrong. I'm not saying that you should try to con the visitors to your organization with some kind of superficial PR job that belies what is really going on. People will see (or feel) through the deception, sooner or later, and that will be their lasting impression. No, what I'm saying is that you should make sure that all efforts to improve the climate of your organization, and your successes in doing so, are visible to visitors.

The *external environment* remains the most difficult of the climate determinants to manage because it is largely out of the control of the organization's leaders. But external factors can, nevertheless, be shaped in ways that allow a desired climate profile to be created. For example, admissions people and hospital administrators can take the extra time to carefully explain to patients changes in Medicaid and what the hospital is trying to do about them, and auto dealers can explain about how their cars comply with the latest EPA regulations.

Similarly, the organization's *strategy* can be communicated to visitors so that they receive the desired motivational cues. If the school has a mission statement that emphasizes student responsibility, it can be posted in every classroom, featured on the letterhead of the school's stationery, and mentioned when school leaders address parents and teachers. In much the same way, hospitals with strategies that focus on TLC can constantly remind nurses that this is a priority and give them the time to deliver it. Provisions can also be made for families and visitors such as comfortable waiting rooms and people to give directions and answer questions.

Unfortunately, the employees who most frequently communicate an organization's strategy to visitors are the least prepared to do so. Most visitors experience the external climate when they interact with the organization's front-line employees. Sometimes these front-line employees are the least paid and are hired and trained with little concern for their strategic role in creating the right kind of visitor climate. For example, banks can spend a lot more time training managers than customer service representatives (CSRs) or tellers, yet it is precisely those first-line employees who "are" the bank to its customer visitors.

An organization's *history* may be more difficult to communicate to visitors, but, if done properly, can help create the desired climate. For example, many high schools use trophy cases and bulletin boards to proclaim their histories and influence a student's experience at the school. One might display the athletic trophies won by the school down through the years. Another might use the same trophy cases to focus on awards won in drama or debate. Still another might use the same visible space to feature famous graduates who have succeeded in the arts, in science, or in medicine. Whether because of the trophy cases, the lobby of the corporate headquarters, or the public statements of a hospital spokesperson, visitors can absorb a sense of the organization's priorities and values from the way its history is portrayed. And if leaders understand this, they can manage visitor climates to arouse the kind of motivation they want.

Organizational arrangements can often have a powerful impact on customers, patients, and students. Do customers get the impression that their concerns have to be passed up through an elaborate hierarchy in order to be addressed? A quick response from an employee empowered to make a decision can be very satisfying to a customer. The New England Baptist Hospital used to give every patient a red rose when discharged. Originally, the rose was a symbol of the quiet care the hospital tried so hard to deliver to its patients. More recently, a customer satisfaction survey was attached to the rose. With the survey, New England Baptist was saying it wanted to learn how to deliver a better visitor experience.

In schools, formal and informal organizational arrangements can be especially powerful determinants of classroom climates. Do the teachers dress informally, putting them on a level with students? Are administrators remote and unreachable, or are they visible in the halls and even in the classrooms? Does the public address system regularly interrupt classroom activities, making a statement that such activities are relatively unimportant? All this says something about the formal processes followed by school administrators. Similarly, those aspects of the reward system that are visible to the school's student visitors impact the climate. Are the top awards given out by the school for academic performance, "citizenship," or something else? School assemblies are organizational arrangements. Does the school hold pep rallies and assemblies for academic as well as athletic achievement? I know of one school that holds an annual "AP Pep Rally" in May before the three weeks of Advanced Placement tests. The event is somewhat tongue-in-cheek, with cheers in Latin and chanted calculus formulas, and speakers occasionally chide students for attending the rally when they should be studying. But the school boasts some of the top scores in the nation and, significantly, among the highest percentage of its students taking Advanced Placement tests.

Organizational arrangements are one of the first things to change when clients want to improve the visitor climate created by their "customer call centers." Companies such as First Data Corporation centralize much of their customer service by building these large centers, usually staffed with entry-level personnel. They are economically efficient, but they can be terribly inefficient when it comes to delivering high-quality customer service. We have learned that the visitor climate created by call center employees depends on a sophisticated approach to call center management. It turns out that managing the internal climate to arouse nAff is the most important motivational priority for a high-performing call center. The technology has to be right. It has to facilitate rapid information processing and open employee–manager communications. The supervision has to be right. Supervisors must be social leaders more than taskmasters. The performance measurement, reward, and incentive systems must all encourage social support and employee interaction, not just speed or number of calls handled. When these internal climate bases are touched, the call center can hit a home run with customers.

Leadership is, of course, the most important means of managing visitor climate, and it is palpable even when the leader has no direct contact with visitors. The importance stems from Litwin's "diffusion of climate," similar to what I earlier referred to as "the cloud chamber effect." Leaders, through their day-to-day practices, create the climate that arouses employee motivation and is passed along to and experienced by visitors. As we've seen, specific practices have predictable impacts on specific climate dimensions. Leaders are the interpreters of the determinants of climate for employees and visitors alike. If they choose to take an activist role, to a large extent they decide what goes on the walls of the buildings, how employees are trained to treat visitors, and what rewards are made available for good visitor management.

I am not aware of research identifying a short "hit list" of leadership practices that determine the healthiest visitor climate profiles. In the future one no doubt will be discovered. There is simply too much riding on visitor climate, and the successful organizations will be the ones whose leaders grasp and apply the practices with the most power.

The Future of Climate: Measurement and Feedback

I am certain that the six dimensions I have used to describe organizational climate will change. The next generation of our climate survey will have to pay more attention to cross-functional and cross-boundary behavior. Organizations of the future will be much more horizontal and climate measures and climate management techniques will have to evolve to remain relevant in such horizontal structures. The organization of the future may be a network of companies working, like a jazz combo, in coordinated independence.

The future of climate assessment and climate management also will involve a greater level of speed, technology, and customized organization-specific assessment. The survey process will be online. Climate questionnaires will be created, modified, distributed, and collected at the keyboard and over the Internet. Firms such as Mercer Delta Consulting, The Forum Corporation, and Sherbrooke Associates are already creating software to help clients customize climate and leadership practices surveys so they can measure unique variables in addition to the standard climate dimensions.

I'm not sure if the future of climate management will include online feedback of the climate survey results. The technology for doing this is already available. The challenge will be to deliver the survey results with the right amount of expert advice and coaching. As I have repeatedly emphasized, climate data are most effectively turned into information and insight with the help of professional guidance. It remains to be seen if we can "package" that guidance into a climate management tool kit or a climate management Web site. It is possible that such a Web site could provide clients with up-to-date climate data, discussion groups on specific climate issues, and online coaching to deal with matters requiring expert guidance.

My own hunch is that because so much of organizational climate is and always will be driven by leadership, it's the leadership component rather than climate itself that will require facilitation. Leadership is so *personal*, and good leadership is so *emotional*. Getting people to learn about their leadership practices requires more than showing them data and interpretations of data. Communicating information about leadership practices or climate data can certainly be done online. But the commitment to change and to turn good intentions into real actions requires more than just having the information. It is fundamentally a challenging, confrontational process that pushes the leader to reexamine *attitudes* and alter *behaviors*. No "hit list" of practices will fully capture the subtlety or the complexity of this task. My guess is there will always be a value-added role for face-to-face climate coaching.

The Future of Climate: Climate in Cyberspace

Everything changes when we look at organizational climate in cyberspace. Or does it? Let's take a look at virtual organizations made possible by the Internet and their visitor climate as experienced by people who "visit" an organization by visiting a Web site.

Web site visits are, typically, brief and fragmentary. *In Deep Branding on the Internet: Applying Heat and Pressure Online to Ensure a Lasting Brand*, authors Marc Braunstein and Edward H. Levine note that users switch page views, on the average, every 12 seconds, and the typical site visit averages only 5 minutes. So in an hour, the visitor encounters about 300 pages of content—huge quantities of information competing for his or her attention. The trick is to transform these visitors, who may just drop in out of curiosity or because of a hot promotion, into customers. To accomplish that, you need to establish a relationship with the visitor. The point is not simply to attract a large number of "hits" at your site, but also to manage the quality of the experiences people have once they have chosen your site.

It's not easy to do. Think of the enormous quantity of Web sites competing for attention. Think also of the social context of the Web site visit. It's not like visiting an auto showroom or a bank branch, where you are surrounded by the organization and its people and artifacts. While seeking out and dealing with a Web site, the visitor is subject to all the distractions of the home or office—the phone ringing, people coming into the room, something going on outside the window, the to-do list nagging at you from the corner of your desk. It's analogous to the difference between watching a movie on a big screen in a theater, complete with Dolby sound, and watching the same movie on your television at home, with the kids crying in the background.

In the typical encounter with a Web site, the interface between the customer and the climate of the organization is narrow and controlled: the screen of the computer, which includes the displays on the Web site, and the paths and processes by which the customer navigates the site. In some cases the customer visits a site to find out about the company or collect information, whereas at other times the purpose of the visit is explicitly to transact business or shop. But even in the former cases, the owner of the Web site is eager for the visitor to engage in some kind of financial transaction with the company. So the design of the Web site, like the design of an organization, guides visitors to make choices. Usually the customer visiting the site never hears a human voice, even via telephone, or sees the face of a member of the organization.

The organization's Web site, nevertheless, creates a climate, in the sense that people who visit come away with measurable thoughts and feelings about the way the organization does business, the aspects of a relationship that are valued by the Web site owner, and the kind of visitor behavior that will be rewarded. Many prospective college and graduate students select the schools to which they choose to apply mainly on the basis of the Web site. As Braunstein and Levine argue, e-businesses are not just selling products. They are selling ideas in the minds of customers. And paralleling the conclusions Cates reached about customer loyalty, there is more value in selling more to the same customers than there is in selling less to a lot of different customers. Thus, deep branding pays. It's the same on the Internet as it is in the showroom. Establish ongoing relationships with visitors, so you become partners in the search for the solution to a visitor's problem.

Virtual Internet-based organizations have similar cyberclimate issues. More and more businesses are outsourcing aspects of their operations to part-time employees or allowing organizational members to work at home. In the extreme, many, if not all communications, can be remote. Personal experience with the organization is largely through e-mails, Web sites, and digital protocols. Because of the highly controlled nature of these interfaces, the climate dimensions that best describe a virtual organization or a cyberspace visitor climate may be different from those that we have used to describe the more traditional work environment. The most important motivational dimensions may even be disguised. Members of a virtual organization and cybervisitors come away from their experiences with "measurable thoughts and feelings," but such cyberclimates have yet to be qualitatively measured. E-businesses use questionnaires to evaluate customer service or customer satisfaction, and companies that have experimented with work-at-home arrangements have utilized standard employee satisfaction surveys. But these are a far cry from the motivational cues we measure with our climate questionnaire.

What, exactly, would such cyberclimate surveys measure? What form do the dimensions of climate take, and what might be the opportunities for motive arousal?

The dimensions, I assume, would include variations of the six features that we came to see as important in our research on traditional organizational climate: Structure, Standards, Responsibility, Recognition, Support, and Commitment. We know that Support would have to be expanded to pay greater attention to cross-functional teamwork and that Responsibility would have to be customized to better fit the realities of the particular organization we are assessing. But assuming these things, of course, is not enough. Speculation in these pages and elsewhere needs to move on to the kind of concrete research that we did on traditional organizational climates. And our understanding of cyberclimate, like organizational climate, needs to be grounded in motivation theory. Here are a few of my thoughts:

- Despite the remoteness, abstraction, and low-touch nature of Internet relationships, they still can be powerful in arousing nAff. Think of the kinds of relationships conducted by e-mail, which combines informal spontaneity (how often do we redraft our e-mails?) with candor and intimacy because you can say things in an e-mail that you'd be too embarrassed to say while looking the other person in the eye. Jennifer Egan's article "<lonely gay teen seeking same>" appearing in the December 10, 2000, *New York Times Magazine* is a moving exploration of the power of nAff and the surprising ability of cyberspace to function as a path to fulfill that need. In the less steamy world of e-business, successful companies can create cyberclimates that arouse nAff. They can do this by emphasizing the sense of community (which is why chat rooms are so important to many Web sites) and by "personalizing" the visitor relationship by inviting communication through non-Internet media. My brother chooses to stay with MindSpring as his Internet provider because the tech support people he talks with on the telephone don't make him feel stupid. They project compassion for his difficulties and work with him to solve his problems.

- Encounters with websites, cyber technology, and the Internet can do much to arouse nAch. The digital world is a world of immediate and concrete feedback. A Palm Pilot is a high achiever's dream come true. Online high achievers don't have to put up with the distractions that so often frustrate them at work. They can accomplish so much more! Just think of how late at night or early in the morning that e-mail was sent by your workaholic, high-achieving colleague! High achievers get a real kick out of shopping for cars on the Internet and finding the best deal. The kick is not simply in saving $100 or so but also in achieving the best deal. Many enjoy taking active control of the process on eBay and Priceline.com. A successful Web site will provide visitors with all the tools they need to help themselves and this stimulates the high achiever's need for high levels of personal responsibility.

- The need for power is more difficult to manage, but it is clearly aroused by cyberspace technology. Users of the Internet and visitors to company Web sites have obvious power over others through their choice of when to use the "Buy" and "Delete" and "Send" and "Reply" buttons. The fact that the visitor is in total control of both the initiation and the termination of the relationship is the ultimate power arousal mechanism. In addition, if we think of nPow in terms of the feelings of freedom and independence described earlier in this chapter, then other opportunities to engage this motive undoubtedly arise. In fact, research shows that the most successful e-marketers adopt an "opt-in" strategy. Rather than spamming customers with blanket e-mail offers, businesses invite customers to opt-in to receiving alerts on deals of particular interest to them. Opt-in arouses nPow for the customer, and paying greater attention to such cyberclimate dynamics offers a fascinating area for climate experts to help Internet sites live long and prosper.

The Future of Leadership

Whether it's in service of a virtual or traditional enterprise, leadership in the future will continue to mean strategically stimulating and directing organizational performance. It will continue to be differentiated from management. And it will continue to generate an enormous amount of interest and press coverage.

I believe that three issues will become an increasingly important part of our conversations about effective leadership: (1) the leader as facilitator, (2) women as leaders, and (3) the emotional price that our best future leaders must necessarily pay for their success. Let me gaze into my crystal ball and comment on each of these issues.

The Leader as Facilitator

Although the old-fashioned "command and control" model of leadership will continue to be important, especially in situations where clarity and speed are requirements, most organizations will find that a facilitation model of leadership works better. In the high-performing organizations of the future, decisions will increasingly be made by bringing people together, pooling ideas and information, and moving toward some form of consensus. This style of leadership is 100% consistent with the expectations of tomorrow's knowledge workers. It is consistent with the evolution of nPow into a far more socialized and less selfish form. And we have the technology to facilitate facilitation, that is, to reduce the bureaucracy of meetings, the time-consuming burden of "bringing people up to speed," and the inconvenience of file drawers filled with papers that record what was decided.

There's another reason why the most effective leader of the future will be a facilitator. With more and more highly specialized knowledge required to complete any given task—not only technological knowledge but also cross-cultural knowledge about the suppliers, markets, and members of the organization—it's unlikely that a single leader will know enough to make the best decision. Sometimes he or she may have to do so, but facilitation will prove to be the wisest method in most situations. Facilitation requires highly developed "people skills."

Women as Leaders

As more and more women move into leadership positions, ongoing research is showing that they bring new sets of competencies to the task of leadership. *Business Week* (November 20, 2000), on the basis of performance evaluations of senior managers, identified four skill areas in which women outperform their male counterparts:

- Motivating others
- Fostering communication
- Producing high-quality work
- Listening to others

In two areas men sometimes earned higher marks:

- Strategic planning
- Analyzing issues

I have studied gender leadership differences for three of my corporate clients and my research reflects a similar split between "people practices" and "analytic practices."

In one company, 360-degree feedback done in 1995 revealed that *subordinates* rate men and women equally strong as leaders, but women have two distinctive strengths:

- They are more open and candid, and they confront conflict more directly.
- They are viewed as being stronger coaches and better at giving feedback.

Women, according to subordinates, also have clear weaknesses:

- The goals that women set are not as challenging as the goals that men set.
- They are less analytical and less well informed about marketplace realities than their male counterparts.
- They have more trouble "letting go" and encouraging innovation.

Peers rate their women colleagues as more "outspoken" and more willing to "stick to their guns" but weaker in communicating an exciting vision and knowing the industry, the market, and business in general. *Bosses* rate men higher across the board, and the only practice in which women rate higher is "acknowledging mistakes and limitations," a finding that says as much about men as it does about women.

My research with another company, also in 1995, led to similar conclusions, except that, over all, women rated slightly higher than men. Women were better at practices involving coaching and other forms of performance management, such as confronting conflicts, communicating views of performance, giving feedback, encouraging collaboration, and demonstrating personal concern. Men scored dramatically higher in "expecting people to correct their own errors" and were seen as outperforming women in being nondefensive, empowering people at lower levels, and demonstrating broad-based knowledge about the industry and the market. In other words, women did better at the "people practices."

My third study, done in 1996 at a rather "macho" organization, generated similar results. Women, many of whom worked in HR, were stronger than men at "people practices" involving coaching and feedback, being supportive, and recognizing rather than criticizing. Men did better with outwardly focused analytic practices, such as staying abreast of industry and market changes, understanding leverage points of the business and the competition, and encouraging innovation.

My conclusions? Even allowing for some stereotyping that went into the evaluations, if women are to continue to break through the "glass ceiling," they need to continue to develop their leadership knowledge and skills in areas that involve the "external competence" practices described earlier. But what's more, if I'm right about the future importance of facilitation skills, guess who is better prepared to lead? I believe that "female competencies" will have a lot to do with the future of leadership. We all should read what Deborah Tannen has to say about gender differences in *You Just Don't Understand* (1991). My own crude summary of Tannen's conclusion is that women care about relationships, whereas men care about establishing and reconfirming their status and situational control. I am willing to bet that organizations in the future will generate more and better results if their leaders are skilled at managing relationships. For many, this means having more women leaders.

The bottom line for me is this: We guys had best get used to the fact that women are superior, by genetics or social conditioning, when it comes to facilitative leadership. They are more likely to be able to successfully navigate their way through tomorrow's organization, and they are better suited to lead these same organizations. And the climates these women leaders will create will be high-performing climates, probably rich in Recognition, Support, and Commitment. Pack it in, John Wayne. Your day has passed. Or better yet, cultivate your womanly leadership skills.

The Emotional Price of Good Leadership

Leadership in the future will be more psychologically demanding. The leaders of tomorrow will be increasingly aware of the importance of the motivational arousal effects of organizational climate. They will be sensitive to the emotional impact of their actions, including negative impacts. Negative climates take a great toll on mental health and can even trigger outbreaks of antisocial or violent behavior. When someone works in a place for 20 years and that place has low Support and more criticism than Recognition and little individual Responsibility, the resentment, blame, and anger that arise can certainly cause an outbreak of violent or self-destructive behavior. Knowing these facts, the leaders of the future will give importance to building and maintaining positive climates that motivate rather than alienate.

This kind of leadership exacts an emotional price. Leaders will have to continue to create positive, motivating expectations, even when they are uncertain about their support from above. They may have to challenge others and absorb their emotional reactions. This will require a whole new level of psychological skill—the ability to manage one's own inner states—in order to be consistently successful. They may not label their most successful leadership behaviors as "practices," and they may not realize that they are manipulating six dimensions of the work environment. But they will know that they have to pay much closer attention to people's needs and moods, their values, and their likes and dislikes.

Leadership is not going to get any easier. It's going to get harder as it gets softer. I believe that the people side of leadership will be the side that matters most. The best leaders of tomorrow will become emotionally involved with the people they are leading, especially when making the personal calls that are an inevitable part of the job. The more effectively leaders manage climate, the better their organizations will perform. So the best leaders will focus on managing climate. Our "hit list" of leadership practices shows what the best leaders of tomorrow will have to do more of. These practices and others like them take a lot out of a person. They require sensitivity, patience, interpersonal awareness, and a lot of personal discipline.

They also involve personal exposure. Opening up. Letting those who are being led see, feel, and sense the leader's vulnerability and his or her frustrations. Strong, silent types will not be as successful as leaders who *use* their own emotions to demonstrate their high expectations, their commitment to goals, and their genuine concern for others. The best leaders of tomorrow won't be able to spend much time alone in their offices.

Leadership in the future, then, is going to be a very emotional experience. On-the-job climates will blend into off-the-job motivational influences. Effective leaders will learn to manage "the whole person." In an elusive way, the best leaders will have to bring their own full emotional selves to the network of relationships that constitutes an organization.

How are future leaders going to cope? I have two suggestions. The first involves a form of therapy. If the future of leadership is going to be so much more personal, emotional, and stressful, then leaders need perspective. They need to see their jobs in a way that feels more manageable. The "cloud chamber" analogy we have introduced in this book provides a useful, almost therapeutic, perspective. Appreciating how motivational cues really work takes some of the pressure off the leader. The leader need not be physically present, personally solve all of the problems, intervene in all of the conflicts, or make all of the judgments to effectively guide and control all of the expectancies and incentives in an organization. If leaders concentrate on engaging in our brief "hit list" of practices described in Chapter 7, they can reduce the complexity of their job and decrease the stress they feel every day. If they can become aware of the context that their actions create, even when they are not consciously "leading," they can focus on strengthening the motivational cues that generate a positive organizational climate.

My second suggestion is to create and utilize more tools. The future of leadership may be more soft than hard. It may be more focused on people than on technology. It may be more a matter of climate management than financial management. But we are developing tools to help leaders lead in that kind of future. The ToolKit in the next section of this book is just a beginning.

The Bottom Line: Motivational Capital

In today's information age we are all aware of the vital importance of intellectual capital, which is the body of knowledge, skills, and perspective that resides in the people of the organization. It's an asset more valuable than the organization's traditional capital assets. But in the future the bottom line may very well be a function of an organization's motivational capital. The reserve of energy, directed toward the work that the organization needs to do in order to compete and win, may be what makes all the difference.

The organizations of the future will be flatter, with ad hoc task forces and virtual teams replacing hierarchy and permanent functional structures. To achieve adequate control, chief executives will have to create and rely on a network of leaders who understand their roles as managers of motivational capital. These leaders will have to motivate their teams to move quickly and effectively into new or changing markets. Speed will be everything and, other things being equal, the highly motivated team will get there first.

The bottom line is this: Leaders who know how to create and sustain high-performing climates and who know how to make the most of the organization's motivational capital are the leaders who will have the greatest personal impact. Like the impact of particles in a cloud chamber, it is normally unseen, but it is very real and very powerful.

Part IV
Climate Management ToolKit

As I have indicated throughout the course of the book, in my work with clients I use a variety of documents to assess their organizational climate and leadership practices and give constructive feedback to them. In the ToolKit I include samples of these documents.

- *The Climate Questionnaire* is the one whose development I describe in Chapters 3 and 4. I have modified it slightly since its original development in 1981, and I sometimes make other modifications according to specific needs and wishes of clients. Occasionally we use a Part III where we invite open-ended responses.

- *The Organizational Climate Report* is typical of the kind of written report I give to our clients. These reports are, of course, accompanied by various kinds of climate feedback workshops and personalized consulting, which are more fully described in Chapter 8.

- *A User's Guide to Your Organizational Climate Scores* is a tool that I often give our clients when we cannot personally explain their climate survey results in feedback workshops. I write different "benchmark" sections for each client. In the sample, I've used a real one with the name changed to "AMZ."

- *The Climate Survey Feedback and Planning Guide* is designed to help leaders at any level of an organization interpret their climate survey data and make plans to improve their personal effectiveness. We advise clients that completing the guide is an important activity. It is their personal property, and the data it contains are confidential.

- *The Practices Resource Guide* helps leaders interpret management practices feedback and provides them with ideas for raising their scores. The comments found in this resource guide were collected from my clients (both managers and subordinates) and from other consultants.

Appendix I

The Climate Questionnaire

It is urgent you complete this survey by return date

Instructions

This questionnaire is designed to collect data about how people feel about their jobs, how they are managed, and how things work in this organization. The results will be used to help your manager solve problems and identify opportunities for improving the organization.

The questionnaire is divided into two parts. In Part I, you will be asked to describe the climate of your organization. By "organization" we mean the smallest work unit that is meaningful to you. In Part II, you will be asked to describe the management practices of your manager.

For each of the statements in Part I use the following scale:

1 = If you DEFINITELY DISAGREE; that is, if the statement definitely does NOT express how you feel about the matter.

2 = If you are INCLINED TO DISAGREE; that is, if you are not definite, but think that the statement does NOT tend to express how you feel about the matter.

3 = If you are INCLINED TO AGREE; that is, if you are not definite, but think that the statement tends to express how you feel about the matter.

4 = If you DEFINITELY AGREE; that is, if the statement definitely expresses how you feel about the matter.

For the results of this survey to be useful, it is important that you provide a truly *accurate picture* of how you see things. We ask that you take the time to answer each question carefully and honestly. This is *not* a test, and there are no right or wrong answers.

Your individual responses will be kept *strictly confidential*. No one's individual answers will be released for any purpose. The only reports will be statistical summaries of the responses of different groups or sets of employees. This questionnaire will be destroyed after it is processed.

- Fax Pages 1–3 to Mercer Delta's independent processing company for processing at 1-555-555-5555. No cover page is needed.
- OR mail Pages 1–3 in the return envelope provided.
- This questionnaire must be received no later than RETURN DATE

Part I: Organizational Climate

This section of the questionnaire is designed to measure how you feel about your work environment. You will be asked to describe the kind of climate or atmosphere that has been created in the organization. By "organization" we mean the smallest work unit that is meaningful to you. When thinking about the organization, you should keep in mind the actual experiences you have had working here.

	DEFINITELY DISAGREE	INCLINED TO DISAGREE	INCLINED TO AGREE	DEFINITELY AGREE
1. In this organization, the rewards and encouragements you get usually outweigh the threats and the criticism.	1	2	3	4
2. I feel that I am a member of a well-functioning team.	1	2	3	4
3. In some of the projects I've been on, I haven't been sure exactly who my boss was.	1	2	3	4
4. Around here management resents your checking everything with them. If you think you've got the right approach, you just go ahead.	1	2	3	4

continued

	DEFINITELY DISAGREE	INCLINED TO DISAGREE	INCLINED TO AGREE	DEFINITELY AGREE
5. In this organization, people are rewarded in proportion to the excellence of their job performance.	1	2	3	4
6. The jobs in this organization are clearly defined and logically structured.	1	2	3	4
7. In this organization we set very high standards for performance.	1	2	3	4
8. People in this organization don't really trust each other enough.	1	2	3	4
9. In this organization, it is sometimes unclear who has the formal authority to make a decision.	1	2	3	4
10. Our management believes that no job is so well done that it couldn't be done better.	1	2	3	4
11. Generally, I am highly committed to the goals of this organization.	1	2	3	4
12. Around here there is a feeling of pressure to continually improve our personal and group performance.	1	2	3	4

continued

	DEFINITELY DISAGREE	INCLINED TO DISAGREE	INCLINED TO AGREE	DEFINITELY AGREE
13. We don't rely too heavily on individual judgment in this organization; almost everything is double-checked.	1	2	3	4
14. You don't get much sympathy from higher-ups in this organization if you make a mistake.	1	2	3	4
15. Around here we take pride in belonging to this organization.	1	2	3	4
16. When I am on a difficult assignment, I can usually count on getting assistance from my boss and co-workers.	1	2	3	4
17. There is not enough reward and recognition given in this organization for doing good work.	1	2	3	4
18. Our philosophy emphasizes that people should solve their problems by themselves.	1	2	3	4
19. We have a promotion system here that helps the best person rise to the top.	1	2	3	4

continued

	DEFINITELY DISAGREE	INCLINED TO DISAGREE	INCLINED TO AGREE	DEFINITELY AGREE
20. Our productivity sometimes suffers from lack of organization and planning.	1	2	3	4
21. I don't really care what happens to this organization.	1	2	3	4
22. You don't get ahead in this organization unless you stick your neck out and try things on your own.	1	2	3	4
23. As far as I can see, there isn't much personal loyalty to the organization.	1	2	3	4
24. In this organization people don't seem to take much pride in their performance.	1	2	3	4

Part II: Your Manager's Practices

In this section of the questionnaire you will be asked to assess the practices of your manager—the person to whom you directly report.

The following statements describe the way a manager might perform his or her job. Please indicate how much you agree or disagree with each of the statements as descriptions of your manager by circling the appropriate number.

Please note below the name of the person being described.

My Manager . . .	STRONGLY DISAGREE	DISAGREE	NEITHER AGREE NOR DISAGREE	AGREE	STRONGLY AGREE
1. establishes clear, specific performance goals for me in my work.	1	2	3	4	5
2. is supportive and helpful to me in my day-to-day activities.	1	2	3	4	5
3. sets challenging performance goals and standards for me.	1	2	3	4	5
4. encourages me to initiate tasks or projects I think are important.	1	2	3	4	5
5. communicates excitement and enthusiasm about our work.	1	2	3	4	5
6. conducts team meetings in a way that builds trust and mutual respect.	1	2	3	4	5

continued

My Manager . . .	STRONGLY DISAGREE	DISAGREE	NEITHER AGREE NOR DISAGREE	AGREE	STRONGLY AGREE
7. recognizes me for good performance more often than criticizes me for poor performance.	1	2	3	4	5
8. clarifies who is responsible for what within our work group.	1	2	3	4	5
9. encourages innovation and calculated risk taking.	1	2	3	4	5
10. relates the total reward system (compensation, recognition, promotion) to the excellence of job performance rather than to other factors such as seniority, personal relationships, etc.	1	2	3	4	5
11. demonstrates personal commitment to achieving goals.	1	2	3	4	5
12. encourages me to participate in making important decisions.	1	2	3	4	5

continued

My Manager . . .	STRONGLY DISAGREE	DISAGREE	NEITHER AGREE NOR DISAGREE	AGREE	STRONGLY AGREE
13. utilizes recognition, praise, and similar methods to reward subordinates for excellent performance.	1	2	3	4	5
14. makes sure tasks and projects are clearly and thoroughly explained and understood when they are assigned.	1	2	3	4	5
15. involves people in setting goals.	1	2	3	4	5
16. gives me feedback on how I am doing on my job.	1	2	3	4	5
17. expects me to find and correct my own errors rather than doing this for me.	1	2	3	4	5
18. goes to bat for me with his or her superiors when he or she feels I am right.	1	2	3	4	5

Appendix II

The Organizational Climate Report

Introduction

This report provides in-depth information on the organizational climate of your work group and an analysis of the management practices that impact this climate. Research studies conducted over the past 20 years have demonstrated that our measures of climate are related to employee motivation and performance.

This report is organized into two sections:

I. Organizational Climate—measures of how people perceive the work environment.
II. Management Practices—measures of how people see their own managers behaving.

Two different kinds of data are presented in this report:

Percentile Score: This is a measure that converts the average raw scores into a relative score by comparing it to a norm base. This score tells you what percentage of the norm base is scored lower than you did.

Spread: This is a measure of how much people answering the questionnaire agreed or disagreed on their ratings. Narrow spread means agreement.

Part I: Organizational Climate

The following scores for each climate dimension were derived from Part I of the questionnaire, which asked people to describe the way things are in the department or work team. The score for each dimension is a percentile score based on the average of the responses of the people who completed questionnaires.

CLIMATE DIMENSION	SCORE	COMMENT
1. Structure	61%	HIGH—people generally understand their job responsibilities and levels of decision-making authority.
2. Standards	29%	LOW—performance standards are not high and people feel that there is little pressure to improve them.
3. Responsibility	47%	MODERATE—people feel generally responsible for results although some decisions are double-checked.
4. Recognition	48%	MODERATE—people feel there is a balance between rewards and criticism in this organization.
5. Support	83%	VERY HIGH—people are very trusting and there is a high degree of teamwork in this organization.
6. Commitment	82%	VERY HIGH—people feel very committed to the organization and its goals.

Part I: Organizational Climate

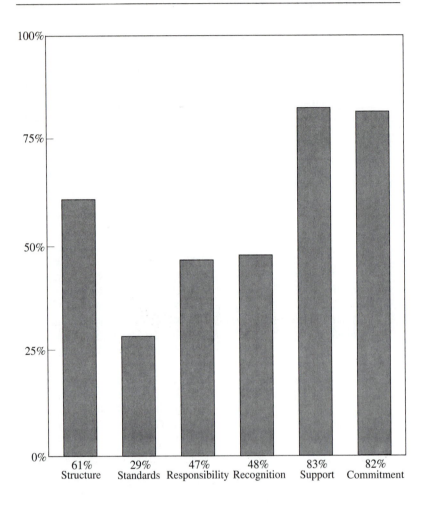

Part II: Management Practices

The following scores for the 18 management practices were derived from Part II of the questionnaire, which asked people to describe the practices of the manager to whom they report. The percentile score for each practice is based on the average of the responses of the people who completed questionnaires. The spread is an indication of the dispersion of the responses. The number in parentheses following each practice is the raw score at the 50th percentile of the norm base.

DIMENSION	PRACTICE	SCORE	SPREAD
Structure	1. Establishing clear, specific performance goals for your subordinates' jobs. (3.75)	76%	Medium
	2. Clarifying who is responsible for what within the group. (3.75)	95%	Narrow
	3. Making sure tasks and projects are clearly and thoroughly explained and understood when they are assigned. (3.50)	72%	Narrow
Standards	4. Setting challenging performance goals and standards for subordinates. (4.00)	67%	Narrow
	5. Demonstrating personal commitment to achieving goals. (4.17)	75%	Narrow
	6. Giving your subordinates feedback on how they are doing on their jobs. (3.67)	94%	Narrow
Responsibility	7. Encouraging your subordinates to initiate tasks or projects they think are important. (4.00)	92%	Narrow
	8. Expecting your subordinates to find and correct their own errors rather than doing this for them. (4.00)	8%	Medium
	9. Encouraging innovation and calculated risk taking in others. (3.67)	87%	Narrow

continued

DIMENSION	PRACTICE	SCORE	SPREAD
Recognition	10. Recognizing subordinates for good performance more often than criticizing them for poor performance. (3.90)	89%	Narrow
	11. Using recognition, praise, and similar methods to reward subordinates for excellent performance. (3.75)	75%	Narrow
	12. Relating the total reward system (compensation, recognition, promotion) to performance rather than to other factors such as seniority, personal relationships, etc. (3.67)	62%	Medium
Support	13. Being supportive and helpful to subordinates in their day-to-day activities. (3.86)	94%	Narrow
	14. Going to bat for your subordinates with your superiors when you feel your subordinates are right. (4.00)	86%	Narrow
	15. Conducting team meetings in a way that builds trust and mutual respect. (3.60)	14%	Medium
Commitment	16. Communicating excitement and enthusiasm about the work. (3.88)	78%	Narrow
	17. Involving people in setting goals. (3.67)	89%	Narrow
	18. Encouraging subordinates to participate in making decisions. (4.00)		

Appendix III

A User's Guide to Your Organizational Climate Scores

What follows is a sample of a climate management tool that we give our clients when we cannot personally explain their climate survey results in climate feedback workshops. The "benchmark" sections, of course, vary from organization to organization. For the following sample, I've used a real one with the name changed to "AMZ." Please note that for this survey, we changed the wording of the questionnaire items and substituted the phrase "work team" for the word "organization".

Structure

Definition

The sense employees have of being well organized and of having a clear definition of their roles and responsibilities.

Specific Survey Items

- The jobs in my work team are clearly defined and logically structured.
- In my work team, it is sometimes not clear who has the formal authority to make a decision.
- In some of the projects I've been on, I haven't been sure exactly who my boss was.
- Our productivity sometimes suffers from a lack of organization and planning.

Interpreting Structure Scores

High Structure (scores of 70% and above) is positively correlated to performance when the work is relatively predictable and routine, when process discipline is important, and when errors or mistakes are very costly. High scores mean more constraints, more bureaucracy, and a greater reliance on formal organizational arrangements. High Structure may stifle creativity and informal activities that are often important to innovation.

Moderate Structure (40% to 60%) is the most common range of scores, showing a degree of flexibility in jobs and responsibilities. With this flexibility, there is often ambiguity and confusion. Moderate Structure can be associated with high performance when individual initiative is required and people are mature enough to tolerate the lack of clarity.

Low Structure (35% and below) will often drive performance when creativity and innovation are required. Low scores mean that employees feel somewhat disorganized, confused, or out of control. Low Structure is particularly problematic when employees are inexperienced, unskilled, or performing work they have not done before. Structure scores below 25% are always too low.

Proposed AMZ Benchmark

Based on my experience with AMZ, I believe that the most appropriate benchmark for most of AMZ's business units would be between 45% and 55%. Many of your businesses are in transition. Leaders are trying to break old work habits and introduce new procedures. Attempting to create a highly structured climate in these circumstances would be counterproductive.

Improving Structure

The key to higher Structure is clarity. Managers need to set clearer goals. They need to discuss assignments in order to clarify expectations, uncover mix-ups and confusion, and eliminate duplication or overlapping responsibilities. Clarity does not have to mean autocracy or heavyhanded, dictatorial leadership (although that does raise Structure scores).

The specific management practices our research has shown will improve Structure scores are:

1. Establishing clear, specific performance goals for your subordinates' jobs.
2. Clarifying who is responsible for what within the group.
3. Making sure tasks and projects are clearly and thoroughly explained and understood when they are assigned.

Standards

Definition

The feeling of pressure to improve performance and the degree of pride employees take in doing a good job.

Specific Survey Items

- In my work team, we set very high standards of performance.
- In my work team, people don't seem to take much pride in their performance.
- In my work team, there is a feeling of pressure to continually improve our personal and team performance.
- Our management believes that no job is so well done that it couldn't be done better.

Interpreting Standards Scores

High Standards (75% and higher) normally drive high performance. High Standards scores are especially important to employees who have strong egos, are "self-starters," and who have high levels of achievement motivation. However, high Standards scores can be painful because people feel pressure to continually improve performance. A high Standards climate is no place for those who want to relax or rest on their laurels. It burns out many people, particularly if Structure and Support are below 50%. (Note: This dimension doesn't measure someone's personal or internal standards. It measures the sense of external standards presented by the organization.)

Moderate Standards (45% to 60%) indicate less pressure. Management still has high expectations, but the sense of pressure is not as relentless. This is the most effective range for most employees in most companies.

Low Standards (below 35%) are generally bad news. In a limited number of situations, they can be positively related to performance when the organization is made up of individual experts or contributors. In these cases (e.g., scientists, attorneys, or "old pros" who are "in a groove" and turn out excellent work no matter what) employees may feel the organization's performance expectations are irrelevant. Low Standards scores normally indicate that management tolerates poor performance and that mediocrity prevails in the organization.

Proposed AMZ Benchmark

AMZ should strive for a relatively high Standards climate profile in all of its businesses. Scores under 50% should be deemed to be unacceptable, and managers should aim at a Standards score of 65% or more. Most of AMZ's business units are subject to significant "uncontrollable" factors and this often encourages managers to feel helpless to impact bottom-line performance. A high Standards climate would counteract this lack of accountability. This is perhaps your most important climate management priority.

Improving Standards

There are basically three management strategies to improve Standards. First, leaders must set the bar higher, raise their expectations, and ask more of people. Often this involves working on Structure because lack of clarity is making it difficult for employees to know what is expected or when a good job has been done. The second strategy is less direct but more important. Leaders must give more performance feedback, and negative feedback must be included. Setting a high goal is only a start; people need to hear when they are falling short as well as when they are succeeding. (See our comments on Recognition, which should be read in conjunction with this advice.) At AMZ the tendency is to deal with poor performance in an indirect and insincere manner. This does little to raise the Standards of the organization. The third "to do" is related to the first two—get rid of underperforming people. Our research shows that the single biggest signal that a company has low Standards is its tolerance for deadwood, especially deadwood at the higher, more visible levels of management.

The specific management practices that have a positive impact on Standards are:

4. Setting challenging performance goals and standards.
5. Demonstrating personal commitment to achieving goals.
6. Giving your subordinates feedback on how they are doing their jobs.

Responsibility

Definition

The feeling employees have of "being their own boss," of not having to double-check all their decisions.

Specific Survey Items

- We don't rely too heavily on individual judgment in my work team; almost everything is double-checked.
- Management doesn't want me to check everything with them; if I think I've got the right approach, I just go ahead.
- You won't get ahead in my work team unless you stick your neck out and try things on your own.
- Our philosophy emphasizes that people should solve their problems by themselves.

Interpreting Responsibility Scores

High Responsibility (70% and higher) scores are positively correlated with high levels of performance in organizations that value and require individual initiative. High achievers are stimulated by high Responsibility. Along with the emphasis on entrepreneurial initiative, high levels of Responsibility are often associated with a certain amount of "ready-fire-aim" behavior. Although this works well in a high innovation and growth environment, it may not work as well in organizations that require close collaboration or complex, interdependent working relationships.

Moderate Responsibility (50% to 65%) may work for some highly regulated industries or where risk avoidance is more important than hitting home runs, especially if managers are new to their jobs.

Low Responsibility (below 35%) means that people don't feel they have freedom of action. Independence is discouraged. This can be associated with moderate to high levels of performance if employees are new (and need close supervision) or if the task requires zero defects (and, therefore, must be routinely double-checked). Generally, low levels of individual Responsibility demotivate people and discourage innovation and creativity. Low scores are hardly ever appropriate for top-management teams, but they can be tolerated at lower levels for short periods of time.

Proposed AMZ Benchmark

Most of your businesses should perform best with moderate to high Responsibility in the 60% to 70% range. Because of the current need for strategic and organizational change, some degree of restraint on independent action is desirable. However, your differentiation strategies will be most successfully implemented with high levels of this climate dimension between 70% and 80%.

Improving Responsibility

There is no one best way to improve this climate dimension. The most straightforward approach to increase feelings of Responsibility involves improving each manager's delegation practices. This, however, often proves difficult. Sometimes it is a skill issue (inexperienced managers don't know how to set objectives and let go of tasks). But more often it is a matter of risk aversion. Experienced managers hesitate to delegate and empower others because they fear that the work will be done incorrectly; or they claim they don't have the time to explain or train; or they have observed a pattern of poor performance whenever they let go; and so on. Improving Responsibility in such cases depends on a three-pronged strategy. First, coaching managers to create the proper framework for empowerment (making sure goals are clear, performance measures are understood and accepted, and people have the necessary skills and resources to do the job). Second, establish appropriate control systems so that managers can truly let go and still remain confident that mistakes will be corrected before they become disasters. Third, employees must be trained to *take* more responsibility. Often, this means hiring more skilled or more confident people, or breaking up old boss–subordinate relationships so that new, more empowering relationships can be built.

The specific practices that we know drive higher Responsibility scores are:

7. Encouraging your subordinates to initiate tasks or projects that they think are important.
8. Expecting your subordinates to find and correct their own errors rather than doing this for them.
9. Encouraging innovation and calculated risk taking in others.

Recognition

Definition

The feeling of being rewarded for a job well done with the emphasis placed on reward versus criticism and punishment.

Specific Survey Items

- In my work team the rewards and encouragements you get usually outweigh the threats and the criticisms.

- There is not enough reward and recognition given in my work team for doing good work.
- We have a promotion system here that helps the best people rise to the top.
- In my work team people are rewarded according to their job performance.

Interpreting Recognition Scores

High Recognition (65% and higher) is a vote of confidence in the company's performance management system. It means that people feel the "cream rises to the top" of the organization and that promotions are fair. It also means that the environment is generally upbeat and positive. It is not a measure of satisfaction with pay (one of the classic dimensions of traditional attitude surveys). Our research has yet to find a high-performing organization that has a sustained Recognition score below 50%. The fact is that people respond best to positive reinforcement, not punishment. High levels of Recognition require a great deal of time and attention to maintain. One rule of thumb might be, "the more boring the work, the higher the Recognition score needs to be."

Moderate Recognition (50% to 65%) is the most normal range. It shows a healthy "pay for performance" equation.

Low Recognition (40% and lower) is a signal that people feel unappreciated or that the performance management system is seriously flawed. Meritocracies motivate most people, and there is little evidence that low Recognition can support high performance. There is some evidence that, in organizations of professional experts (such as law firms or bench scientists), high levels of Recognition aren't necessary for high levels of performance. The logic seems to be similar to the logic we explained regarding Standards: Experts sometimes feel that formal performance management and extrinsic rewards are less meaningful than "doing a good job" or "serving the client." I would never let people benchmark Recognition below 50%. That would be saying a punitive climate works best, and we have tons of research to show this isn't the case.

Proposed AMZ Benchmark

I think you should benchmark your Recognition score for most of your business units in the moderate-to-high range between 55% and 65%. Although this is somewhat lower than many other high-performance climates, it reflects the realities faced by AMZ in the coming year. You are not in a high-growth mode. This restricts the amount of positive rewards you can dispense. Furthermore, I understand that the parent company has placed significant restrictions on your ability to implement incentive compensation programs deep into the organization. Until you have the ability to dramatically increase the "pay for performance" equation, Recognition will suffer.

Improving Recognition

Important starting points for improving Recognition are your performance appraisal and informal recognition practices. Appraisals need to be perceived as thorough, fair, and timely. All managers should be trained in day-to-day coaching tactics in order for them to develop habits of delivering candid feedback balanced with plenty of positive reinforcement. In the long term, the formal reward and promotions systems need to be adjusted so they more clearly support the idea that AMZ is a performance-driven meritocracy.

The specific management practices we focus on are:

10. Recognizing subordinates for good performance more often than criticizing them for poor performance.

11. Using recognition, praise, and other similar methods to reward subordinates for excellent performance.

12. Relating the total reward system (compensation, recognition, promotion) to the excellence of job performance rather than to other factors such as seniority, personal relationships, and so on.

Support

Definition

The feeling of trust and mutual support that prevails in the organization.

Specific Survey Items

- If you make a mistake in my work team, you don't get much sympathy.
- When I am doing a difficult job, I can usually count on getting assistance from my boss and co-workers.
- People in my work team don't really trust each other enough.
- I feel that I am a member of a well-functioning team.

Interpreting Support Scores

High Support (70% or higher) is related to high performance in organizations where collaboration and teamwork are required and expected. It is also correlated to performance in situations where close boss–subordinate relationships are needed. As companies downsize and reengineer their core processes, these attributes are becoming more, not less, important. Our Support dimension also picks up a measure of trust. We have had several clients question the use of the word *sympathy* in one of the Support items. Our research shows rather conclusively that the absence of sympathy from senior management leads to a "we–they attitude" and a lack of organizational cohesiveness and mutual trust.

    Moderate Support (45% to 60%) is the normal range for high-performing organizations. There is enough teamwork and trust to solve problems, but it's not so overly nurturing as to discourage individual responsibility.

    Low Support (35% and below) is not always a major performance inhibitor. Many operations work quite well without high degrees of mutual teamwork, trust, and support. For example, high-performing (and world-class) consulting organizations often score on the low end of our Support scale (usually not as low as 30% but often below 50%). Effective R&D organizations can also be relatively low in this dimension. Low Support generally means there is mistrust and cynicism in the air. These negative feelings, although not always blocking high levels of short-term performance, tend to be a longer-term demotivator.

Proposed AMZ Benchmark

The target level of Support should vary from business to business and from level to level at AMZ. I would recommend that it never fall below 50%, but the benchmark might be as high as 75% or 80% for those operations that have highly integrated work processes (such as one of your factories or one of your senior business teams). Support scores of 60% to 70% would be appropriate for most of your organizations. The benchmark level of Support will, in part, depend on the level of Responsibility required. High levels of independence (Responsibility) often conflict with high levels of Support, so trade-offs must be made. Standards also count. The higher the Standards benchmark is, the higher the Support benchmark should be. Pressure without Support leads to dissatisfaction, turnover, and low levels of sustainable performance.

Improving Support

The key to increasing the Support scores is effective coaching. Our research shows that close, open, and inclusive interpersonal relationships drive higher feelings of trust, teamwork, and support. Although training can have some impact on coaching practices, world-class companies make effective interpersonal skills one of their most important criteria for selection and promotion. AMZ should do the same.

The specific management practices that have the greatest impact on Support are:

13. Being supportive and helpful to subordinates in their day-to-day activities.
14. Going to bat for subordinates with your supervisors when you feel they are right.
15. Conducting monthly team meetings in a way that builds trust and mutual respect.

Commitment

Definition

The sense of pride employees have in belonging to the organization; the degree of commitment to the organization's goals.

Specific Survey Items

- Generally, I am highly committed to the goals of my work team.
- People take pride in belonging to my work team.
- I don't really care what happens to my work team.
- As far as I can see, there isn't much personal loyalty to my work team.

Interpreting Commitment Scores

High Commitment (70% and above) is positively correlated to high performance in organizations that are demanding and achievement oriented. Commitment is a measure of the bond between employees and the company and the strength of the psychological contract. High levels of this dimension, therefore, provide an organization with a reservoir of motivation and goodwill that can be drawn upon in difficult times. New ventures are most successful with scores in this range.

Moderate Commitment (50% to 60%) characterizes most high-performing companies. It means there is a healthy degree of loyalty bonding employees to the company, but it's not blind loyalty.

Low Commitment (below 35%) is a clear warning sign that employees are disaffected, discouraged, and demotivated. There are situations in which Commitment is not directly related to performance. For example, we have studied successful professional organizations (teachers, engineers, or technical experts) in which the loyalty of the professional employee runs more to the profession or the client than it does to the particular organization.

Proposed AMZ Benchmark

Given the demands that AMZ is currently placing on itself and its employees, I believe Commitment should be benchmarked at a high level of 65% or 70% for all of your business units. This will provide you with sufficient organizational "glue" to see you through the pain of the changes you are trying to implement.

Improving Commitment

It is seldom possible to work directly on improving Commitment. Higher Commitment scores are usually a function of working on the first five climate dimensions. For example, goals need to be clear (Structure), roles need to be clear (Responsibility), Standards must be perceived as being high, rewards must be worth something (Recognition), and people must want to be part of the team (Support). When all of this happens, climate scores for the list dimension will improve.

The two managerial strategies that most directly impact the feelings of employee commitment involve the demonstrated commitment of the leaders and the leaders' willingness to let employees participate in running things. The specific practices we use to drive commitment deal with these strategies:

16. Communicating excitement and enthusiasm about the work.

17. Involving people in setting goals.

18. Encouraging subordinates to participate in making important decisions.

Appendix IV

The Climate Survey Feedback and Planning Guide

Introduction

This *Feedback and Planning Guide* is designed to help you interpret your climate survey data and to help you make plans to improve your personal effectiveness. Although it will not require a great deal of your time, completing the guide is an important activity. It is your personal property, and the data it contains are confidential; only you will see its contents.

Benchmark Setting

Introduction

Organizational climate is the set of perceptions shared by people in the organization about how things are run and how they feel about the organization as a place to work. This worksheet is provided to help you determine what type of organizational climate is *necessary or required* for your work unit to function effectively. Certain aspects of organizational life place demands on the work unit and, in turn, create requirements for different types of climate.

> the *strategy* you are attempting to implement
>
> the *people* who work for you
>
> the *nature of the work* performed
>
> the *organizational context* in which you work

I. Sizing Up Your Organization's Strategy

The work climates of high-performing organizations fit or match the business priorities and strategies of the organization. Think about what your work group or organization is trying to do. Think about how it will "win the game" it is playing. The following eight areas are meant to stimulate your thinking about strategy. Although they are not an all-inclusive description of strategy, they will help you determine which dimensions of organizational climate should be emphasized.

STRATEGIC EMPHASIS	CLIMATE REQUIREMENTS
1. Innovation and Individual Initiative	■ *Lower* Structure ■ *Lower* Responsibility
2. Disciplined Execution	■ *Lower* Recognition ■ *Higher* Commitment
3. Technology and/or Process Excellence	■ *Higher* Structure ■ *Higher* Standards
4. Personal or "High-Touch" Service	■ *Higher* Recognition ■ *Higher* Support
5. Speed and Overall Efficiency	■ *Higher* Structure ■ *Higher* Support
6. Quality and Customized Products or Services	■ *Higher* Responsibility ■ *Higher* Recognition
7. Clarity and Consistency of Effort	■ *Higher* Structure ■ *Higher* Commitment
8. Flexibility and Ability to Change Quickly	■ *Lower* Structure ■ *Higher* Responsibility

II. Sizing Up Your People

High-performing organizations have climates that complement the needs of the employees of the organization. Your benchmarks for each climate dimension, therefore, should be established with these needs in mind. Think about the climate that would best motivate your people. Think about their personalities, likes and dislikes, experience levels, and skills. The following questions should help you size up your people and the climate profile that best suits them.

1. How experienced or skilled are they?

Highly Skilled	⟶	*Higher* Responsibility
Very Experienced		*Lower* Structure
Learning New Skills	⟶	*Higher* Structure
Less Experienced		*Lower* Responsibility

2. How entrepreneurial, ambitious, and competitive are they?

Driven to Succeed   ⟶   *Higher* Standards
                                            Lower Responsibility

More Collaborative   ⟶   *Higher* Recognition
and Less Competitive   *Higher* Support

3. How important are relationships and social needs?

Relationships Are   ⟶   *Higher* Recognition
Very Important   *Higher* Support

More Concerned About   ⟶   *Higher* Standards
Results Than People   *Higher* Commitment

4. How concerned are they about status and being "in control?"

High Needs for Control   ⟶   *Higher* Structure
                                            Lower Responsibility

More Relaxed About Power; ⟶   *Higher* Recognition
Willing to Follow Others   *Higher* Support

III. Sizing Up the Nature of the Work

The best climate profile fits or matches the work to be performed by the members of the organization. Think about the different jobs in your work group. Think about what kind of environment would be best suited to these jobs. The following guidelines should help you think through the relationship between the nature of the work and climate.

WHEN THE WORK:	THE CLIMATE REQUIRES HIGHER:
▪ Is routine	▪ Structure
▪ Is able to be programmed	▪ Responsibility
▪ Requires discipline	▪ Commitment
▪ Has "one best way"	

WHEN THE WORK:	THE CLIMATE REQUIRES HIGHER:
▪ Is highly variable	▪ Responsibility
▪ Can't be predicted or programmed	▪ Support
▪ Requires creativity	▪ Commitment
▪ Has no "one best way"	

IV. Sizing Up the Organizational Context

Your climate benchmarks need to be established with a realistic appreciation of what's possible, given the organization's history and resources. Think about the kind of climate that *can* be created with your existing resources, not just an ideal climate that would be impossible to establish. The following four questions should get you started.

1. Which climate dimensions have *historically* been the strongest?
2. Which dimensions seem to "fit" most naturally with the *leadership styles* of the top managers of the organization?
3. Which dimensions seem to match those of your organization's *strongest competitors* (and, therefore, are proven to work in your industry)?
4. Which dimensions do you *personally* feel most comfortable emphasizing?

Instructions

In the space provided below, draw the climate profile you feel is *required* for consistent, high levels of organizational performance. Benchmark each of the six climate dimensions based on the size-up you have just completed.

Climate Benchmarks

% 100 80 60 40 20 0					% 100 80 60 40 20 0
Structure	Standards	Responsibility	Recognition	Support	Commitment

Organizational Climate

Climate Feedback

Organizational Climate Profile

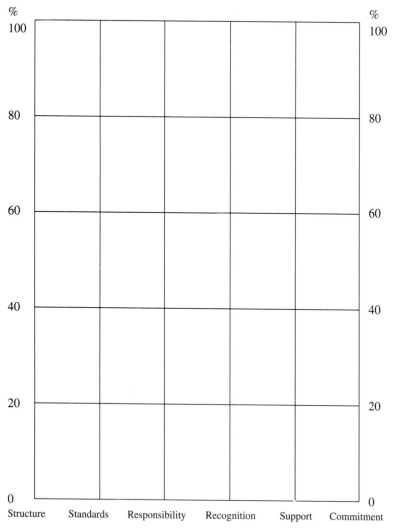

Climate Data Analysis

---

1. What are your reactions to the climate feedback?

2. What are the biggest "gaps" between your benchmarks and the actual scores?

3. Are there any surprises? If so, what are they?

4. What issues seem to be in the data? What are the possible causes?

ISSUES	POSSIBLE CAUSES

Management Practices

Management Practices Feedback

Practices That Impact the Performance Dimensions

STRUCTURE	YOUR SCORES
1. Establishing clear specific performance goals for your subordinates' jobs.	_____
2. Clarifying who is responsible for what within the group.	_____
3. Making sure tasks and projects are clearly understood when they are assigned.	_____

STANDARDS	
4. Setting challenging performance goals and standards for your subordinates.	_____
5. Demonstrating personal commitment to achieving goals.	_____
6. Giving subordinates feedback on how they are doing on their jobs.	_____

RESPONSIBILITY	
7. Encouraging your subordinates to initiate tasks or projects that they think are important.	_____
8. Expecting your subordinates to find and correct their own errors rather than doing this for them.	_____
9. Encouraging innovation and calculated risk taking in others.	_____

Practices That Impact the Development Dimensions

RECOGNITION	YOUR SCORES
10. Recognizing subordinates for good performance more often than criticizing them for poor performance.	_____
11. Using recognition, praise, and other similar methods to reward subordinates for excellent performance.	_____
12. Relating the total reward system (compensation, recognition, promotion) to the excellence of job performance rather than to other factors such as seniority, personal relationships, and so on.	_____

SUPPORT	
13. Being supportive and helpful to subordinates in their day-to-day activities.	_____
14. "Going to bat" for subordinates with your supervisors when you feel your subordinates are right.	_____

15. Conducting team meetings in a way that builds trust and mutual respect. _____

COMMITMENT

16. Communicating excitement and enthusiasm about the work. _____
17. Involving people in setting goals. _____
18. Encouraging subordinates to participate in making important decisions. _____

Practices Analysis

Use the following charts to identify significant themes in your data from among the highest- and lowest-rated practices. Then determine what actions you'll take to address them.

My Leadership Strengths (Highest Scores)

No.	Practice	%

My Leadership Weaknesses (Lowest Scores)

No.	Practice	%

Initial Thoughts to Improve My Leadership Effectiveness

Action Planning

Action Planning

In the space below, describe the *three issues or problems* that are highlighted by the climate and practices feedback you have received. Then list the *immediate actions* you can take to address each issue.

ISSUE 1	ACTION ITEMS

ISSUE 2	ACTION ITEMS

ISSUE 3	ACTION ITEMS

Feedback Meeting

Introduction

One of the most important decisions you will make with regard to the data you received is how to share them with your employees. We recommend that you conduct a meeting to discuss your group's climate and your management practices.

Before you begin planning, consider the following guidelines.

- Your people *expect* to hear something from you. They completed questionnaires and, at a minimum, you should thank them for the effort.

- Your report is your *personal property*. You need not show it to anyone. Yet, if you want to implement changes in your unit's climate or in your use of certain leadership practices, you will need your team's support. Sharing the data in a feedback meeting is an excellent way to begin gaining such support.

- *Plan* your approach.

  - Decide whether and how to involve your boss.
  - Think about what to share with your team; generally choose *issues* arising from the data rather than actual numbers; select discussion items you and your people will feel comfortable discussing.
  - Decide who will attend the meeting. Invite all team members, even if not all of them participated in the survey.
  - Consider how to handle meeting logistics; be sure you and your employees will have enough time for a meaningful discussion.

- *Prepare* for the meeting carefully.

  - Identify your own objectives and prepare an agenda.
  - Consider scripting your opening remarks to ensure clarity and correct understanding.
  - Consider what questions you will ask your people to obtain their insights and clarification. Avoid questions that seem judgmental or accusatory. Instead, ask open-ended questions, take notes, and respond nondefensively.

- *Don't overwhelm your people* with jargon or data. Unless they are familiar with the concepts used in the climate survey you should plan to talk to them in everyday language.

- *Collect more data during the meeting.* Ask for clarification of the "messages" you received via the feedback report. Consider asking your team for their views of the *importance* of specific practices, and use this to test your own improvement priorities.

- *Don't simply "announce" your action plan.* In discussion, try to confirm or modify your initial priorities, and remain open to new ideas and suggestions.

- *Plan realistically for what you can accomplish during the feedback meeting.* Work to raise and get help on a limited number of worthwhile issues. If there are many major issues you'd like to discuss, start with a small number of manageable ones. The others can be addressed in later meetings.

Appendix V

The Practices Resource Guide

This booklet will help you interpret your management practices feedback and provide you with ideas for raising your scores. The comments found in this resource guide were collected from clients (both managers and subordinates) and other consultants.

A page is dedicated to each of the 18 management practices that were in Part II of the climate questionnaire. Once you have determined which practice you want to try and improve, turn to the specific page for that practice.

- On the top of each page you will find a list of "work habits," behaviors, or attitudes that *might* lead a person to mark you low on that practice. Hopefully, this list will help you think more objectively about your leadership style and give you hints about what your subordinates "see" (or what led them to score you the way they did on the climate survey).

- The bottom half of each page contains ideas for specific corrective actions that ought to help you raise your scores. These are general suggestions. You will need to adapt and tailor them to your situation. Once again, these ideas for action are meant to stimulate your thinking; they are certainly not guaranteed prescriptions for managerial effectiveness.

The suggestions in this resource guide can be shared with the members of your work group and used as part of your climate improvement plan.

1. Establishing Clear, Specific Performance Goals for Your Subordinates' Jobs

A Low Score May Indicate:

- You don't sit down with your subordinates and develop annual or periodic goals.
- You aren't spending adequate time explaining the details you expect from subordinates.
- You are assuming your subordinates know what you want and toward which goals they should be working.
- What you say is important differs substantially from week to week (or project to project).
- You never write out performance objectives.
- You have articulated only vague or general goals.
- You are very "hands off," forcing subordinates to create their own performance goals and plans.

Ideas for Action:

1. Meet with each subordinate on a regularly scheduled basis to develop and review specific objectives and accountabilities. Ask detailed questions to measure progress. If questions arise, provide guidance and direction.
2. Make sure subordinates know exactly what you mean when you say you want "the job done well."
3. Quantify your expectations and your standards of performance as much as possible. Create a written set of performance objectives for each of your subordinates.
4. See if you and your subordinates can complete this sentence for all major project assignments: "The primary goal of this project/assignment is . . ."
5. Focus on deadlines for subordinates' work. On major tasks or long-term projects, set up intermediate "benchmark" deadlines.
6. Ask subordinates to create a written goal statement for each of their major accountabilities. If these aren't what you expected, meet privately with each subordinate to discuss and refine the goals.

2. Clarifying Who Is Responsible for What Within the Group

A Low Score May Indicate:

- People are overwhelmed by the pace of change in the organization. They are confused or anxious.
- You have a number of *new* players on the team. Roles and relationships need to be sorted out.
- Lines of authority and responsibility are confusing and you are unwilling or unable to clarify things.
- You aren't sorting out projects and helping people understand their jobs.
- You give the same task or assignment to two different people.
- You tend to be "action oriented" and don't take the time to sort out organizational overlaps, duplications, and so on. (When subordinates bring those to your attention, you are likely to say things "just make it happen. . . .")
- There are few, if any, written job descriptions or accountability statements that describe what people really do in your work group.

Ideas for Action:

1. Prepare an Authority–Responsibility Chart for major initiatives. Identify who has primary responsibility for doing each task (use a circle) and who is responsible for providing support or advice (use a square). Then indicate who has what kind of decision-making authority: final authority to make decisions about that task (use an "F"), review authority—the right to review the work or give input but not actually make the final decision (use an "R"), and veto or approval authority—the right to overturn or approve someone else's decision (use a "V"). Just trying to draw up this kind of chart should help the team clarify working relationships. A sample of a completed chart is on page 266.

2. Publish an organization chart for your work group that includes a brief description of each person's duties and responsibilities.

3. Ask your subordinates to identify areas of organizational overlap or confusion. Clarify each area that is mentioned.

Project: XYZ

Team Members ↓	Critical Tasks ⟶					
	1	2	3	4	5	Etc.
A	R	(F)			R	
B	V		R	(F)		
C	R	R		(F)		
Etc.						

4. If the nature of your group's work requires that peoples' responsibilities and job assignments frequently change, establish mechanisms to resolve the confusions and conflicts that arise. For example, use weekly staff meetings, regular one-on-one sessions with you, or encourage subordinates to work out such conflicts with each other.

———

3. Making Sure Tasks and Projects Are Clearly and Thoroughly Explained and Understood When They Are Assigned

A Low Score May Indicate:

- You have people who are new and are in need of a more directive and "hands-on" management approach.
- You don't take the time to explain what you want.
- You tend to overload people with too many projects and fail to clarify which ones are most important.
- You don't ask for feedback (e.g., "is that perfectly clear?") when you give an assignment to your subordinates.
- You have too many ideas; you are always giving your subordinates "ideas" and they often assume these are "instructions."
- You give the same assignments to different subordinates and don't explain why or how these people should coordinate with each other.
- Your group is understaffed and people are stretched too thin.

Ideas for Action:

1. Meet for 30 minutes with each subordinate to review his or her assignments and answer any questions that arise.
2. When giving assignments, pause and ask for feedback. For example, ask the subordinate to repeat your instructions. Then go over those aspects of the assignment that are most troublesome.
3. Whenever possible, write out the key tasks involved and the overall objectives of projects assigned to subordinates.
4. Ask subordinates to give you a brief project plan before they undertake an assignment. Use this to clarify areas of potential confusion.
5. Have more frequent meeting with subordinates and ask for project updates. This will give you an "early warning system" to identify missed or confusing assignments.
6. Slow down. Don't give important assignments "on the run."

---

4. Setting Challenging Performance Goals and Standards for Your Subordinates

A Low Score May Indicate:

- People don't know what your expectations and standards really are.
- You are overly lenient and forgiving when subordinates miss deadlines, turn in sloppy or incomplete work, or otherwise underperform.
- You fail to set high personal standards and act as a role model for your subordinates.
- You establish conflicting goals or send mixed messages about what you want.
- You are seen as reserved, quiet, or withdrawn and people have difficulty reading you.
- You set standards that appear to be impossible to achieve.
- You "undersell" or underestimate the capabilities of your people.

Ideas for Action:

1. Be more open and spontaneous with your people. Engage them more in discussions about the work, their performance, and your personal goals.

2. Clarify your expectations. Review the goals and performance standards for each of your subordinates.

3. Ask your subordinates where there is waste of inefficiency in your operations, and how this waste can be eliminated. Act on all of their ideas that make sense.

4. Be more demanding. Tighten up budgets and deadlines. Don't accept below-standard work. Insist that subordinates improve their work habits.

5. Meet with your subordinates to discuss specific goals and standards for each of their key projects. Summarize these in writing and use this summary as a control system to measure progress.

6. Have more frequent performance review sessions. Use these sessions to clarify and reiterate your expectations.

7. Don't hand out gratuitous praise. When performance is poor, make sure you clearly communicate your opinion and insist on improvement.

---

5. Demonstrating Personal Commitment to Achieving Goals

A Low Score May Indicate:

- You are preoccupied and don't seem to consistently care about achieving some of your group's goals.

- You don't seem to be very enthusiastic about the work or the goals of your group.

- You aren't translating formal goals and objectives into personal challenges. You're not personalizing your group's performance targets.

- You are perceived to be lazy and lack a high sense of urgency about your group's work.

- Your behavior doesn't match your words. You aren't acting as a role model (e.g., you show up late for meetings, you leave work early, etc.).

- You accept failure too easily.
- You don't push yourself or your people to "be the best." You seem to settle for less than top performance.

Ideas for Action:

1. Be positive and enthusiastic about achieving goals; avoid pessimistic remarks about organizational roadblocks affecting achievement of your goals; avoid sarcasm when talking about performance problems, inadequate work performed by others, and so on. Frequently ask subordinates how you can help, and remain as positive as you sincerely can about the achievement of goals.

2. Discuss organizational goals frequently, and reinforce their importance in day-to-day contact with your people.

3. Be aware of the *symbolic* nature of your actions. Strive to show others how personally important goals are by making highly visible and symbolic gestures (e.g., showing up on a weekend to work on a project, etc.).

4. Exhibit the kind of behavior you would want your subordinates to exhibit, particularly in times of stress or pressure.

5. Publicly state your commitment to your group's goals, emphasizing the negative consequences if the goals aren't achieved, as well as the benefits of goal accomplishment.

6. Increase the number of visible rewards (e.g., wall charts, recognition programs) so that everyone can see how you feel about what counts.

---

6. Giving Subordinates Feedback on How They Are Doing on Their Job

A Low Score May Indicate:

- You are too distant and removed from the day-to-day work your people do.
- What feedback you give is too general ("nice job") rather than specific and clear ("I especially liked . . .").
- You don't test to see if subordinates understand what you're saying when you discuss their work or their performance.

- You send mixed messages; your subordinates don't know what your feelings or opinions about their work really are.
- You never put feedback in writing.
- Your feedback is too brief and/or too infrequent.
- You *assume* that subordinates already know how they are doing and how you evaluate their performance.

Ideas for Action:

1. Meet for 20 minutes with a subordinate and provide him or her with an unambiguous and candid assessment of performance.

2. Ask subordinates how they think they are doing. State your own point of view. Then discuss openly with your people the *quality* of your feedback and ask for suggestions about improving it.

3. Collect performance data throughout the formal review cycle. Keep individual files updated with relevant letters, memos, and notes. These data should be as objective as possible. Be sure that similar documentation is kept for *all* subordinates— avoid the appearance of singling out certain ones.

4. Plan for time in your own schedule to give subordinates more frequent ongoing performance feedback; establish checkpoints during task or project planning at which your people will expect to sit down with you and review their performance and progress.

5. Prepare for each performance discussion; be able to provide concrete examples of good performance (specific things that subordinates did well and that you want them to keep doing) and concrete examples of performance that needs improvement. Discussion of poor performance should be clear, without fuzziness, or hinting. If possible, provide subordinates with specific ideas on how to perform more effectively next time.

6. When performance problems come to your attention, verify that they are real before taking action. As a first step, get the facts, and make sure your information is accurate, complete, and without exaggeration.

7. Make sure your formal performance appraisal discussions are consistent with the informal feedback you have provided to subordinates. Ask your subordinates if *they* feel inconsistencies exist and be prepared to openly discuss such matters.

7. Encouraging Your Subordinates to Initiate Tasks or Projects They Think Are Important

A Low Score May Indicate:

- Innovation is not viewed as a priority in your work group.
- You do not delegate enough decision-making authority.
- Your subordinates are afraid to take any initiative without your explicit approval.
- You are too detailed in your instructions and discourage people from taking any liberty.
- You are overcontrolling and overmanaging. People feel you don't trust their judgment; only your ideas count.
- When subordinates try things on their own, you are not supportive.
- You try to "fill up" each subordinate's work day with your projects rather than allowing subordinates to manage their own time.
- There are too many rules in the workplace. People feel over-regulated and constrained.

Ideas for Action:

1. Sit down with subordinates and review the projects they are currently working on and those they would like to work on. Develop a list of activities and projects *they* feel are top priority. See how many items can be approved and made part of your subordinates' responsibilities.
2. Ask yourself if you have set up a system where your people can be effective without your intervention. Don't "smoke your own exhaust"; check to see that:

   - You have the right people matched to tasks and projects.
   - You have early warning systems to alert you to major problems without your having to look over your people's shoulders.
   - You have provided your subordinates with all needed information and have answered all of their questions.
   - You aren't holding back the real decision-making authority or all the most interesting parts of the work.

3. Examine the kinds of decisions you and your subordinates must make on a day-to-day basis to be successful; also consider less frequent decisions (perhaps larger in their implications) that must be made. Define yourself the decisions you feel you must make, those your people can make alone, and those on which you must work together. If possible, test your conclusions with your subordinates to be sure your analysis is consistent with their views.

4. Communicate to your people which decisions you want to be involved in and which you feel they must handle alone. Set up a consistent, simple process for handling routine decisions (e.g., as part of a weekly staff meeting) and implement it. Refuse to deviate from the process without strong reasons, and insist your people follow it.

5. Once in a while, "get out of the way." Let subordinates do a task from start to finish without *any* intervention on your part.

6. Set a date for follow-ups with subordinates and make sure to leave them alone until that date.

---

8. Expecting Your Subordinates to Find and Correct Their Own Errors Rather Than Doing This for Them

A Low Score May Indicate:

- You are impatient; you can't wait for results and constantly nag subordinates.

- Your standards are much higher than those of your subordinates.

- You have special knowledge or experience about doing the work and this leads you to be overly intrusive and directive.

- You ask for frequent progress reports, updates, status reports, and so on, and your subordinates feel you don't trust them to monitor their own performance.

- You like to meddle; you enjoy being personally involved in the details of your subordinates' work.

- You don't have confidence in your people. You feel they will let poor-quality work go by.

- You don't have an understood and accepted management control process in place. Performance requirements are unclear, thus forcing you to personally supervise all aspects of your subordinates' work.

Ideas for Action:

1. Spell out your expectations and performance standards clearly. Put them in writing.
2. Once you have done this, "let go." Allow your subordinates to deliver the results you've called for but give them the freedom to do it their way (not just your way).
3. Force yourself to *not* ask for frequent updates and progress reports. Ask your people when *they* want to review performance and negotiate a mutually acceptable monitoring system.
4. Tell your subordinates the kind of errors that concern you the most. Then step back and allow them to "self-correct" for 60 or 90 days. Challenge them to find and correct 100% of the important errors.
5. Take a vacation. Physically "back off" for a while and see if your subordinates respond by doing high-quality work.
6. Use teams more often. Delegate some of your supervisory responsibilities to members of these teams. Step aside and let team members do the problem solving.
7. Identify your most trusted subordinate and have him or her do more supervising of the technical or project work. This tactic may increase everyone's sense of responsibility.

---

9. Encouraging Innovation and Calculated Risk Taking in Others

A Low Score May Indicate:

- You believe that most of the new ideas required for success come from people other than your direct reports.
- You emphasize zero defects and are viewed as having a low tolerance for mistakes of any kind.

- Goals and performance standards are unclear and people don't understand the parameters or boundaries within which they can take risks.

- Innovation is not a priority—for you or your organization.

- You have punished or criticized people in the past for deviating from established practice or suggesting new ideas.

- People feel overworked, underbudgeted, and generally so "stretched" that there is little opportunity to innovate.

- You have too many ideas. Your aggressive innovativeness discourages others from pushing their own new ideas.

Ideas for Action:

1. Identify and review with subordinates areas where the risks of experimenting with new ideas and creative approaches are acceptable and/or where group performance is most in need of improvement. Discuss the consequences of failure and mistakes in the different areas in which your group works, and differentiate between the mistakes that are catastrophic, those that are regrettable, and those that are tolerable.

2. Specify areas (using the preceding analysis) in which subordinates may act freely to try new ideas or resolve performance problems. Clarify your own role in this process and the actual amount of freedom you want subordinates to have. Define the approval process, if any, you want them to follow.

3. Publicly emphasize the need for innovation and risk taking. Tie this back to your organization's key objectives and strategy (just saying it isn't enough!).

4. Praise the next person who tries something new and *fails*. Go out of your way to avoid criticizing when your people deviate from normal practices.

5. Hold a meeting to identify areas where your operations need to be changed or where innovations would add the most value. Use this information to put appropriate boundaries around innovation and risk taking.

6. Give out a monthly or quarterly reward for the "best new idea." Publicize the first few rewards so that people better understand your support for new ideas.

10. Recognizing Subordinates More Than Criticizing

A Low Score May Indicate:

- You are overly critical.
- Your performance standards are so high that your subordinates rarely, if ever, meet your expectations.
- When you praise a subordinate, you always add a "but. . . ."
- You are unaware of what's involved in doing good work at the level below you. Your subordinates, therefore, feel you don't appreciate their performance.
- Your positive reinforcement is not timely (it's too late).
- You only dole out rewards when you have to.
- All your rewards are formal and structured, never spontaneous and informal.
- Your impatience and dissatisfaction with some of your subordinates' performance are widely known. Your criticism tends, therefore, to be more public than your recognition.

Ideas for Action:

1. Make a point to provide positive feedback to each of your subordinates once a week for the next month. You may praise their effort, the results they've achieved, a past success, whatever—but find a genuine reason to recognize each subordinate.

2. Clarify your performance expectations. Have a candid discussion with each subordinate about his or her current level of performance so that realistic reward criteria are developed.

3. Avoid always having to "raise the bar" by finding something wrong. Be more accepting and communicate more unadulterated positive recognition.

4. Spread positive recognition around as much as possible. When the group does good work, try to make everyone feel good about it.

5. Keep your criticism private. Avoid critical public comments about a person's individual performance.

6. Find "winners" as often as possible. Publicly recognize and reward these people.

7. Spend more time with your people. Be more social—don't always talk about work or performance issues. Try to build *personal* bonds with your subordinates.

---

11. Using Recognition, Praise, and Other Methods to Reward Subordinates for Excellent Performance

A Low Score May Indicate:

- You rely only on the formal reward system (salary, bonus, promotions) and underleverage informal rewards.
- You fail to discriminate and single out truly excellent performance.
- There is little informal interaction between you and your people.
- You are out of touch or unaware of your subordinates' performance.
- You are aloof. You aren't perceived to be an enthusiastic supporter of your people.
- Your standards are very high. Your subordinates feel you are never satisfied.
- Nobody who reports to you has ever done excellent work.
- You don't hold enough team meetings, or the meetings you hold are too informal. There are too few opportunities for informal conversations.

Ideas for Action:

1. Clarify expectations of rewards with your people. Make them aware of policies and guidelines, and try to provide them with a realistic perspective on what rewards they can expect.

2. Brainstorm creative nonmonetary rewards you could use effectively with your people. Examples include:

   - Providing lunches/dinners for high performers, project teams, and so on.
   - Awarding plaques, certificates or small gifts to mark significant achievements.

- Assignment of special projects that carry high visibility and/or responsibility.
- Informing senior managers (through memos, casual conversations, etc.) of subordinate's effective performance; copying the subordinate on such memos.
- Nominating high performers for special developmental experiences; allowing them to represent the work unit as conferences, and so on.

3. Identify employee preferences and, when possible, gear rewards to them.
4. Apply nonmonetary rewards consistently, and handle them seriously, as you would a salary increase or promotion. The award itself may be fun or lighthearted, but don't let subordinates lose sight of the fact that it is, in fact, recognition for high performance and that you and the company value and reward high performers.
5. Provide unusual rewards such as parties or special meetings to attract attention to top performers.
6. Make sure rewards are deserved, not just blowing hot air. Otherwise people will learn to ignore what you say.

---

12. Relating the Total Reward System (Compensation, Recognition, Promotion) to the Excellence of Job Performance Rather Than Other Factors

A Low Score May Indicate:

- You play favorites.
- Deadwood is tolerated and poor performers seem to be rewarded in your organization.
- There is a weak "pay for performance" norm operating in your organization.
- Your subordinates feel that the wrong people have been promoted.
- The criteria for rewards and recognition are not understood and accepted.
- You are spending an inordinate amount of time with a few of your subordinates, making the others feel less important.

- You are perceived to be overly conservative and set in your ways.
- You are too formal. Everything is "by the book" and people don't feel you care enough to "break the rules" to recognize outstanding effort or performance.

Ideas for Action:

1. Provide each of your subordinates with a detailed explanation of your organization's compensation and promotion policies and practices. Allow time for a discussion. If there are questions you can't answer, see that someone from the personnel department provides an answer.

2. Go out of your way to explain the reasons why people are promoted. Avoid "badmouthing" or criticizing newly promoted people or "the system" that promoted them.

3. Be aggressive and unrelenting in upgrading your organization. Remove or demote people who are consistently underperforming and who can't be developed. Create improvement plans for underachievers who have potential.

4. Make sure you spend adequate personal time with each of your subordinates. Avoid the appearance of having favorites.

5. Fight hard to see that your group gets its fair share of organizational rewards. Let your subordinates know that you intend to "pay for performance."

6. Work with human resources to find ways to reward your high performers. Brainstorm with them both formal and informal recognition programs.

7. Try using more team or group rewards. Try letting the group have a voice in distributing rewards. Sometimes they will discriminate more effectively than you will.

---

13. Being Supportive and Helpful to Subordinates in Their Day-to-Day Activities

A Low Score May Indicate:

- You seem to be unavailable when important questions or issues arise.

- You think people learn best when it's "trial by fire." You've let them burn one too many times.
- You are "too busy" and discourage your subordinates from "wasting your time on minor matters."
- When interacting with subordinates, you do all the talking, always dealing with your agenda and not theirs.
- You fail to ask subordinates what help or assistance they want.
- You are removed from your subordinates' day-to-day activities and *can't* provide the help they require.
- You duck tough questions, letting subordinates take the flak on the assumption you can always fix it up later.

Ideas for Action:

1. When someone asks for help, provide it, but then make a point of asking whether they feel helped.
2. Examine each of your subordinate's technical competence and emotional makeup; list each of your subordinate's strengths and weaknesses, and review his or her general self-confidence, independence, and so on.
3. If possible, ask the subordinate how he or she likes to work best (e.g., closely supervised, at arm's length, etc.). Then ask the subordinate to assess the kinds of support he or she wants from you.
4. Agree to provide the amount and kind of support your subordinates need but only to the extent you have time to do so and are comfortable in doing so. Do not commit to amounts and types of coaching that are unrealistic or, for whatever reason, unlikely to occur. Clarify what you will provide to the subordinate and when; assist the subordinate in finding other kinds of help (training, counseling, etc.) you are unable or unwilling to provide.
5. Periodically test the level of coaching and support you're providing and increase or decrease as necessary. For example, when assigning a new task or project, ask routinely what you can do to help. Review the level of support you provide to more experienced people to be certain you're not overmanaging them.
6. Get around the office regularly. Be available in an informal way.

14. "Going to Bat" for Subordinates with Your Supervisors When You Feel Your Subordinates Are Right

A Low Score May Indicate:

- Your subordinates don't believe you will aggressively stand up for their interests.
- You are overly political.
- You shy away from unpopular positions and are prone to go along with what your superiors want.
- The quality of your relationships with your manager and the higher-ups in the organization is unclear or unknown to your subordinates.
- You have failed to explain the reasons *why* you haven't actively supported your subordinates' positions.
- Your subordinates feel very strongly about one or more issues and you seem to be standing on the sidelines or uncommitted.

Ideas for Action:

1. Meet with your subordinates in order to identify those issues where your advocacy is important. In this meeting, concentrate on listening, not defending a point of view or explaining *why* something can't be done.
2. Communicate fully the reasons why you haven't supported your subordinates' positions in the past.
3. Take the time to explain the boss's and the organization's strategies, priorities, and so on to your subordinates. Provide them with a context so your personal position is more understandable.
4. Be more open with your people. Give them more information about the decision-making process in the organization.
5. Be more of an advocate and a champion of your subordinates' ideas. Take more risks with the higher-ups in the company.
6. Allow your subordinates to deal directly with your supervisors. Give your people firsthand exposure to the business and political realities you deal with.

15. Conducting Team Meetings in a Way That Builds Trust and Mutual Respect

A Low Score May Indicate:

- You dominate meetings. You use meetings to push your own personal agenda and fail to let people participate.
- You pay inadequate attention to *process*; and seem concerned only about *content* or *results*.
- You don't hold frequent meetings.
- You never act as a facilitator in meetings by drawing out ideas from people, seeking a consensus, or moving the group on to other topics.
- You are overly critical in meetings. You criticize others or spend time arguing your own position or otherwise devaluing the ideas of others.
- You allow, or even encourage, conflicts and disputes to take up time in staff meetings.
- You tend to personalize arguments and problems, thus allowing discussions to become more focused on personalities than on results.

Ideas for Action:

1. Run more frequent meetings.
2. Run better meetings. Here are a few ideas:

   - Invite all relevant parties and check with invitees to be sure no one who ought to be present has been left out.
   - Set specific time limits, establish ground rules for debate on controversial topics (e.g., a prohibition on interrupting speakers or on sarcasm).
   - When appropriate, assign prework.
   - Stop the meeting from time to time and ask, "How are we doing? Where are we on the agenda?"
   - Consider using a facilitator to keep the conversation on track with the group's permission to refocus if the meeting starts to ramble.
   - As the meeting progresses, take notes (or have a recorder do so) of important points that are brought up.

- Note and restate action items (i.e., who will do what after the meeting) and any overall conclusions that are reached.
- Take time at the end of the meeting for an overall summary, and test to be sure the other participants agree with it.

3. Improve your understanding of each of your subordinate's objectives and personal issues. Try to be more sensitive to these in team meetings.

4. If team members have different goals, don't argue with them or pit one person against the other. Try to formulate *superordinate goals*, ones that transcend individual objectives. Focus people's attention on the importance of these overriding goals. Try to emphasize collaboration, not competition.

5. Play an active role in following up on decisions made in team meetings. Schedule additional meetings, talk to key people, and so on, as necessary to implement decisions in a timely manner.

16. Communicating Excitement and Enthusiasm About the Work

A Low Score May Indicate:

- You are very quiet and reserved.
- People don't know how you *feel* about the group's work or its performance.
- You are cynical. People view you as being frustrated and having a negative attitude.
- You are critical of some of the organization's past priorities and the decisions that its managers have made.
- You are new to the job and are seen as tentative and insecure.
- You are discouraged.
- Your subordinates believe they are giving 110% and you haven't provided adequate recognition and "pats on the back."
- People don't think you are committed to the goals of the organization.

- There are major strategic issues that are unresolved and you are seen as being in a "waiting" mode.

Ideas for Action:

1. Try to be more expressive.

2. Share your professional feelings with your subordinates. Tell them how important the organization's work is to you and how committed you are to achieving the organization's objectives.

3. Suggest new recognition programs that emphasize the importance of accomplishing results. These don't have to be highly structured or formal. Use these awards or events to restate your personal commitment to the organization's goals.

4. Allow yourself to get angry or emotional when you are disappointed about a person's performance. Let others know you have a *personal* stake in success or failure.

5. Assemble a group to formulate a "vision statement," a description of the collective aspirations of your management team. Paint an exciting picture of the organization's future. Show how each person's job fits into this vision. Communicate your own excitement about achieving the future vision.

6. Confront the strategic issues that you feel may be paralyzing the organization. Bring them out in the open and actively work to resolve them.

7. Look in the mirror—if you can't get more excited and committed about what you are doing, think about moving on.

8. Take a vacation. Sort out any personal problems or internal conflicts that might be getting in the way of your enthusiasm for the job.

17. Involving People in Setting Goals

A Low Score May Indicate:

- Individual or departmental goals are imposed on people from "above."
- People feel there aren't any clear goals.
- Goals are changed without involving people.
- You don't hold enough team meetings to discuss goals, work processes, or priorities.
- In goal-setting discussions, you do all of the talking.
- Your department's goals aren't properly coordinated with those of other groups or functions.
- You are so busy with other matters that you pay inadequate attention to goal setting and getting people's real input on goals and priorities.
- You are too formal. You seldom have informal discussions with people about the group's goals or strategies.

Ideas for Action:

1. Ask your people how they feel about their personal goals. Clarify those that appear vague or confusing. Encourage your people to contribute their point of view before finalizing each person's goals.
2. Before setting next year's (or next month's, etc.) goals, make sure you ask your people for their input and ideas.
3. Circulate a written summary of your departmental goals and ask people to comment. Ask your people which goals are unreasonable, which might be raised, and ask them to identify the biggest *barrier* to goal accomplishment.
4. Ask your people to set their own goals before providing them with your or the organization's input.
5. Make a point of "pushing back" against goals imposed on your group that you feel are inappropriate.
6. Encourage your people to openly communicate their ideas and feelings about individual and departmental goals.
7. Emphasize where goals are flexible and where they're not. Allow people to negotiate and discuss those goals and areas where there is flexibility. Be clear about areas where there is no flexibility.

18. Encouraging Subordinates to Participate in Making Important Decisions

A Low Score May Indicate:

- You push too hard for your own solution to problems.
- You intimidate your subordinates and they shy away from confronting you or arguing with you.
- You are perceived to be secretive. Many decisions are made behind closed doors and your subordinates are informed only after they have been finalized.
- Even when you discuss decisions and issues with your subordinates, they don't believe they have any real influence.
- Decisions you feel are unimportant are thought to be important by your people.
- One or more of your subordinates tend to dominate group meetings. This reduces others' sense of participation.
- You are too action oriented. In your desire to get things done, you are viewed as being autocratic and uninterested in others' opinions and input.

Ideas for Action:

1. Be much clearer in *explaining* your point of view and the reasoning behind your decisions and approach to problems. Ask subordinates to challenge your logic and reasoning.

2. Have a private discussion with key associates to test your understanding of their goals and their roles in your department. Think about the role you want each subordinate to play and how you impact their ability to accomplish their goals. Identify the areas of potential conflict and candidly discuss these (before the conflict erupts into "warfare").

3. Involve the right people as early as possible when major decisions must be made. If possible, involve everyone affected. If this is not possible, weigh the speed and efficiency of making the decision alone or in a small group with the need for "buy-in" and commitment among the rest of your people. (Obviously, if the decision has been forced on you from above or if your mind is already made up, you should avoid the pretense of involving others.)

4. Ask your subordinates to list the key issues facing your organization. Ask for their point of view on the decisions that must be made. Listen to other people's views and ideas encouragingly. Listen to everybody before making up your mind or allowing the group to evaluate any approach.

5. Clarify which decisions are more important and which are less important. Encourage your people to actively discuss these relative rankings.

6. Even if your people can't participate in making the decision, try to work through detailed action plans on important implementation issues with all involved.

7. Get in the habit of allowing more give-and-take in staff meetings. Don't let any one subordinate dominate discussions. Before closing off debate on an issue, make sure everyone who wants to contribute an idea has been heard.

References and Suggested Readings

Agryris, C. (1991). "Teaching smart people how to learn." *Harvard Business Review* 91301, May-June, 99–109.

Alexander, R. (1979). *Darwinism and human affairs.* Seattle: University of Washington Press.

Atkinson, J. W. (1958). *Motives in fantasy, action, and society.* Princeton, NJ: D. Van Nostrand Company.

Atkinson, J. W. (1964). *An introduction to motivation.* Princeton, NJ: D. Van Nostrand Company.

Atkinson, J. W. (1966). *A theory of achievement motivation.* New York: John Wiley & Sons.

Bandura, A. (1985). *Social foundations of thought and action.* Englewood Cliffs, NJ: Prentice Hall.

Bass, B. M., & Stogdill, M. (1990). *Handbook of leadership: theory, research, and managerial applications* (3rd ed.). New York: Free Press.

Braunstein, M., & Levine, E. (2000). *Deep branding on the Internet: Applying heat and pressure online to ensure a lasting brand.* Roseville, CA: Prima Publishing.

Collins, J. C., & Porras, J. I. (1995). *Built to last.* New York: HarperCollins.

Comer, J., & Edmonds, R. R. (1989). *Conversations between James Comer and Ronald Edmonds: Fundamentals of effective school improvement.* Dubuque, IA: Kendall/Hunt.

Conger, J., & Benjamin, B. (1999). *Building leaders.* San Francisco: Jossey-Bass.

Davis, S. M. (1984). *Managing corporate culture.* Cambridge, MA: Ballinger.

Deal, T. E., & Kennedy, A. A. (1982). *Corporate cultures.* Reading, MA: Addison-Wesley.

Deci, E. L. (1975). *Intrinsic motivation.* New York: Plenum Press.

Deci, E. L. (1995). *Why we do what we do.* New York: Penguin Books.

Eccles, R. G., & Nohria, N. (1992). *Beyond the hype.* Boston: Harvard Business School Press.

Edmonds, R. R. (1981). Making public schools effective. *Social Policy.* September/October, 56–60.

Gardner, J. W. (1990). *On leadership.* New York: Free Press.

Goleman, D. (1995). *Emotional intelligence.* New York: Bantam.

Goleman, D. (1998). *Working with emotional intelligence.* New York: Bantam.

Grove, A. (1995). *High output management.* New York: Vintage Books.

Grove, A. S. (1983). *High output management.* New York: Random House.

Hamel, G. (2000). *Leading the revolution.* Boston: Harvard Business School Press.

Hamel, G., & Prahalad, C. K. (1994). *Competing for the future.* Boston: Harvard Business School Press.

Hargrove, R. (1995). *Masterful coaching.* San Francisco: Jossey-Bass.

Katzenback, J. R., & Smith, D. K. (1993). *The wisdom of teams.* Boston: Harvard Business School Press.

Kearns, D. T., & Nadler, D. A. (1992). *Prophets in the dark.* New York: Harper Books.

Kotter, J. P. (1988). *The leadership factor.* New York: Free Press.

Kotter, J. P. (1990). *A force for change: How leadership differs from management.* New York: Free Press.

Kotter, J. P., & Heskett, J. L. (1992). *Corporate culture and performance.* New York: Free Press.

Lawler, E. E. (1998). *Strategies for high performance organizations.* San Francisco: Jossey-Bass.

Lawrence, P., & Lorsch, J. (1967). *Organization and environment.* Boston: Harvard Business School Press.

Lawrence-Lightfoot, S. (1983). *The good high school.* New York: Basic Books.

Lewin, K. (1938). *The conceptual representation and the measurement of psychological forces.* Durham, NC: Duke University Press.

Litwin, G. H., & Stringer, R. A. (1968). *Motivation and organizational climate.* Boston: Harvard University Press.

Litwin, G., Bray, J., & Brooke, K. L. (1996). *Mobilizing the organization.* London: Prentice Hall.

Locke, E. A., & Latham, G. P. (1990). *A theory of goal setting and task performance.* Englewood Cliffs, NJ: Prentice Hall.

Lombardo, M. M., & Eichinger, R. W. (2001). *The leadership machine.* Minneapolis: Lominger Limited.

Lorsch, J. W. (1985). "Strategic Myopia: Culture as an Invisible Barrier to Change." In R. H. Kilman, M. J. Saxton, R. Serpa and Others, *Gaining control of the corporate culture.* San Francisco: Josey Bass.

McCall, M. W. (1998). *High flyers: Developing the next generation of leaders.* Boston: Harvard Business School Press.

McCall, M., Lombardo, M., & Morrison, A. (1988). *The lessons of experience.* Lexington, MA: Lexington Books.

McClelland, D. (1961). *The achieving society.* Princeton, NJ: D. Van Nostrand Company.

McClelland, D. (1975). *Power, the inner experience.* New York: Irvington Publishers.

McClelland, D. (1987). *Human motivation.* Cambridge, UK: Cambridge University Press.

McClelland, D., & Winter, D. (1969). *Motivating economic achievement.* New York: Free Press.

Mercer Delta Consulting. (1998). *Creating a High Performance Operating Environment: The Leadership Challenge.* New York.

Mercer Delta Consulting. (1998). *Teamwork at the Top: Designing and Leading Effective Executive Teams.* New York.

Nadler, D. A. (1998). *Champions of change.* San Francisco: Jossey-Bass.

Nadler, D. A., & Tushman, M. L. (1997). *Competing by design: The power of organizational architecture.* New York: Oxford University Press.

Nadler, D. A., & Spencer, J. L. (1998). *Executive teams.* San Francisco: Jossey-Bass.

O'Reilly, C. (1989). "Corporations, Culture and Commitment: Motivation and Social Control in Organizations." *California Management Review* 31/4, summer, 9–25.

Peters, T. J., & Waterman, R. H. (1982). *In search of excellence.* New York: Warner Books.

Schein, E. H. (1965). *Organizational psychology.* Englewood Cliffs, NJ: Prentice-Hall.

Schein, E. (1980). *Organizational psychology* (3rd ed.). Englewood Cliffs, NJ: Prentice-Hall.

Schein, E. (1992). *Organizational culture and leadership.* San Francisco: Jossey-Bass.

Schein, E. (1999). *The corporate culture survival guide.* San Francisco: Jossey-Bass.

Schneider, B. (Ed.). (1990). *Organizational climate and culture.* San Francisco: Jossey-Bass.

Stringer, R. A. with Uchenick, J. (1986). *Strategy traps and how to avoid them.* New York: Lexington Books.

Tagiuri, R., & Litwin, G. (1968). *Organizational climate: Explorations of a concept.* Boston: Harvard University Press.

Tannen, D. (1991). *You just don't understand.* New York: Morrow.

Thomas, K. W. (2000). *Intrinsic motivation at work.* San Francisco: Berrett-Kohler.

Tichy, N. M. (1997). *The leadership engine.* New York, NY: HarperCollins.

Tichy, N. M., & Devanna, M. A. (1986). *The transformation leader.* New York: John Wiley & Sons.

Tichy, N. M., & Sherman, S. (1993). *Control your destiny or someone else will.* New York: Doubleday, Currency.

Tornow, W. W., London, M., & CCL Associates. (1998). *Maximizing the value of 360-degree feedback.* San Francisco: Jossey-Bass.

Ulrich, D., Zenger, J., & Smallwood, W. N. (1999). *Results-based leadership.* Boston: Harvard Business School Press.

Index

Harshbarger, Scott, 87–89
Harvard Business School, 21, 53
Harvard Graduate School of Education, 180
Health care organizations, 184–203
    climate survey for, 191–192
    commitment at, 199–201
    conflicting missions for, 186–187
    economics at, 187
    high touch environment at, 188–189
    integrated delivery network at, 190–191
    intervention in, 201–202
    lack of control at, 187
    leadership challenges at, 189–190
    level and quality of services at, 187
    prognosis for, 202–203
    recognition at, 196–198
    reducing defections in, 211
    responsibility at, 195–196
    role diversity at, 188
    speed or pace of activities, 187
    standards at, 194–195
    structure at, 192–194
Herzberg, 28
High achievers. *See also* nAch (need for achievement)
    motivation of, 29–31
High-performing organizations, links between strategy and climate in, 91
High-tech start-ups, 37
Hinduism, 23
Historical forces in organizational climate, 13–14, 82, 95–97
Historical values, 95
Home Depot, 208
Horizontal organizations, 33
Houlihan, Margaret, 184, 185
Humana, Inc., 60–61
Hummer, Jim, 39

IBM, 17
Identity, 56
Individual responsibility, 176
    emphasis on, 47
    encouraging high levels of, 115–116
Individuals
    distinction between settings and, in organizational climate, 4–5, 6
    expectancies and incentives of, 42